Gib Bodet, Major League Scout

Gib Bodet, Major League Scout

*Twelve Thousand Baseball
Games and Six Million Miles*

By GIB BODET
as told to P.J. DRAGSETH

Foreword by Tommy Lasorda

McFarland & Company, Inc., Publishers
Jefferson, North Carolina

Unless otherwise indicated, photographs are from the Gib Bodet Collection.

Library of Congress Cataloguing-in-Publication Data

Bodet, Gib, 1932–
    Gib Bodet, major league scout : twelve thousand baseball games and six million miles / by Gib Bodet as told to P.J. Dragseth ; foreword by Tommy Lasorda.
        p.   cm.
    Includes index.

    ISBN 978-0-7864-7240-6
    softcover : acid free paper ∞

    1. Bodet, Gib, 1932– 2. Sports agents—United States—Biography.   3. Baseball players—Recruiting—United States.   4. Baseball players—United States—History.
    I. Title.
    GV742.42.B63A3 2014
    796.357092—dc23
    [B]   2013042894

British Library cataloguing data are available

Front cover © 2014 Hemera/Thinkstock

Manufactured in the United States of America

McFarland & Company, Inc., Publishers
    Box 611, Jefferson, North Carolina 28640
        www.mcfarlandpub.com

From Gib Bodet:

To my wife of sixty years, Jean, who was always supportive of the idea I could establish myself in the game of professional baseball as a scout, and who was often both a mother and dad of our three great kids, Mike, Lynda, and Jeff, during long absences from home.

To the players, the few who are chosen to play professionally and the many not chosen who play just for the love of the game.

To the many scouts I have worked with and competed against who are rarely given the credit they so richly deserve.

To America's great game, baseball. It all starts with amateur baseball, for that's where all the players start, and where they came from.

Finally to those major league organizations who know there is no substitute for developing your own players because that creates constant winning. To quote Casey Stengel, "If you don't believe it, look it up."

From P.J. Dragseth:

To my dear husband Rich, who still prefers going fishing to attending a baseball game. I forgive you.

Acknowledgments

Special thanks to P. J. Dragseth, with whom I collaborated on this book. Her ideas, always constructive, helped immeasurably as we put together the message that I wanted to deliver. She enabled me to relate my forty-plus years of experiences in scouting with a book that covers what's good, bad, and indifferent in the world of a baseball scout.

— Gib Bodet

Table of Contents

Foreword
by Tommy Lasorda

Scouting is the backbone of baseball, and the scouts are the unsung heroes of our game. Without their dedication to finding players, perseverance through hardships, personal sacrifices and love of baseball, we fans would not enjoy the game as it is today.

I have had the privilege and honor of working and sharing a wonderful friendship with Gib Bodet for decades. His contributions to the Dodgers are second to none. He is an outstanding scout with a keen eye for talent, a baseball lover with a passion for players, and a fan of baseball with stories and experiences that will connect generations of fans with their heroes while giving tremendous insight into how a baseball organization works.

Tommy Lasorda (left) and Gib Bodet at the Scout of the Year Awards when Gib was honored in 2009.

Preface
by Gib Bodet

I think my first thoughts about writing a book were in the late 1990s. I had made a scouting trip up through the New England states and called on an old friend, Tony Viglione. I remember Tony saying, "You know, Gib, you have a lot of very good information about your career and scouting in general that should make a very good book." At first I didn't take it too seriously, but over time I did, and Tony and I started putting together tapes during my scouting trips to the Northeast. We sat in his kitchen with a little tape recorder on the table and he asked questions and I answered them, and we discussed every phase of baseball. That was the beginning of the book.

In 2012 I celebrated the end of my forty-third year in professional baseball. Where did all of this start for me? Well, I was born in New Orleans and attended six schools from New Orleans to Dallas to Albany, Georgia, to New York City. I eventually landed in Fair Lawn, New Jersey, in 1942, and that's where I first met my dear friend Tony Viglione seventy years ago when we attended Roosevelt School, which was a grammar school in Fair Lawn, New Jersey.

We were approximately a forty-five minute ride from New York City. We took a bus to get there and then a trolley to go to Yankee Stadium or the Polo Grounds. We didn't go to Ebbets Field much because that was in Brooklyn, and that was a long way away. That made us approximate to such players as Joe DiMaggio, then a great star with the Yankees, and visiting players of that era like Ted Williams, Hank Greenberg, and Bob Feller. As a matter of fact, I cut school on a Tuesday, April 30, 1946, to go to a ballgame and got to see Bob Feller pitch a no-hitter in Yankee Stadium, one of three that he pitched in his career.

That's where I grew up and that was my initial contact with the sport. There was no organized youth baseball in our town, but we had playground baseball, and Tony and I spent a lot of time playing baseball, often with just three on a side. That creates imagination for young players. It seems to me nowadays with all this coaching and over-instruction, kids rarely play on their own.

Actually, as a young kid my favorite sport was football, followed closely by baseball and basketball. I got busted up playing sandlot football as a high school kid and had two shoulder separations and two broken collarbones, which inhibited my ability to play football. But I recovered from that and played high school baseball and basketball.

After high school came the army. Jean and I had been married in 1953 when we were quite young, just nineteen. I was too young for World War II, but not too young for the Korean War. Guys in my age group I grew up with all had the experience of going into the service. My last year as a ballplayer in high school was 1951. Although I had thought of a pro baseball career briefly in high school when the scouts came around, nothing came of it. But I played ball in the service, which was an interesting experience. I played on some very good teams against some very good players in both basketball and baseball.

Jean and I were stationed in Europe. One of my coaches in the military suggested I become a coach if I wanted to get into baseball after the service. I thought about it but essentially filed the idea away for future reference. Our son, Mike, was born during that time, and our twins, Jeff and Lynda, came three years later.

When my sons were old enough to play Little League baseball I got into it and coached Little League ball for a few years, then coached American Legion ball, then helped a local high school coach for a year and coached a scout league team. All of that reinvigorated my interest in professional baseball.

I got my start with the Boston Red Sox in 1969, and went from there to the Detroit Tigers, the Montreal Expos, the California Angels, and the Kansas City Royals. Finally, in 1979, I got a job that many people were interested in getting but very few got, and that was as an area scout with the Los Angeles Dodgers. Every baseball job I got as a scout was because I got better offers and changed clubs based on my reputation of being a hard worker. I became a regional cross checker in the West Coast circa 1991, and then national cross checker in 1997. The duties of the cross checker are to see potential prospects recommended by other scouts and determine whether or not the organization should draft them.

Of course in the beginning you don't have the choice territories and so forth, but as an area scout I was scouting in California, a warm-weather baseball region, where an awful lot of future big league players are found. During my tenure as a cross checker with the Dodgers I recommended players like Todd Hollandsworth, Paul Konerko, Eric Karros, and Mike Piazza, among others. Konerko later became minor league player of the year, was traded, and has gone on to a great career with the White Sox. Eric Karros was National League Rookie of the Year in 1991, Mike Piazza in 1992, and Todd Hollandsworth was drafted in 1991 and won the award in 1995. I'm quite proud of that. We had a run where we had nine rookies of the year, 1979–1996, and as an area scout I had quite a bit to do with three of them.

In addition to that, other Dodgers I've been involved with are David Hansen, who holds the all-time record of hitting seven pinch-hit home runs in one season. In addition to that I signed Mike Munoz, a left hand pitcher with the Dodgers and others for ten years. And then as a cross checker I recommended Shane Victorino; Clayton Kershaw, who won the Cy Young Award in 2011 and 2013; Chad Billingsley; Scott Elbert; Matt Kemp, who came in second for the National League MVP in 2011 behind Ryan Braun and is now a dominant major league player; and James Loney. With Detroit I found Jason Thompson. Dick Wiencek signed him. With Kansas City I signed infielder Brad Wellman, who was later traded to the Giants. I was always proud of that signing because Wellman was an undrafted player. When an undrafted player is signed and makes it to the big leagues, you feel that's quite an accomplishment. Incidentally, when I worked with Kansas City, Johnny Schuerholz was the scouting director. He's a very smart guy who put together a very talented scouting staff. He later became an extremely successful general manager with the Atlanta Braves.

I also signed a player by the name of Alan Wiggins when I worked for the Angels. He was predominantly a base stealer. He didn't have much power, but boy, he could steal bases. As a matter of fact, Al played in a World Series. And there were others I recommended as a cross checker, like Xavier Paul, a fine outfielder with the Cincinnati Reds now, who enjoyed a pretty good year in 2012.

So that gives you some background, which covers quite a long period of time. When you consider I started scouting when players like Bob Gibson, Tom Seaver, and Carl Yastrzemski were playing in the big leagues and worked up through Clayton Kershaw, Matt Cain, and Albert Pujols, you realize that covers over four decades in which I saw over twelve thousand ballgames and traveled over six million miles.

Two big reasons for this book are Tony Viglione, who offered a lot of thoughts and suggestions about content, and all the encouragement from my wife Jean. When I was overly busy with a lot of travel and felt I didn't have time to devote to a book, she constantly said, "You know, if you don't get something down in black and white, somebody else along the line will come up with a book that won't be half as interesting as a book you could have done because of your experiences in the game." That was a big jolt and a restart for me.

What am I trying to do in the book is share my baseball experiences that will give readers some insight into the scouting profession and what it takes to be a successful scout. To my amazement, people still often tell me they would love to be a scout and get paid to watch baseball games. They have no idea of the knowledge, patience, and experience required to do this very demanding job.

In addition to remembering my baseball experiences and baseball stories, some of which were serious and others that were comical, this is an attempt to look closely at the ins and outs of scouting. We want to spotlight what scouts look for on the positive side and the negative side as we make decisions on players. I also discuss my views on paid instruction, agents good and bad, and scouts good and bad.

Recently, when P.J. and I were going over some material, she related an experience she had many years ago when she was doing some research with some key major league players. When talking with Reggie Jackson, she asked him about a realistic age when a youngster could start thinking seriously about making the decision to choose pro baseball for his career. Although he didn't realize it, Reggie's firm reply was focused directly on the duties and responsibilities of the scouts. He said, "You don't choose baseball. Baseball chooses you."

Introduction
by P.J. Dragseth

Do you remember the 1969 Miracle Mets who went from worst to first in the National League and took the World Series in five games? Or perhaps Kirk Gibson's heart-stopping home run off Dennis Eckersley in the bottom of the ninth in Game One of the 1988 World Series rings a bell? If you're a student of the game, perhaps you may recall May 26, 1959, when Cardinals pitcher Harvey Haddix threw twelve perfect innings but lost the game after an error in the thirteenth. And who can forget the antics of the Babe, the prowess of Ty Cobb, the astuteness of the great Connie Mack, the rise and fall of Pete Rose, the tragedy of Lou Gehrig, the determination of Ron Santo, the appeal of Dizzy Dean and the Gashouse Gang, the fifty-six game streak of Joe DiMaggio, the disappointment of the Black Sox Scandal, and so many other amazing facets of baseball?

Furthermore, how many of us follow our own team inning by inning, one game at a time, as we live and die with every step forward and every setback? We read about yesterday's games in the sports pages, discuss and argue about them in coffee shops, and look forward to the next match-up.

The sport has its own history that has been traced as far back as the American Revolution in a soldier's diary that mentioned a "game of base" played at Valley Forge; it has its own legends, such as the Ernest Thayer poem "Casey at the Bat" written in 1888; it has the feats of such great players as Ty Cobb and Cy Young. It has its own traditions like "Take Me Out to the Ball Game," written in 1908; the first seventh-inning stretch taken by President Taft on Opening Day of the 1910 season; the pregame playing of the "Star Spangled Banner" long before it was named out National Anthem in 1931; and of course peanuts and crackerjacks. These were all part of watching the best athletes of their eras play the great American game as it earned its place as part of Americana.

If you remember any of these things or thousands of others, thank a scout!

Baseball scouts have been called the backbone of baseball, the ones who put the teams and the talent in touch, the ivory hunters who beat the bushes to find the talent that populates the diamond. These professionals bring their own unique baseball backgrounds and expertise as they work behind the scenes, preferring to remain anonymous as they evaluate, judge, and recommend players. What they do and how well they do it is the foundation of every organization.

In the 1850s two men were born whose exploits would change the game and the way it recruited and signed players: Timothy Paul "T.P.," or "Ted" Sullivan and Lawrence ("Larry") Sutton. The two contemporaries both performed scouting duties, but in different ways and for different reasons. Sullivan, who initially traveled by covered wagon and later by train, found and signed hundreds of players for teams he established and operated in dozens of leagues he organized in the Northeastern United States, the first of which was Sullivan's Semipro Alerts in 1878. He was eventually dubbed "the best hustler of them all" by the *Sporting Weekly Journal*, published in Philadelphia at the turn of the last century.

Larry Sutton, on the other hand, was a longtime employee of the *Newark Star Eagle* newspaper and a part time umpire who recommended players for the Brooklyn Robins-Superbas-Dodgers initially as an unpaid "watcher." Later he was hired by club owner Charles Ebbets in 1909 after recommending Zack Wheat, a player with Mobile in the Southern Association, who was then purchased by Ebbets for $1,200. That made Sutton the first paid scout in the game. Though he kept his job at the newspaper and eventually became part owner, he was a very successful scout.

Organizations gradually saw the value and eventual necessity of employing the skills and knowledge of scouts. In the beginning only a few organizations could afford a scout or two while most did without. However, their expertise was recognized over time as all clubs saw the need for good scouts. Eventually a division of labor among scouts came about. Briefly, there are two basic categories, named for the type of players they scouted. Amateur scouts covered amateur players. That group consists of area scouts, area scout supervisors, cross checkers and national cross checkers. Professional scouts cover all levels of pro ball, checking out players for possible trades and deals, as well as doing advance scouting at the major league level, noting the strengths and weaknesses of teams to be faced in future series.

To this day scouts travel far, dedicate long hours to their task, and work anonymously without glory or high salaries as they bring players to this game that we love. They truly are the unsung heroes of baseball.

Gilbert "Gib" Bodet is one of these amazing men. He began as a baseball scout in 1969 and completed his forty-fourth year finding and evaluating talent in 2012. That in itself is unique. But what designates his place in the realm of rarified air among his peers is that 2012 marked his thirty-third consecutive season with the Dodgers. Not many scouts spend that many years with one club.

Bodet received the prestigious Scout of the Year Award–West Coast in 2009. This is a great honor because the award is given by his fellow scouts, one from each of the three major scouting regions in the country. In 2012 Gib Bodet was one of the recipients of the Legends of Scouting Award presented by the Professional Baseball Scouts Association at the annual "In Spirit of the Game Awards Banquet." He must be doing something right!

In this book he offers the readers an inside look at the scouting community through the eyes, experiences, and colorful memoirs of one of its most influential members as he recalls the ups and downs, the ins and outs, responsibilities, duties, skills, stresses, disappointments, satisfactions, and pride of being called "scout."

Beyond this he is dedicated to helping parents of young players as he discusses what scouts look for in high school and college players; explains to parents what to expect if their son is a prospect; expresses definite views about over-instruction for young players; and cautions parents about picking instructors and checking their backgrounds to ensure they get their money's worth. In all of that his goal is the satisfaction of assisting young players as they learn this game and strive to get better as they approach draft eligibility.

He remembers his mentors along the way, including the legendary Joe Stephenson of the Boston Red Sox. He recalls scouts he has worked with and competed against over the years as these peers developed mutual respect and lifelong friendships in a profession that's more than a career. It's a lifestyle.

Bodet played high school baseball and semi-pro ball, and was scouted by the New York Giants and Boston Red Sox as he dreamed of playing in the major leagues someday. But that was interrupted when he was drafted into the U.S. Army during the Korean War. He was on active duty in the U.S. Army from 1952–1955 and then served in the reserves through 1961 when he got his final discharge. As an army athlete he was considered outstanding in both basketball and baseball, USAREUR COMZ, yet he never played pro baseball at any level afterward. Instead, he spent many years coaching and instructing youngsters while his own two sons, Mike and Jeff, progressed through amateur baseball from tee-ball through high school and American Legion.

What kind of a man is he? How does he work with young players? Of all his experiences, the following story is my personal favorite and certainly demonstrates his patience and knowledge when it comes to teaching youngsters about the game:

> I remember when my boys were very young playing Pee Wee and Little League baseball and all that. We had a kid playing on a team with my younger son, Jeff, and I had actually developed a warm spot for him. I think there was no dad in the family and his mom worked hard. He really wasn't a very talented little player but he tried hard. He was a kind of chunky, strong little guy who really didn't have baseball actions and wasn't really that coordinated. He later went on to become a very good high school football player.
>
> Well, one game we played with those little kids was a high scoring game. Late in the game with the score tied, the other team had a runner on third when the batter came up and hit a fly ball to centerfield. Amazingly, this little guy caught the ball, and the runner tagged up at third and tried to score. Our little centerfielder reared back and threw the ball fifty feet over the backstop. Game over.
>
> When this little guy came off the field he was really crying and I felt so sorry for him. I said, "Elliott, come over here." I bent down and put my arm around his shoulder. "Listen. Let me tell you something. You know how long I've been in baseball?"
>
> He was crying and nodded his head. "Yeah, yeah."
>
> And I said, "Do you know how many kids are in this league?" Of course he didn't. "Two hundred fifty kids. And I will tell you one thing. We lost this game. But we have another game tomorrow and we'll win that game. But do you know how many kids in this league could throw that ball over the backstop?"
>
> Then he stopped sniveling a little bit. "How many?"
>
> "There's only one guy I know who could throw that ball over that backstop."
>
> "Who's that?"
>
> "Just you, Elliott."
>
> I think he was eight or nine years old and he looked at me and gave me a huge grin, and I think he went home happy.

During those years others noticed his patience, positive approach, and baseball acumen with youngsters and suggested he consider becoming a minor league coach or a scout. When he was first approached by the Montreal Expos about a scouting career, he didn't feel he was ready. By 1969 he made the leap and was hired as a part time scout with the Boston Red Sox. The story of that hire is unique, as well as the events of his moves to the Detroit Tigers, Montreal Expos, Anaheim Angels during the Gene Autry era, and the Kansas City Royals before he found his baseball home with the Dodgers in 1979. From then until this very day his work ethic, manner, and expertise have taken him up the ladder to his current high-ranking position as National Cross Checker and one of the hardest workers and most respected scouts in baseball.

Gib Bodet has dreamed of this book and mentally prepared for it for a long time before the actual project began. He has accumulated many experiences and stories from people he has met, worked with, and learned from along the way. As readers will see, even more important to him is a desire to impart the knowledge of scouting he has garnered in an effort to reach out to parents of young players who aspire to play pro baseball. To do that he discusses the lifestyle and components of scouting itself, their trained eyes as they look at young players, the tools they seek as they evaluate potential prospects, and the ins and outs of the scouting process. Why? He wants to help parents be aware of what to expect and be better prepared when their son is scouted, drafted, and signed. This book is written from the heart with the sincerest hope of enriching and entertaining all who read it.

Today Gib Bodet is among a senior group of "old school" scouts whose number decreases every year due to advanced age and declining health. They learned scouting by playing the game; a majority of them played professionally, though most never made the major leagues; they were mentored by the experienced scouts who went before them; and they learned by experience that the best way to evaluate players is by watching them play in games and not by looking at lists of statistics. "After all," as he often says, "the game is played on the diamond and not on paper." Without a doubt this vanishing breed of dedicated senior scouts has made a place for themselves in the annals of the game as the anonymous heroes whose legacy is the continuation of the game from generation to generation. Gib Bodet represents them well.

When Gib asked me to work on this book with him I was proud and honored. His dedication to his profession and his concern for fair and positive interaction with young players and all players is genuine. Without bragging or tooting his own horn, he relates his satisfaction as he watched players he scouted and cross checked progress through the ranks of professional baseball.

My Road to the Dodgers

As a youngster I knew what scouts did but never actually thought about being one. I had a couple of scouts show some interest in me as a high school player, but I had never really thought much about it until a few years later, after I had completed my second year in the service stationed in Europe during the Korean War and tried to lean on my experiences there.

The first coach I played for in the military was Sergeant Bob Morton. He was very much a disciplinarian and I can remember him having team meetings about three times a week. I remember a specific player, Sergeant Chang from Hawaii, who was the highest ranking member of the team but not one of the better players. During one meeting Coach Morton said, "Look, my MO is this: I treat everybody alike. Now, has anybody got anything to say?" Sergeant Chang wasn't afraid to speak up and he said, "We get it that you want to treat everybody alike, but we ain't all alike, so keep that in mind. We ain't all alike."

I remember that so vividly. I picked up on that and tried to include that in my scouting. Players are not all alike. They do not have the same skills. And obviously, when you are making a judgment, you have to take into account a lot of different things.

The second year there I played basketball for a coach named Al Espinoza, a guy from California. At one point he asked me what I was going to do when I got out of the service and I said, "Gee, I have no idea. I would love to play professional baseball." But at that time I was married and had a son, Mike, who was born in Europe, and the reality of playing low minor league baseball wasn't in the picture for me. So I said, "I really don't know what I'm going to do, Al."

Al said, "You've got pretty good baseball smarts, so why don't you become a coach?"

Well, I filed that in my memory and never thought too much more about it. Soon after that we had twins, Jeff and Lynda, and as the boys got a little bit older they got involved in Little League baseball. Actually, that was the start of my civilian baseball adventures that eventually led me to get into pro baseball.

It initially happened by accident. As I watched the boys' practices there were volunteer coaches who really didn't know much about what they were doing. Some of them tried strict methods of teaching with little kids that I really didn't like, such as screaming at them or berating them if they didn't do well. Half the time the little 7-or 8-year-old kids would be crying. So I volunteered to help out and coached them as Little Leaguers, and as they got older I coached them as PONY leaguers and American Legion baseball. I discovered early on that I really enjoyed working with these youngsters and passing along the things that I was taught as a young player. If they don't get a good foundation as young players and go into a higher level of play, they get passed over easily by kids who have had decent instruction.

Eventually I got involved with a scout league team. For those of you who may not be familiar with scout league teams, they are teams sponsored by major league teams, run by scouts who are usually helped by high school coaches or part time scouts. The Twins, Expos, Dodgers, Red Sox, and Yankees were some of the major league sponsors. The clubs consisted of junior college and high school players that would be eligible for the next calendar draft. Games were played in the fall, generally September through December. In those days we had a winter draft held in January that involved mostly junior college players. It gave better high school players an opportunity to play with and against older players, which is always beneficial for them.

Often in youth baseball, the bigger, stronger player is dominant. Strength alone in baseball needs technique added. Harnessing power and strength helps develop young players. Remember: Strength without technique can't compare to strength with it. Technique is taught and has nothing to do with size.

During that time thoughts of what Espinoza said lingered. So I decided to write letters to every organization to share my thoughts and see if they had any spots where they could use me and my outlook about young players. I actually never really expected much interest, and said I would be willing to get into scouting or coaching a scout league team or maybe coaching in the low minor leagues.

Getting a job scouting is something that just sort of evolved. I never thought too much about scouting initially, but when I did get involved I had written letters to fifteen or twenty clubs. I got some replies that really encouraged me along the way. But one in particular always comes to mind. I've always been very appreciative of a response to my letter to Dallas Green, who at the time was with the Phillies in a front office job. I knew well who Dallas Green was. He sent me a very encouraging letter that said, "We don't have a job for you now, Gib. But you will get a job. I can assure you of that."

That was followed closely by a nice response from Neil T. Mahoney of the Boston Red Sox. He showed some interest in me when I was a kid player in northern New Jersey when I had gone to a workout conducted by an old Red Sox scout by the name of Caleb "Socko" McCarey. At that time Neil Mahoney was the East Coast Scouting Supervisor. He was there that day and had me fill out some paperwork and while I was doing that we chatted a little bit. So when I sent these letters after the Korean War, seven or eight years after my workout, I sent a letter to him saying I hoped he may remember me. Lo and behold, he responded and said he definitely remembered! That was a nice moment.

He referred me to Joe Stephenson, who was the head Red Sox scout in California at that time, and that was the beginning. I started out working part time with the Red Sox with Joe as my teacher and mentor, and we formed a lifelong friendship. Having the benefit of Joe Stephenson's knowledge and skill was such a basic part of my experience that I have a special affection for him. It was the best way to get my feet wet in scouting.

Initially I worked with him as a bird dog in the Southern California territory. He was a big man, a cigar smoker. Whereas some guys held the cigar like it was some kind of status symbol, with Joe it looked somehow like it was part of his uniform. He was a very good-natured guy who had spent some time in the major leagues during World War II in a rather unique career. He was a catcher and had three cups of major leaguer coffee for a total of twenty-nine games between 1943 and 1947 with the New York Giants, Chicago Cubs, and Chicago White Sox.

When I first met Joe and had some conversations with him, he made me feel very much at ease. I told him that the lion's share of my experiences as a player had been playing in the service. I said, "To some extent I'm a little uneasy about that because there are guys like you who had been major league players."

And he said, "Listen. I played in the minor leagues briefly and was twenty-two when I got to the major leagues. But that was only because of World War II, when so many of the good younger players had been taken into the service."

I think Joe and his wife had six kids, and one of them, Jerry, became a scout after a brief major league career with the Red Sox. He and Ken Brett were among the youngest pitchers in baseball at the time. They broke in when they were nineteen. Today I'm working with a third-generation Stephenson scout, Joe's grandson, Brian, who is a sharp young guy.

If there was a quality that Joe had that sticks out in my mind, it's that he was probably the most logical scout and logical individual that I think I have ever worked with. I remember he told me, "Don't have a concern because maybe this guy played in the big leagues and you didn't. It's still about judgment. Just stick to your guns. If you don't have an opinion and you're a scout, then all you'll be is a guy who just echoes what a guy a level higher than you in the scout pecking order says. I don't want that. When you see a player and you like him, I want you to tell me about him."

And that was the kind of association I had with Joe through all the years I knew him. He treated me a little differently than the normal scouting pecking order can create. By that I mean the highest level guy will say, "What you say is ... and what you mean is...," and I hate that. Speaking the King's English is not how I make my living, but I think I'm halfway reasonable about my opinions.

I remember this from the first time I met Joe. He said, "If you see a good looking woman walking down the street, it doesn't matter how old we are or who much we love our wives, we're not blind. So if you see a good-looking woman walking down the street, you probably say to yourself, 'Now there's a pretty girl,' right?"

And I said, "Right."

And he said, "Do you have to ask anybody if she's pretty?"

When I said no, he said, "Well, that's the way it is with ballplayers, kid." He said, "A good scout will see a player and say, 'You know what? This is a live one.'" That was one of his favorite expressions. "This is a live one. Keep your eye on those live ones."

It's the same general principle. If I see a good player, I don't need to run and get validation from half dozen other scouts. You'll find in our business as that there are guys who will form an opinion about a player and then they will go to other scouts that they're friendly with who may work with other clubs and say, "You know, I really like so and so. What do you think?"

He told me he never operated that way and he didn't think it was wise. He said, "If you need to have your player validated by another scout with the New York Yankees or whatever club, then you shouldn't be scouting." That was Joe. He was a terrific individual. He was his own guy, a loner as a scout.

I think the first player that I was ever able to draft was an eighteen-year-old outfielder from Apple Valley, California, by the name of Rick Berg in 1973. He was an exceptional runner and a good left-hand hitter. He never got to the big leagues, but he did make it to the AAA with the Pawtucket

Red Sox in the International League. He played several years in the Red Sox organization before he retired.

During that same time Joe was interested in two particular players that I had scouted for him and recommended, Jack Clark and Kevin Bell. Both had played on a scout team that I had coached, and both were extremely impressive. We didn't get either one. The Giants drafted Jack Clark in the thirteenth round as a pitcher and Kevin was passed in that draft.

I had worked Kevin out myself and Joe said, "Go ahead and try to sign this guy, Gib." He gave me fifteen thousand dollars to sign him, which was actually pretty good money. Translated from that point in time, probably somebody who would be taken in maybe the fourth or fifth round would get that money, whereas a player taken in the first round in that era was getting sixty or seventy thousand.

But Kevin decided not to sign. You really never know until you get to know a player well. I knew Kevin well, and I knew his mom and dad well. I had him on teams from the time he was a ninth grader until he was a senior, but he was reluctant to go out. Then six months later he was the first player picked by the Chicago White Sox in the 1974 January junior college draft. He did get to the big leagues but was hurt very badly in a collision at the plate with Manny Sanguillen that really mangled Kevin's knee. He was hobbled after that.

Kevin Bell's parents were probably a model that you wish all parents who have youngsters playing in competitive sports would be. They were just absolutely terrific. Win, lose or draw, whether Kevin had three hits or made two errors, they were always the same, very encouraging to him and very encouraging to other kids, too. His dad was a fireman and just a first rate guy. He had played pro ball in the Cleveland organization, I believe, and when I went in to try to sign Kevin, he knew the money we were offering was very fair and he knew that professional baseball could certainly be more than just a walk in the park.

That was basically my first step with a scout that I knew exceptionally well, Joe Stephenson. But it was certainly not the end of my interaction with him.

In 1974 the Scouting Bureau came in and a lot of clubs went from 20 or 30 scouts in the fold to just 5 or 6. This was the idea of Joe L. Brown, who was then the general manager of the Pirates. He sold major league baseball on it as an economy measure, and lot of scouting jobs were eliminated. Scouting jobs were not easy to get, even for people with big time credentials.

My next stop was with Detroit as an area scout. On one occasion I branched out of my area because I had heard there were very good players in

Orange County in California. I remember this quite well. I had seen an afternoon game and then went to this particular night game at El Modena High School, right in the middle of Orange County. One of the first things that Joe always said was to get to know who the scouts are with other clubs. He had a pretty good evaluation process that he would use. There are scouts that are just information gatherers, but the best scouts are top flight evaluators. Our competition comes from the exceptional evaluators group.

When I walked into ballparks, I had a tendency to look around and see if there were any scouts there. So when I got to that high school night game, I noticed a lot of people there but I didn't see a single scout. And lo and behold, I saw a catcher that I really liked. It was forty-some years ago. He had a sturdy catcher's build, had a good arm, and he swung the bat well, threw well, and had good hands. He was a little rough around the edges, but I thought about Joe's term and said to myself, "Here's a live one."

It got to about the sixth inning and his team was winning easily, but he was facing a pitcher who wasn't quite a prospect, but maybe the type of player a college coach would latch onto. And he swung the bat well against this guy. One of the things we look for is how well the guy competes against good competition. Incidentally, this kid was a left-hand hitter. And so I thought, "Boy, this is great."

I wasn't working for the Red Sox any more and was particularly pleased that this was right in the middle of Joe Stephenson territory. I would have taken great delight in drafting this guy, then I thought, "Joe's not around. He's not going to see this guy, and it's fairly late in the season." I thought maybe I would put one over on my old pal. So I made my way through all the people in the seats behind the backstop. Now usually scouts look at a left-hand hitter from a side view because it gives you a little bit better perception of how he triggers the bat, and the swing plane of the bat and all that semi-technical stuff. So I was really feeling great, thinking I was going to watch this kid hit for the last time and then ease out of the park. He hit a line drive that the right fielder caught, so I was going to edge out of the park and get into my car and go home. It was probably 10:30 at night. But as I got a little bit further down the line I saw this trail of smoke coming up from a group of people, and at the end of the smoke trail from his big El Producto cigar was Joe Stephenson!

He saw me and didn't miss a beat as he said, "Hi, Gib, what are you doing here?"

So I used a line that he used a lot when some smart-ass scout asked him what he was doing at a game. I said, "I noticed the lights and decided to come over and see what's going on."

He had a big grin on his face, and asked, "You're kind of far from home, aren't you, Gib?"

And when I nodded in agreement, he said, "Well, it's a little too late to stop over to the bowling alley." That's what we used to do, stop at the bowling alley when I worked directly under him. We'd eat and have a couple of beers and discuss the players I had seen in that given week or so. Then he nudged me and winked and said, "Gib, if I miss them I'm not going to miss them this close to my house." And he laughed. I'll never forget that.

But that was essentially his MO and it tells you a lot about scouting. You do make friends and you do have friendships with guys who work with different clubs. Joe was very professional about it with his friends who were in scouting. But basically he was a loner on players.

Another experience I had with him was during Easter week when the kids were on school vacations. In a lot of areas they have tournaments and I had been to a couple of tournaments that day and decided to go to La Palma Park, which was on the border of Anaheim and Fullerton. I'll never forget this. I was walking into a game that was well into the fifth inning and out of the ballpark comes Joe. At that time Glenn Hoffman, who is now a coach and the brother of Trevor Hoffman, was a shortstop at Savanna High School and a well-known prospect, so he had been getting a lot of attention. Anyway, Joe's coming out and I'm going in and he said, "What are you going in there for?"

Well, I didn't mind telling him I wanted to take a look at Hoffman because everybody knew about him. Joe said, "Don't worry about Hoffman."

"Why's that?"

And he says, "Gib, he can't play shortstop."

Hoffman had a kind of rangy build and he wasn't considered a very good runner, but he had real good hands and a plus arm. So I said, "Why shouldn't I worry about him?"

And Joe says, "Have you ever seen a guy play shortstop with feet like that?"

And I said, "To be honest with you, I didn't notice that."

He said, "This guy wears size thirteen shoes, Gib. His feet won't work, not at shortstop. It just won't work. Come on, let's go have a beer at the bowling alley."

So we went over to the bowling alley and I sat there with him for maybe half an hour and we chewed the fat. But then the draft came around that year, 1976, and the second selection by the Boston Red Sox was none other than Hoffman of Savanna High School. Later that summer when I saw Joe and asked him, "What happened to that shortstop with the big feet? I see you drafted him."

And he says, "Hey, kid, if I didn't think you could scout I wouldn't have tried to steer you in the other direction." That was Joe. And for all the years I knew him he not only was a fun guy to work with, he was a fun guy to compete against. I don't think he had a mean bone in his body, yet you sensed that when you got into serious conversations about players, you got the feeling this guy has the ability to boil things down to the basics. And the basics were highly important to him. The makeup of the player, of course, to Joe and others, was very important, but he had the ability to get to all the tools.

In that era scouts did a much more thorough job of getting to know the kids. Joe came from an era that preceded the draft that didn't start until 1965. I can remember Joe telling me about his following certain kids in the off season. He told me about one particular player, I think it might have been Ron Fairly, going back that far. Fairly was a basketball player, considered a pretty good high school player, but that certainly was not the equal of his baseball ability. I asked him, "What did you want to see him play basketball for?"

And he said, "It's good to see how multisport kids compete in the sport that's not their best. I wanted to see how he handled things in competition when he wasn't the key guy and how he reacted to the key guy on his team." There was a lot of depth in Joe's thought process. Even though Joe didn't sign Fairly, the new Los Angeles Dodgers did in 1958 and he went on to play twenty-one seasons in the big leagues.

How well Joe Stephenson would have fit into the current realm of scouting where everything is so computerized is arguable. But I think by and large, if he were working for a director or someone who realized that he's a very talented evaluator, it wouldn't matter whether he was punching out a computer with one finger or whether he wrote his reports in longhand like we used to do years ago. If he were working for someone today who recognized how talented he was, they'd probably say, "Hey, Joe, stick with whatever it is you're doing and go on from there because you're surely doing it right." He was a very smart guy and a special guy in almost any category you can think of.

When I scouted for Detroit I signed a youngster out of California State University-Northridge by the name of Jason Thompson in 1975. Years later I had a friend look up Jason Thompson online to see what the records say about who signed him. It listed Dick Wiencek, who was the Tigers' scouting director at that time. He had a reputation as one of the all-time scouts as far as the number of players signed was concerned.

Well, sometimes baseball's record keeping is sloppy. I handled everything on the Thompson deal, even the signing bonus. And what happened is, when Jason came back from Hawaii, where he had played in an all-star game, I called him and told him we had drafted him in the fourth round. So he and his dad came in to discuss signing.

He was a fourth-round pick, as I remember, and to show you how times have changed, the agreed signing bonus was $15,000. I scouted the kid, wrote the reports, and handled all of this and Wiencek saw him one time. He did like him, but the problem we had with it was that he didn't see him until very late in the season and I had been on the kid all year. The bottom line was this. Because he had access to the front office, when the kid came back to California from Hawaii and went home, Dick tried to sign him for less money than was agreed on with me. I got the okay for the money from Bill Lajoie, who was running the Tigers' scouting department at the time.

Jason and his dad felt betrayed and it made me look bad. They wouldn't sign for the money Dick offered and they walked out. I later learned they said they wanted the $15,000 I offered them and Wiencek said, "Bodet isn't running the Tigers," or something like that. Finally Detroit ended up settling with the Thompsons. That situation taught me more about how the behavior and ethics of some scouts can impact others. But I guess that happens in every profession.

Jason had a nice eleven-year big league career. He wasn't a star but he was a pretty good player for the Tigers, where he played five good years, and after a season with the Angels he played five very good years with the Pirates. He played his final season with the Expos in 1986.

From Detroit I went to Montreal, where I worked with and for the infamous Bob Zuk, who was well known in scouting circles for signing great players the likes of Wilver Stargell, Reggie Jackson, Freddie Patek, Gary Carter, and an endless line of fine players, several of whom went on to become Hall of Famers. Working with Zuk was a different bag of tricks from Joe Stephenson, that's for sure. But it was an ongoing learning process for me, and to this day I carry things I learned there about working with young players.

He was essentially the polar opposite of Joe. He was a very demanding guy, and a very good evaluator of players who signed some of the very best over the years. And he worked for many teams. He was difficult to handle. But he did have a sort of grudging respect for Joe Stephenson. So when I worked for Montreal I think he was pleased to get me away from Joe simply because I had spent time around Joe, and at that point in my career some considered me a hard worker who would run around and go anywhere to see any possible player. Anyway, occasionally Zuk would say things like, "How do you think Joe would react to a player like this?"

Zuk, a big cigar smoker who was a big heavy-set guy with opinions on everything, was constantly in a hurry to go from one place to another, and he was never ever on time. A day didn't go by in his life when Zuk didn't come up with some kind of a crisis. He started out as a part timer for Oakland when they were in the Pacific Coast League and ended up scouting around forty years.

So we get to a point in this one particular draft and he said he had a conversation with Joe and he had seen Joe at some high school or college game and Joe said to him, "Zukie, I've got you this year. I have a guy hidden out you will never ever find and he's one of the better players I've seen over the years."

Zuk knew better than to ask for the kid's name, so he starts pumping me. "I knew he wouldn't have told you, but what schools does Joe like to concentrate on?" Well, Joe lived in the middle of Orange County and had signed players from Orange County over the years, but Joe was not averse to going out of the area. It was the way he scouted. When he found a kid at first it was visual — what did he see — and then he wanted to get to know the kid's makeup.

Those things you don't acquire by flash scouting, which is where we determine if a kid can run and hit and has a good arm or whatever, and decide if we will write him up as a prospect. No. That wasn't Joe's style. Zuk knew Joe's style and he was almost obsessed that year by trying to find out who this kid was that Joe had hidden out. So he kept after me about it and I told him, "look, I had a very loose routine with Joe. I lived in the San Gabriel Valley about 35 miles from where Joe lived, and that was an area that was producing some real fine players. And there were a lot of young families with teenage kids. Baseball was very prevalent out there.

Here's an example of what I mean. In 1973 I went to a high school game in West Covina, California, and saw Charter Oak High School play Edgewood High School. Out of that one game ten or eleven kids were drafted. Both Roenicke brothers came out of that school. Gary Roenicke was a first-round pick selected by Zuk for Montreal that year. Ron, his younger brother by two years, was later drafted by four different clubs but didn't sign until 1977, when he was selected in the first round secondary phase by the Dodgers. Gary spent twelve seasons in the major leagues at first base, third base, and in the outfield. Ron, who we used to call "Rags" because he was such a sloppy dresser, played for eight seasons and is now the fine manager of the Milwaukee Brewers.

But Zuk was beside himself to find out the name of Stephenson's hidden player. And I was no help to him because I honestly didn't know what schools Joe concentrated on. Joe always told me, "Go where you don't think I'd go."

Anyway, I recall this particular sequence of events simply because I must have spent seventy-five percent of my time going to games in Orange County assigned by Zuk, who always told me, "Let me know if you see Joe there."

Now, this may seem disjointed but it's pretty clear in my mind. I remember this quite well. In 1976 Glenn Hoffman had been selected by the Red Sox in the second round of the draft. Keep in mind in that era they weren't drafting fifty or a hundred guys, meaning fifty or a hundred rounds in the draft. In the last ten to twelve years that number has been reduced to fifty in the entire draft. But I can remember when clubs would pick a hundred players with no intent to sign more than ten or maybe twenty.

Anyway, I was at a game at Anaheim Stadium. I didn't have any pro coverage at that time, but I was down there watching a game. And who did I bump into but Joe Stephenson, and sitting next to him was Bob Zuk. I was working with Zuk at that time. Both Zuk and Joe were very cognizant of contemporary big league teams. So Zuk says to Joe, "You know, I was really surprised you took Glenn Hoffman in the draft."

Joe answered, "Why do you say that?"

And Zuk continued, "Well, you know, I had considerable interest in him," as a way of endorsing Joe's selection.

Joe didn't give a hoot in hell what Zuk thought, but he used to love to toy with him. So Joe says, "I had an interest in him and got to know the family pretty well."

Now Zuk, I will tell you this, if he came into your home he would call and make an appointment and be very polite and very nicely dressed and carry a leather attaché case. It was his persona of a big powerhouse scout and he more often than not overwhelmed the parents and the player. I think he intentionally intimidated people. Working with him was an unpredictable and unbelievable experience, but it was educational. I must tell you there were things he did and said that were very, very sharp. On the other side of the ledger were the times when I said to myself, "I would never say that to a parent. There was no way in the world I would say that to a parent."

It was different with Joe. He would come into the house he would be nicely dressed: nice slacks and a shirt open at the collar, and a sport jacket. Once he was there for five minutes you felt like you had known the guy your whole life. He was good at making fun of himself, and the game, and scouting, and he always told me the worst thing you could say to the family was that scouting was an exact science. Actually, he said, "Scouting isn't a science at all. What we're doing is establishing who the kids are and what their potential may be."

That's what scouting really is. I don't think it's tough to tell who they are and I don't think it's tough to tell what their potential is if you know what you're doing and what to look for in players. Joe was good at that, and of course parents know their son better than you do and they want to tell you all the things he accomplished in Little League. Joe was always very attentive to that. He had been in the game for a good many years and had come up the hard way and had kids who played the game. He was just an easier guy to know and to relate to. And Zuk wasn't.

So getting back to the three of us watching batting practice, and taking a leaf out of Joe's notebook, Zuk, who always spoke quite formally, said, "Yes, I knew the Hoffmann family quite well and I know that's always important."

Then he asked Joe, "Did you have any previous interaction with the Hoffmann family?"

And Joe told him he had known them a little, but he liked the kid and thought he'd play in the big leagues one day.

And Zuk said, "Well, I just wanted you to know I knew the family very well and was very interested in Glenn."

Later, just prior to the game starting, one of the ushers went down on the field and sang the national anthem. He had a real nice voice and they announced this was Glenn Hoffman's father, who had been an usher at Anaheim Stadium for many years and from time to time he sang the anthem.

Zuk said, "I didn't realize he did that."

So the game started and about the third inning along comes Glenn Hoffmann's dad. He walked up and Joe greeted him pleasantly, and Zuk didn't know who he was. So they began talking and Joe says, "I'd like to introduce you to Gib Bodet. He used to work for me but now he works for Montreal." And we exchanged pleasantries and so forth.

Then Joe said, "And this gentleman here, oh you already know him."

So Glenn's dad looked at Zuk and said, "I don't believe I've had the pleasure. And your name is…?"

Mr. Hoffmann obviously didn't know Zuk from a bar of soap, and Zuk was mortified. He was certainly embarrassed because he had been caught in a humongous lie. Hoffman sort of strayed away, and Joe, with his good-natured humor, took a long drag on his big cigar and said, "You know, Bob, it occurs to me that you didn't make a very good impression on Mr. Hoffman when you got to know him because I don't think he knew you from the man in the moon." Zuk was so embarrassed. He stumbled around and made some weak attempt to explain it away, said he had to go make a phone call, and he disappeared into the crowd. What a beauty. What an interaction there! One guy was having a lot of fun and the other guy was constantly trying to top Joe.

Joe was very comfortable in his own skin. He was very likeable. And he was very proficient. Zuk was proficient, an excellent evaluator of players. But he came out of a different era and he had a different personality. That's what it was.

We had a lot of players under contract to Montreal and we used a field at Edgewood High School in West Covina, California. It was a pretty large field and it was centralized. We had a lot of inner-city kids who were under contract, like Ellis Valentine and others we worked out there in the winter. As the season was approaching I'd hit fungos or throw batting practice.

Zuk ran the whole program. So when we worked out on a Sunday morning I got there at eight o'clock and made sure the field was ready to go, and then Zuk had me drive around to pick up kids who didn't have cars. So quite often I'd meet the inner city kids around seven in the morning in L.A. and drive them out to West Covina, which was about thirty miles away, but not a big deal on a Sunday. I took them home after the workout. Godfrey Evans, one of the infielders we had under contract, often helped because he had a car. One thing that rubbed me raw was that Zuk was a real taskmaster who wanted everybody there on time but he was constantly late. Always late. More often than not he was at least fifteen minutes, up to two hours late!

I remember one time we were supposed to start the workout at nine. I had been into the Watts area to pick up some of the inner city kids, had gotten the field ready, and the kids were all there on time. Gary Carter was there and Dennis Blair, plus Ellis Valentine and a bunch of other kids, but no Zuk. So part-time scout Chet Reese and I were dealing with all the kids, and they knew something was up.

We used to have squad games against one of Zuk's part-time scout teams run by Steve Hill, who drove fifty miles each way from the area in the San Fernando Valley with his van full of players for his team. So quite often we'd have the two groups of kids playing against each other. Now Hill's kids were unsigned players playing for Crenshaw High School and different schools like that who didn't have any kind of off-season program. Steve put them on his team and he had a van, plus I think an older son of his had a vehicle, and that's how they would bring the kids out. They played the group of signed players we had.

My assignment was that if any scout from another team showed up, take all Steve Hill's good kids out of the game. I remember saying, "Well, who am I supposed to replace them with?"

"Replace them with some of our pro kids," Zuk said. And it was one confusion like that after another. Anyway, he shows up at this workout at eleven that was supposed to start at nine and I'm burning. Usually we were reacting to him, but this time he was reacting to me. He knew I was hot. He comes walking through that gate in left field and he was huffing and puffing and he came up to me. Before he could say anything I said, "Hey, Bob, let's get one thing straight. I don't mind if you're late, but two hours late with all these kids out here that Chet and I are supposed to handle and Steve Hill's got his team full of guys and nothing can start till you get here, and then you're telling me that if the Mets scouts Harry Minor and Roger Jongewaard come, I'm supposed to take the better high school players out of the game? Okay. What's the problem?"

"The problem, my dear Gib, is simple. I was accosted by a ruffian truck driver." I mean it was constant. He used that line again maybe a year later when we came back from San Diego. Another time, when there were long lines to get gas in the 1970s and people got their gas and then stood in line to pay in the store, Zuk cut into line at the store and took a couple of cigars and dropped a bill on the counter and a truck driver told him to get to the back of the line. It probably never happened, but he constantly "multitasked" and always had a story to cover himself.

That was Bob Zuk. Success was there. If you look at the number of players that he signed over the years, it's highly impressive, and maybe as many as four of them went to the Hall of Fame. And yet he worked for all those teams. Why? Because he was so hard to deal with!

I remember one time going with him and he had a beer box in the back of his white Cadillac. I knew he wasn't a drinker, so I made a joke and said, "A beer box is a little out of character for you, Bob." If you're old enough, you may remember those long-necked bottles.

"Here, you drive," he said, and he opened up the box and it was jammed with papers. Well, we had to detour by the main post office in Los Angeles to send that box of stuff to Montreal. He had not turned in his expenses for six months and they were jumbled in the box, unorganized, and there were tons of receipts. He used to shuffle back and forth between San Francisco and Oakland and Portland and Seattle a lot, so you can imagine the mess. There were probably hotel bills and receipts from airline flights. It probably involved thousands of dollars and he had turned nothing in when they told him he would have to turn in documentation if he wanted to get reimbursed. Hence he was sending them the beer box full of documentation.

As a matter of fact, I was told at one point that the sale of a club was held up until his claim for money for expenses was satisfied. And he also kept a speed gun at one time and major league baseball got involved because he was keeping the speed gun until he had at least some kind of reimbursement. He had that problem every place he worked. And in spite of his success he had constant battles with the clerical people wherever he went.

But I learned a lot from Bob Zuk by watching him and by listening to his direct advice that often came across as a scolding, but only because that was his style.

In addition to scouting, Zuk had a very successful photography business on the side. Having a side business was not uncommon for scouts of that era. You have to realize that thirty to forty years ago a highly paid scout might have been paid fifteen or twenty thousand dollars a year, and there were a lot of scouts making less than ten thousand dollars a year. As a result, to make ends meet, a lot of scouts were teachers or had small businesses. I knew of guys who scouted in the Northeast back then, and one owned a hardware store, another owned a small tavern, several sold real estate. They were raising families and did these things simply to pay the bills.

Zuk was a fascinating, multifaceted guy who was the most disorganized person I have ever met in my life! Yet, behind all that he had a very sharp mind in some respects. I think of it quite often now in dealing with contemporary scouts. He tried to get all of us to use the same language. Though essentially impossible, it was a good idea in terms of writing reports on players. As an example, when you say, "Boy, this guy can really run," and the average running time from home plate to first base is 4.3 seconds, Zuk would say, "But you have down 'he's a 4.3 runner,' so don't say he can really run. A 4.3 runner for a right handed hitter is an average runner, and that is 4.2 for a left handed hitter. So say he's an average runner. Really run, or really throw, or really anything means he's above average in those departments." He tried to get us to use the same terminology.

Well, that was true unless it was someone he really needed. There was an educator in San Diego, I believe his name was Bob Guess, and he used those terms all the time. Zuk never corrected him because he didn't have anybody else down there. But that was Bob Zuk.

Did everything he said make sense to me? Not really. There were things that I would never have done that Zuk did. A quick anecdote on Zuk is a time we went in to sign a player from a very affluent family, and I thought his abrasive personality may alienate the parents. He didn't. They were self-made, hard-working people whose son was a left-hand pitcher, a prospect. His father was a retired Air Force officer who had a very good job at Vandenberg Air Force Base, and his wife was involved in education; I think she was a principal at a local high school. After ten or twenty minutes in the house, Zuk said, "Well, we'll give you a chance to talk about it as a family."

And the father said, "There's really no need for that. We want our son to go to college."

Zuk said, "Regardless, I'll give you a call in a day or two."

This was in Southern California, so we went up to Andersen's for a bowl of their famous split pea soup, and I told Zuk, "I'm discouraged. I don't think there's any chance of signing this kid."

Zuk said, "We may not sign him, and our only chance is that the kid would help us convince his parents. We'll give him a couple of days to do that."

I said, "I don't think so." So Zuk went through a long list of privileges this kid had and the latest kind of innovative exercising equipment he had in the garage to make him better. There were things like stretching devices to develop his arm.

"Well, Bob, I just don't see it."

Zuk said, "Well, we'll see whether your negativity is correct." That was kind of the way he talked if you disagreed with him. And sure enough two days later when Zuk called them, the kid had talked his parents into it. Why? No doubt because of Zuk's observation. There is no question of that. At that point in my career I had not been in enough homes to try to relate to how a youngster can influence his parents to get them to react favorably. But Zuk had noticed it.

I never forgot that. Although I didn't get along particularly well with him, I did have a respect for his ability. In this case he made a good read on the parents and the youngster, and we did include the college scholarship plan in the signing bonus.

Another experience I remember quite vividly represents the flip side of the coin. In the 1976 draft, as I recall, maybe of the first six players we got four or five of them. And then a little bit further down in the thirteenth round I got a player by the name of Ed Irvine out of Jordan High School in Long Beach, California, which is a great hotbed for athletes in almost every sport. He was an outfielder and we wanted to make a second baseman out of him. He was a very likeable kid who played very hard and he had what the scouts call "tools." He could run and throw and had a quick bat.

That particular year we were having a hard time trying to sign any of the players we drafted. The first player we selected was Bobby James, a big hard-throwing right-hand pitcher from out in the San Fernando Valley. Zuk prided himself on being able to sign anybody. Of course, in his past he had signed Reggie Jackson and Willie Stargell, who were big league stars by that time, and Gary Carter had become a real good major league player, and that's just a few signees from his list. We did sign James, but as for the others, Zuk was very frustrated.

I remember picking him up at LAX (Los Angeles Airport) after he flew in from a trip trying to sign a player in Northern California. Anyway, he wanted to know how I had done with Ed Irvine. And I said, "I'm having trouble signing him. At first I thought I was making good progress. He's a very smart kid who has a full ride baseball scholarship to the University of Arizona."

So I think I had offered Eddie $7,500. Keep in mind this was 1976 and that was a fair amount for that time.

Zuk said, "I'll show you how to handle him. How much was his ultimate counter-offer?"

"Seventy-five thousand," I said.

I can still remember this. I was driving the car and he said, "WHAT?"

"Seventy-five thousand. I went in and thought I was making progress with him but he said he needed time to make a private phone call."

So while Ed did that I went down to a local diner and got myself a snack, and returned in an hour, which he had asked me to do, and the counteroffer was $75,000. So I told him I would like to come again and bring my boss and we'll talk some more. He said that was fine.

So here we were, Gib Bodet, who had been scouting just a few years, accompanied by the legend of the scouting world, Bob Zuk. Well, we drove over to Eddie Irvine's house in Long Beach. This is not the high-rent district. He lived in a very hard and tough neighborhood. But, and I remember this well, you could eat off the floor in his home. It was very sparsely furnished but it was just as clean as a whistle. As I recall, Eddie was the oldest child and I think the only boy in the family. His mother worked.

Anyway, we get back to the house, and Zuk immediately takes over the conversation. I remember they had a kind of false fireplace in the living room and one large easy chair which Zuk immediately occupied. Eddie's mom had come home from work and offered some coffee and refreshments. She made it clear that this decision was Ed's. She said, "He's capable of making his own decision about whatever he wants."

Zuk immediately launched into his usual, "If you're not aware of it, I have signed the great Wilver Stargell. I've signed Reggie Jackson. I've signed Gary Carter, who is now the best catcher in the National League, with the exception of Johnny Bench." And he went on and on and on. And the kid was just standing there, kind of leaning on the mantel of that fake fireplace, and he listened to him.

I'll never forget this as long as I live. Zuk finally ran out of material and said, "Now, Edward, I want you to tell me what you told Mr. Bodet about the signing bonus."

Ed calmly answered, "Seventy-five thousand," and continued leaning up against that fake fireplace.

Ignoring the kid's response, Zuk said very quietly, "I have a slight hearing impediment," and leaned in closer to the kid. "Come here," and motioned with his finger like you would do with a puppy, and said, "Come here."

So Eddie took a couple of steps toward him and Zuk said, "I want you to tell me again, what was that number?"

Eddie said, "Seventy-five thousand," a little louder.

Zuk's comeback once again was, "Sorry, my hearing is a little defective and I can't be correct in what I thought I heard you say. What was that number again?" And he repeated the puppy-calling motion.

Now this was a good and respectful kid. This was not an antagonistic youngster. He was just a very good high school athlete who was from a tough section and he had to grow up tough. Despite that, he was as straight as an arrow. But he wasn't going to be talked to like he was some kind of a fool. And that's what I thought was the way Bob was treating him.

Zuk tried one last time and said, "Come here." It was almost a command.

The kid walked right over to Bob, no more than six inches from Bob's ear, and he screamed, "Seventy-five thousand dollars!"

Zuk was still in the recliner, and with that he instantly reclined and his feet flew up so fast that he almost flipped the chair over backwards. I nearly choked trying not to laugh. I've thought about that over thirty-five years and I've never quit laughing to myself about it. Obviously, we didn't sign Eddie Irvine. He ended up going to the University of Arizona and after three good collegiate seasons he was selected in the seventh round by the Milwaukee Braves, and he signed. I want to say he got around thirty-five or forty thousand dollars. He spent his entire career with Milwaukee minor league affiliates, even made it to AAA at one point, and retired after five years with a .276 career batting average.

I left Montreal when Bob Zuk and Bobby Mattick, a very well known scout who signed Frank Robinson, Curt Flood, and Vada Pinson, left and went to Toronto. When that happened I was left without a job because I worked for and with Zuk. I became available. That fall I got a call from Walter Shannon of the Angels saying he had heard I was available he asked if I would go to Anaheim Stadium and interview for a scouting job they had. So I went over there and talked to Walter and he hired me.

I always had a great admiration for Walter Shannon. Walter went to Milwaukee with Harry Dalton and company, better known as "the Dalton Gang," and they won a pennant over there when they had Paul Molitor and Robin Yount. Success followed Walter Shannon for sure, and a lot of people around him. I liked his approach. I liked him. And this gave me a chance to make a

Jason Thompson was a pleasure to work with and went on to a fine career.

little more money. Being a local individual was a good thing in his eyes because people get to know you. My scouting area was to be Southern California. That was all very attractive to me. I worked over there for a couple of years with Walter.

When Walter hired me with the Angels, he said to me, "You know, one of the problems we had was that you beat us out of a player, Jason Thompson, when you got him with Detroit. That annoyed Mr. Autry very much. You know, owners sometimes only see the tip of the iceberg, and Jason, a local boy, had gone to the big leagues after being passed by the Angels and the Dodgers." He told me he had talked to Mr. Autry about it and said, "We have a chance to hire the guy that dug up this kid and recognized his potential." And that's how I got hired.

All right, a year goes by and that first year I was with the Angels was the year I recommended Alan Wiggins and he was the first player we picked in the junior college winter draft. He did get to the big leagues, but not with the Angels. He ultimately got there in a roundabout way.

Jason came to the big leagues in a relatively short time. They started him in AA, the next spring he went to AAA, and within a little more than a year he was in the big leagues and started hitting home runs in Tiger Stadium at a rapid pace. I think he had possibly seventeen home runs within just two months. Ultimately, he really cooled down as veteran pitchers adjusted to what he could hit and what he couldn't hit. Then he struggled in that first year after that. But he overcame those problems and became at one time a productive RBI man. Jason hit over 200 runs in his career.

The irony of that whole issue was this: at the conclusion of that first year I scouted with the Angels, the major league team had a lot of big name players on it. They had traded for some, and a couple had come through their minor league system. Their pitching was absolutely super. Their two top pitchers were Nolan Ryan and a young Frank Tanana. In that rotation Frank Tanana was number one and the great Nolan Ryan was number two on the staff. But they had difficulty scoring runs. Their defense was spotty, and the big league club really didn't do much at all.

Autry became very disillusioned with the people who were running the club. He fired general manager Harry Dalton, the scouting director Walter Shannon, the farm director Tom Sommers, and all the scouts who worked for Walter Shannon. In essence I was hired because of my ability to come up with a guy like Jason Thompson, and yet, because Thompson had been one of the key guys who was a thorn in the side of Autry and the Angels, I ended up getting fired, too. The attitude from Autry was basically one of, "I'm getting rid of everybody and that's the way it is."

The reason I mentioned how and why I was hired and then fired by the Angels is that it's an illustration of what can happen in baseball. Scouts and cross checkers quite often become a victim of who their sponsor is. It can be an asset or a liability. When the person who brings you into an organization who is in favor at the time loses his status so to speak, then you're liable to have someone come into the organization and decide to get rid of the scouting director and all of his people. And that is essentially what happened with Walter Shannon and the rest of us with the Angels.

Most of those guys I worked with at that time went to Milwaukee. Dalton went there as general manager, and Shannon as the scouting director. And those guys, within a couple of years, won the American League pennant and went on to play in the World Series. Al Kubski and I were hired by Kansas City, another up and coming American League team.

While I was with the Angels another interesting scout I worked with was Loyd Christopher, who ultimately became a very good friend. Our history goes back many years. I lived in the New York area as a kid about a half hour from New York City and we used to take the bus or the trolley to go to games at the

Polo Grounds and Yankee Stadium. My main contact with the game was *The Sporting News*, called the *St. Louis Sporting News* in those days because that's where it was published. When I was in the service with guys from all over the country, we used to live and die with *The Sporting News*. It covered every league.

Now let me backtrack. As a kid, I loved the Chicago Cubs. But I later turned to the Yankees because I had a particular favorite with them, Joe Gordon. But when they traded him to Cleveland I became an Indians fan. I was probably thirteen or fourteen years old at that time, and had just started paying close attention to the game.

The Cubs were my team: Don Johnson, Lenny Merullo, Phil Cavaretta, and pitchers Claude Passeau and Hank Borowy. I knew it well and loved that team: Peanuts Lowrey, Handy Andy Pafko, Lou Stringer, Loyd Christopher and others. Loyd Christopher had been a big star in the Pacific Coast League with Los Angeles, and his brother Russ pitched with the Philadelphia Athletics. I kept a close eye on Los Angeles players because the team was owned by the Cubs and they were the guys who would go to my team.

As a player Loyd was in the game forever. He was a long-legged outfielder who had a big bat in his years in the Pacific Coast League which were interrupted by brief cups of coffee in the big leagues when he appeared in a total of sixteen games in 1945–46 with the Red Sox, Cubs, and White Sox. Unfortunately he had a series of serious injuries, which kind of hung him up in the Pacific Coast League.

Thirty years later or whatever it was, I was convinced to go to the Angels by Walter Shannon, a man I grew to like and admire very much. And lo and behold, one of their key scouts was Loyd Christopher, who lived in Richmond, California. When I first got there I only slightly knew a couple of scouts and Loyd sensed that. I took to him particularly because he paid attention to me.

We had a workout at Anaheim Stadium, and prior to the workout my best prospect was a young right-hand pitcher by the name of Tehan, but it's not the guy in the big leagues now by that name. Anyway, one of the other scouts at our pre workout meeting wanted to know how tall he was, and I told him 6' 0", about 180 or whatever, and he said, "I don't like six-foot-right-handed pitchers."

And he went on and on. Nobody said too much about it and Loyd was sitting over there and all of a sudden he said, "I'd just like to interject something here. Let's not rule out six-foot pitchers. If we do we'd have to rule out Bob Feller or Tom Seaver," and he mentioned somebody else.

And I thought, "WOW. Now I've got somebody on my side." Then we had the workout. There were a lot of kids that day and we had an interesting workout.

Workouts are interesting. You can get on and off a player from a bad workout. Some of them were nervous. I remember working a player and he lost his breakfast. I tried to help him out a little bit and asked, "What do you think? Maybe you ate something that didn't agree with you?"

He said, "No. It has nothing to do with anything I ate. I'm just so nervous I can hardly stand it." It's easy to forget high school players are still kids. I remember we gave him warm Coca-Cola and crackers because when I came back on the ship in the service that's what was done to control the sea sickness.

But that wasn't the issue. The issue was the conversation that happened before the workout with a scout with years more experience than I had; I think it was Nick Kamzic, who was a scouting legend. He didn't like six-foot pitchers regardless of Loyd's two cents. Then we watched the kid throw in the bullpen and Loyd didn't say much. When we walked away from there even Kamzic was impressed. Finally, when the kid threw well in the bullpen and showed a pretty good curve ball and the delivery of his fastball (remember, speed guns were almost nonexistent back then), I was pleased with how well he did. As we walked away Loyd said to me, "I betcha Nick's view of this kid went from six-foot to six-foot-two throwing in the bullpen."

It told me something about who Loyd was. That year we drafted a catcher from a junior college in the Bakersfield area. He was a hard nosed guy who told me up front that if we didn't give him a baseball contract right away he would work in the oil fields in Oildale making $90 a day. He was going to make a lot more money working in the oil fields than playing ball, but he wanted to give the game a try. Well, nobody with the Angels had seen him but me, and I was the new kid on the block.

So what happened was Walter Shannon said, "Well, you know, Gib, we're pretty deep in catchers and we'd hate to take him away from a job that pays $450 a week working in the oil fields." His mother was a secretary in the facility in Oildale. He wasn't a hardship case or anything.

But Loyd popped up and said, "I have to go right through Bakersfield in a week or two. I'll tell you what. I'll work him out and I betcha I'll see the same things Gib saw."

That made me feel about twenty feet tall because he didn't really know me. But he was a loner and I think it was his inclination to stick up for me. He could tell I was uncomfortable. He stood up for me with the pitcher Tehan and he went up to Bakersfield and worked this catcher out himself. He used to drive a sort of hatchback Toyota, and in the back he had balls and bats and all kinds of equipment he used to work kids out. He worked the kid out and that afternoon he called Walter Shannon and said, "Walter, let's make sure we draft this kid. He is a prospect. Gib was right on the money on him."

In my mind, at that moment Loyd Christopher gave me credibility. And I think nowhere in any of these issues does a scout look for more than that. It's one of the stages you go through. First of all, you're trying to impress someone enough to get the job. Then you get it. Then, basically, it's an "I wonder if they listen to me" stage. I've seen some guys where that stage is the lion's share of their existence. Then the next stage is, will you get somebody who's important in the pecking order to ask you, "What do you think about this guy?" And that's essentially when you've been accepted. Loyd treated me this way when I worked with him.

I got to know him well over the years. He stayed with the Angels most of his career. He is really one of the class characters and I developed great affection for him. Let's say you went to a high school or college game. He'd stand around and talk to the scouts, but the second his team went on the field to take infield, he'd say, "See you later, boys." He had a folding chair he liked to take and he went down the line away from everybody, and he'd sit there, watch the game and make his notes. And he did the same things at the pro parks.

When I went to work for the Dodgers I remember having Salt Lake as a team in the Pacific Coast League I scouted. I always looked forward to going there because Loyd had that area as part of his pro coverage. When I saw him there, we passed the time of day telling the old stories about our time together with the Angels. He was always very attentive. "How's your wife? How's the kids?" He knew my boys played football and he was warm and so genuine in his concerns. It reflected on the players that he got. You were never worried about any player he ever drafted and signed as far as makeup was concerned because the kids he drafted and signed reflected his makeup.

And that's interesting because he had a very warm feeling for Dennis Eckersley, a pitcher he drafted and signed when he worked for Cleveland. Although he's in the Hall of Fame now, he had some bumps along the way in his career with alcohol. And I think Loyd felt as much for Dennis Eckersley as those of us with the Dodgers felt about Bob Welch. We knew he was a good guy with a good heart with a lot of ability, but there was something he had difficulty controlling and it was alcohol.

When the dust settled in Anaheim, Al Kubski and I went over to Kansas City and I worked there into the 1979 season. Kansas City was an interesting experience. I was really fortunate because there, as with almost every place I worked, they were very much player oriented. They loved developing their own players. They had good scouts and they procured excellent players. When

I worked with them they had players like Willie Wilson and George Brett and Frank White. They did procure players in deals, but they had plenty to deal because they had a terrific farm system. Of course that enabled them to get players like Famous Amos Otis and John Mayberry.

I would have to say one of the most interesting guys that I ever worked with that I learned quite a bit from was the one and only Ross "Rosey" Gilhousen. I worked with Rosey when our scouting director was Johnny Schuerholz. Rosey is one of the first scouts, who started in the 1930. Probably the most famous player he ever signed was George Brett. When I worked with Rosey he was a little chubby guy who looked like a mature Winston Churchill but a little bit shorter.

He was not the easiest guy to work with, but behind all his feistiness and quirks, he knew a world of information and a lot of it helped me over the years. He would keep you on your toes and he was a kind of a cunning little character, but he was one of the all-time unforgettable characters in baseball.

After I worked with Rosey I used to run into him fairly regularly. He used to call me "Sarge" because he knew I had spent time in the service and had picked up a habit that was part and parcel to the era I grew up in. Let's say that you were driving a car and stopped to ask directions, and people might say, "Hey, Bud, how to you get to such-and-so?" But in the service "Bud" was replaced by "Sarge," and he started calling me Sarge even though I told him I didn't make sergeant until I was ready to muster out. But I had used that term from time to time.

One of the classic experiences I had with Rosey happened in Sarasota when we were there for meetings. Rosey was the hub of the wheel so we had to meet in his room. Rosey wasn't a big drinker but he did like martinis. So if you were having a glass of beer he'd say, "I'll have a martini with a twist." On this particular day he poured his little chubby body into a pair of walking shorts and was wearing big furry slippers, and he was reclining on a chaise lounge on the balcony of his room. So I was the first guy to get there and Rosey was lounging out there with those shorts and no shirt on — what a sight! Geez, I can still see it. He was kind of leaning back and had his martini resting on his stomach. It was comical but nobody dared laugh.

Rosey was a combination of a lot of things. I remember him asking me about a player, I can't recall who he was, and Rosey said, "Can he run?"

And I answered something like, "Well, he's a 4.2 runner," which, if he's a right-hand hitter, makes him a better than average runner.

And he says, "I didn't ask you for a running time, kid," and he got serious.

I said, "You asked me if he could run."

"I didn't ask you for the time. I asked you 'can he run?'" He said, "You don't need a blankety-blank stopwatch to tell if a guy can run. There are three types of runners: flyers, average runners, or base cloggers. I don't need a stop watch and you've been around athletics your whole life and you were a player, and you shouldn't have to tell me that. So, again, can he run?"

"Okay," I said, "he can run."

"Then the next question is, can he steal a base? Can he run?"

I remember one of the Dodgers scouts did exactly what I had done with Rosey years earlier, and Tommy Lasorda came back at him with, "I don't give a damn what his time is, can he run? Can he steal a base?"

Sometimes we've gotten so refined with the nomenclature and the rest that's part of scouting that we get carried away with the detail of it. That was Rosey and that was his tip to me as I learned more and more about scouting. Just keep it simple. Keep it simple.

Incidentally, there was no love lost between Joe Stephenson and Rosey. I think one of them beat the other one out of a player in the years prior to the draft. It seemed to me that they tolerated each other competitively, but they didn't have warm feelings toward each other.

In late August 1978, I signed a high school player by the name of Brad Wellman for Kansas City after his graduation in June. He enrolled in Chabot Junior College in California in September, then went to spring training the following February. He played shortstop-second base and got to the big leagues in 1982 after he was involved in a big multiplayer trade with the Giants in which he was sent to the Giants with Rennie Martin, Craig Chamberlain, and Atlee Hammaker in exchange for Bob Tufts and Vida Blue. It was one of those deals that worked well for both organizations. Anyway, Wellman made it to the big leagues with the Giants that year and went on to an eight-year career.

In 1979 I had been offered a contract by Kansas City scouting director John Schuerholz, but I hadn't signed it yet when I heard there was a job available with the Dodgers and one with the Philadelphia Phillies. I remembered a nice letter I had received in years past from Dallas Green giving me a lot of encouragement early on in my career when I was looking for a scouting job. So because of his encouragement I thought I would try the Phillies first and write a letter to Dallas. At that time I was living in Covina, California, and had been out walking my dog. When I got home my wife met me at the door and said, "The Dodgers called and want you to call them back."

I did call them back and they said they wanted to interview me for a job. They interviewed me and that's how I went to work there in October

1979. Just to give you an idea of how thrilled I was about it, I took the job without even knowing what it paid! I found out a day or two later. The irony of that whole thing was answering the question, "Why the Dodgers?" It was a no-brainer! Everybody wanted to work for the Dodgers and the O'Malleys.

The O'Malley Era

The O'Malley Era was a very special time in Dodgers history. It began in Ebbets Field in Brooklyn and continued through the westward movement of the Dodgers and Giants to California for the 1958 season and beyond.

By the time I got to the Dodgers I had scouted for ten years and had established myself as a scout who had a solid idea what a prospect was. At that point in time, the Dodgers were the O'Malleys and everybody wanted to work for them. It was a choice job and I worked under Peter O'Malley for nearly twenty years until he sold the club in 1998.

The O'Malley Era, a time when there were still some family-owned major league clubs, was a unique time for the Dodgers and for me. You could say it began in 1950 when Peter's father Walter O'Malley initially purchased controlling interest in the organization. By the time I started with them, Walter had recently died and his two children, Peter and his sister Terry Seidler, jointly owned one hundred percent of the club, and her husband Roland Seidler, a very successful investment banker, sat on the board of directors. But you rarely saw Terry at Dodger Stadium other than at games. She was a truly loyal fan and a terrific lady.

I think Peter had started out at the bottom working as a sort of intern for his dad and ultimately worked in the minor leagues as a general manager at Spokane and other minor league affiliates as he learned the ropes. He worked his way through the ranks and became well grounded in how the game was run, and ultimately became the chief operating officer and president. And he's a very intelligent guy, very well spoken, soft-spoken, and a classy individual. I will never forget the way I was treated there. And nobody I know who spent any time there at all has anything but the highest respect and admiration for him.

Walter O'Malley had set the tone and the foundation for the family's reputation in baseball. Early in the fifties he established a philosophy of stability through mutual employer-employee loyalty and respect that was maintained throughout his and Peter's tenures at the helm. Everyone who ever worked for the O'Malleys agreed that the association with the family was outstanding. They were great employers constantly concerned with the staff and their personal lives.

I remember at organizational meetings Peter O'Malley always said, "Remember, my door is always open. If you have anything that you want to discuss in any area with me, my door is always open and I will always make time for you."

There's no other way to put it. The O'Malleys were special. When I was hired our scouting director, Ben Wade, took me down to a room right outside the press room called Room 40, a place where a lot of the executives ate. Naturally I didn't know any of them, so Ben introduced me around to such guys as the farm director Bill Schweppe and others. Everybody was congenial, talking baseball, and in walked Peter. Ben introduced me to him and Peter sat down at our table. He was very cordial and you didn't feel intimidated. I probably should have been intimidated, but he made me feel very comfortable. Then he started talking to Ben.

At that time an old major league catcher and longtime Dodger scout, Bill Brenzel, had died up in the Northwest. He was a particular favorite of Peter O'Malley because he helped Peter when he had been the general manager at Spokane many years earlier. He said, "Ben, are you going to Bill Brenzel's service?"

Ben said, "No, Peter, I can't. Remember I have that appointment?"

Peter nodded. "I want you to cancel that. I would go myself but, as you know, I've spent a lot of time in Japan over the years and I have another trip scheduled and I simply cannot cancel at this late notice. But I want you to go up there and I want you to look up his widow and daughter. Her name is Pat Vercelli. Tell them not to worry about anything. Anything that comes up, anything they need, we'll take care of it."

And I thought to myself, "Are you kidding me?" It was something I'd never seen done before. Here's Peter O'Malley, owner of this huge organization, and he was very concerned for the family of an old timer he had known for quite a few years. Peter wanted Mrs. Brenzel and their daughter to be reassured that he would be there if she had any kind of problems. He was and still is so highly respected by everybody. I'll never forget that experience. Years later Pat Vercelli said that Peter apparently postponed his trip for a day or two because she remembered him at her dad's funeral.

They were terrific people to work for. After we won the 1981 World Series, Peter and his sister Terry Seidler took everybody who worked for the organization and their spouses to Hawaii for four or five days. To my knowledge he invited everybody on the payroll, everyone who worked at Dodger Stadium from the groundskeepers to the telephone operators, and everyone in the ticket department, the minor league people, the scouting department, and all the support people who run an organization. We had gorgeous rooms in one of the big hotels right on the beach at Waikiki. We paid for absolutely nothing. Everything was on the Dodgers: rooms, meals, the health club, the spa, the golf course. We just signed. It was extremely generous and we all enjoyed that. And, as I recall, they gave us a few hundred dollars apiece for incidentals. It was a terrific gesture and of course everybody had a wonderful time and appreciated it.

In 1988, the last time we won the Series, we were all taken to Rome. There were hundreds of people and their spouses. We spent five or six days in Rome and went on several tours while we were there and it was wonderful. I will never forget that because it was total consideration for the little guy, the working guy. To be honest, I don't remember any publicity whatsoever about either trip. It was a private gift from the O'Malleys to the Dodger personnel.

I remember when we were all gathered at Dodger Stadium and boarded

Jean and I on the boat going to see the Arizona Memorial in 1988 when the O'Malley family took all Dodgers employees to Hawaii to celebrate our World Series win.

buses to take us to the airport. The bus was almost full. At the last minute a car pulled up and Terry and a couple of her sons (she had ten children) got out. Manny Mota and his wife were sitting across the aisle from Jean and me at the front of the bus, and we got up to give her a seat. But she said, "No, no. You stay right where you are. I want to sit in the back of the bus because I know that's where all the action is in baseball." She always had fun and was absolutely terrific.

And another thing I remember is this. You do have situations that you experience over the years where you run into people who are highly placed in the game. Often if you're talking to somebody in your own organization, you are dropped immediately so the other person can be greeted. That's life. I don't expect to be dragged around to meet team owners or be introduced to the Commissioner of Baseball or whatever.

It couldn't have been more than three or four days after we won the World Series in 1988. In those days I was an area scout and had several minor league players who were local to Los Angeles and I was going to pick up equipment to have a workout with them at the stadium as I did frequently during the offseason with our visiting clubhouse manager, Jim Muhe, whom we all called "Beau James." After I gathered up what we needed I was walking upstairs on the club level and there came Peter O'Malley talking with John McHale, who was a real big-time powerhouse executive with Montreal at that time. He was walking in and involved in an animated conversation. I was walking right toward him and said, "Hi, Peter."

He said, "Hi, Gib, I want you to meet John McHale." So I shook hands with him. And Peter said, "Gib is one of our scouts. Judging by the big smile on your face, it was great winning, wasn't it, Gib?"

I said, "You can't beat it, Peter." He then asked McHale to go down to Room 40 and he'd meet him there soon, but he wanted to talk with me for a minute. Peter and I got into a conversation and, to be honest with you, I don't even remember what it was about. But just to be recognized at that point in time by Peter O'Malley meant a lot to me.

I've always thought what an unusual situation it was with the O'Malley family and the Dodgers compared to what we see quite often in the game now. Naturally I don't expect other organizations to operate like the O'Malleys because that's who they were and that's why we remember them as being so special. Back then, they thought of everything and every employee as "the Dodger Family." That's the way they wanted it. It was an ideal scenario.

When I worked for the Angels earlier we knew who Gene Autry was and people who were close to him told me he was a great guy. I have to go along with what they say, but you sure couldn't beat the O'Malley family.

To further illustrate the character of Peter O'Malley, I want to tell you the story about Danny Opperman. In 1987 we had the eighth overall pick in the draft, and Danny, out of Valley High School in Las Vegas, Nevada, was our first pick. It was the same high school that Greg Maddux attended. Greg was a senior when Danny was a freshman. I think Danny was the best pitching prospect that I ever scouted. But circumstances intervened and he never won a game in the major leagues.

He threw stuff as good as Greg Maddux and he had terrific command when he was a freshman. In fact, I don't believe he ever lost a game in high school and he pitched all four years. We had a lot of good reports on him. I was the area scout at that time and I thought, "There's no way this guy won't be a big winner in the big leagues."

He was a strike thrower. He was a good athlete and a good hitter, and he played third base when he didn't pitch. At any rate, he complained of some soreness in his elbow at the conclusion of the high school playoff game he pitched in his senior year, but his coach didn't take him out. Instead he moved him over to third base and brought in a relief pitcher.

I visited Danny at his home a week or two later and talked with his parents. We discussed his sore arm, which he said was doing fine. He got some medical data from a sports medicine guy he had been seeing in Las Vegas. Of course, he stopped pitching when the school year ended and he graduated, but he was scheduled to play some American Legion ball. He said he had been playing some catch and his arm felt good, but they didn't want to rush him back.

Anyway, before the draft I had him come into Los Angeles to be examined by Dr. Jobe, the man who invented and performed many Tommy John surgeries. Dr. Jobe gave him a clearance, saying he was sound as a dollar, and it would be okay for us to go ahead and pick him. I asked Dr. Jobe to call the ballpark and tell the scouting director Ben Wade what he told me and he did.

And Danny paid for his own plane ticket, as a matter of fact, and the reason for that was because he had a baseball scholarship to the University of Texas, and had been cautioned by the coach there to pay for his own ticket. That way, if he decided not to take baseball's offer, and baseball had paid for his ticket, that could invalidate his scholarship. So he paid for his own ticket and other expenses. We selected Danny in the first round in 1987, and there were some negotiation problems for awhile but eventually he got signed.

At that time the general public didn't know Danny Opperman from a bar of soap. He reported to our rookie club at Great Falls, Montana, and was going to make his professional debut on the road. But in the course of warming up for that game he blew out his elbow. Of course there was a huge negative story in the press, who said that our progressive and intelligent organization knew he was hurt, and yet we had just given him first round money, $160,000. The press asked, "How could they take a guy who had this happen in his first game in pro ball and now needs a Tommy John?"

He did have a Tommy John surgery on July 20, 1987. Then the press, out to prove something, started talking to scouts in other organizations. A few of them said, "Oh, yeah. We knew there was something wrong with his arm." And that was accepted. They said the Dodgers knew something was wrong with his arm. But they were all out in left field. Nobody knew there was anything wrong. All you have to do is ask the kid. Did anybody have him examined other than the Dodgers? No. Was he considered to be the best high school pitcher in the country? Yes. And so Peter said, "Well, we did everything that was correct."

Carl Loewenstine has scouted for the Dodgers since 1980.

I told Ben I thought I had an idea of how to handle all the negativity and he said I should pass my idea by Peter. I said, "First of all, they're lying, but we can't do anything but stick to the truth. Basically, what we should do is stress that we took him to the best arm man that there is. What else was there for us to do? We were reassured by Dr. Jobe."

I told this to Peter and I remember this so well. Peter listened without interruption and said he didn't like it.

"Why?" I asked him.

And O'Malley said, "I'll tell you why I don't like it. That's part and parcel of the game for another organization to say they knew something we didn't know. But as long as we took all the necessary precautions, that's good enough for me. And to stress that we just played off Dr. Jobe, I don't like it because basically what that makes it sound like is that he made a bad diagnosis, and as a result we went ahead from it and selected the kid based on the facts we had. So let's just drop it. If they want to keep writing stuff like that, let's stop trying to influence the press. We know we did the right thing and let's not get into a name calling thing." And the issue ended. And as I look back on it, I have to say, "You know what? That's about as classy a way to look at it as possible."

Incidentally, Danny never did pitch in the big leagues, but he did recover from the Tommy John and spent four years in the minor leagues. In his last game at AA he threw a one-hitter in the playoffs. After that he experienced arm trouble again and had a second Tommy John. But he never fully recovered,

Fernando Valenzuela. There was no one like him.

and although he spent a little time in two seasons with our AAA club in Albuquerque, he was never the same and still had pain in his arm. So he retired.

Peter's love of the Dodgers was not because he grew up in the organization. It was part of his terrific love for the game. He was instrumental in so many areas. He was constantly trying to develop baseball in foreign countries because he thought it would strengthen the game. He was some kind of a visionary. In the late eighties-early nineties, maybe a year or so after we won the World Series in 1988, we had an organizational meeting and he said the game was becoming so bloated and so overextended in terms of its financial situation that he didn't know how much longer he was going to be able to continue to own the club. In 1998 the O'Malley Era ended when Peter sold the Dodgers.

All the praise that has been heaped on them as employers was certainly justified. He was always cognizant of the value of scouting and his player development team. He recognized value in all the people in the organization and he let the department heads run their departments.

In those days the Dodgers gave one-year contracts, but two-year contracts were starting to creep into scouting in a few other organizations. However, none of us were ever concerned about it because of the stability of the Dodgers. The club had had two general managers over a forty-year period. They were Buzzi Bavasi and Al Campanis. They had two farm directors for about forty years, actually three, but it was essentially Al Campanis, who became general manager when Buzzi Bavasi went down to San Diego. Fresco Thompson was farm director, and when he died he was succeeded by Bill Schweppe. He was a wonderful farm director, and a terrific guy who had been with the Dodgers for many years. Most of the Dodger people had been with the club back in Brooklyn prior to the move to California. So there was a great history that encompassed the upper echelon people.

When I joined the Dodgers in 1979 they had a terrific scouting department. Scouts like Ed Roebuck, John Keenan, Dick Teed, Reggie Otero, John O'Neil, Tommy Mixon, Boyd Bartley, Gail Henley, Jim Garland, Ralph Avila, Tony John, Joe Campbell, Ron King, Dale McReynolds, Dick Hanlon, Lew Morton, Don Gutteridge, Guy Wellman, Dale Jones, Mike Brito, and Carl Loewenstine, an exceptional scout and very likeable man who would do anything for a fellow scout, came over from the Phillies in 1980 and is still with the club. I apologize if I may have missed a few others. All of them had been scouting from ten to thirty years at that time. Dennis Haren was there, but he had only been scouting a couple of years. As any good organization will tell you, there's no substitute for experience.

It was a colorful group intensely loyal to the Dodgers. Ed Roebuck, who became

Larry Sherry pitched in the big leagues and was a pitching coach with the Dodgers. We played a lot of golf over the years.

probably my best friend in the game; Ronnie King, who helped me get Dave Hansen and Mike Munoz; the irrepressible Reggie Otero, an old first baseman born in Cuba, who lived in Florida and always talked about himself in the third person. He'd say, "Reggie thinks," or "Reggie likes." And the one I remember most was "Reggie likes Tino," because in one draft he was plugging for Tino Martinez, who became a Mariner and then a member of the New York Yankees. He was a beauty. Sadly, Reggie passed away in 1988 when we were playing the Mets and

Don Gutteridge was in this game for seven decades as a successful player and scout. He was scouting for the Dodgers when I arrived.

ing the Mets and struggling like hell to beat them so we could get into the World Series to face Oakland, who was supposed to walk all over us. Reggie watched us win a game on TV, had his usual scotch and water, went to bed, and he didn't wake up. He was special.

I also worked with Dick Teed, who was a very fine scout for many years; Mike Brito, who brought us Fernando Valenzuela; Boyd Bartley, the scout who found Orel Hershiser. And there were Tony John and Joe Campbell, who both scouted in the South. They were terrific guys and good hard workers and good evaluators. Dale McReynolds, our Midwestern scout, discovered Bob Welch, Steve Howe, and many others; Gail Henley was a West Coast scout. Guy Wellman was a force in the Midwest, along with Johnny Keenan, who signed both Davy Lopes and Billy Russell. Tommy Mixon was a very good evaluator who had been a player in the Dodgers' minor league system. He had been a very fine college basketball player, although he was probably about five-eleven. At one point he was drafted by the Detroit Pistons in the NBA. These scouts were all very knowledgeable and I apologize if I omitted anyone.

Here's yet another testament to Peter O'Malley's class. In 1979 when I joined the Dodgers, the presence of Roy Campanella, affectionately known as "Poochie" by the Dodgers, was still very evident. He was certainly a great catcher, named MVP three times, and he was inducted into the Hall of Fame in 1969. But he had an automobile accident the year the Dodgers left New York, in which he suffered a broken neck that left him wheelchair-bound for the rest of his life. By the time I met him he was a happy man very involved in community activities. Peter O'Malley kept him with the Dodgers to work with young catchers at Vero Beach and offer thoughts and suggestions on how they could improve their game.

And there was also Ron Perranoski, who I knew when he was a couple of years behind me at our high school in Fair Lawn, New Jersey, before he went to Michigan State and then started his big league pitching career with the Dodgers. He started his career with the Dodgers as a minor league pitching instructor and then became the big league pitching coach when Red Adams retired. That left his minor league job open and the Dodgers hired Larry Sherry. Sherry, a fine major league pitcher and MVP in the 1959 World Series, became the minor league pitching coach. Larry was an intense competitor on and off the field, an excellent instructor, and a good friend. We played a lot of golf together.

Larry's older brother, Norm, was a catcher and at one time they were battery mates on the same team. It was said in jest that when the two had conferences on the mound, teammates could hear them revert to their older brother-younger brother days arguing about what to do in the game situation.

In 2012 a conglomerate that included Peter O'Malley, his sons Kevin and Brian, and his nephews Tom and Peter, purchased the San Diego Padres, and I wish them nothing but success.

The Life of a
National Cross Checker

There's probably nine hundred baseball scouts in the world who work for big league ballclubs. Baseball scouting is a highly specialized field. It's intriguing to a lot of people to think a guy makes his living judging some seventeen-year-old kid or predicting some twenty-year-old college kid could turn into a star or at least turn into a big leaguer.

I began as a part time scout in 1969 and covered an area. Scouts' areas are usually in the general geographic framework of where you live, or at least within a few hundred miles of home either way. And when you become a full time area scout, your responsibilities are greater and your area, of course, is increased, but still in a geographic proximity to where you live. I did that for close to twenty years. Then I became a regional cross checker which, for me, meant that I went to see the best players in the western United States, Arizona, California, Washington, Oregon, Idaho, and Hawaii at the invitations of our scouts in those areas.

Roughly twenty years ago I was promoted to a national cross checker. In that position I travel across the entire United States, including Hawaii and Puerto Rico, to see the best players recommended by area scouts. But you certainly don't see all the players, and there are occasions when you will see a player who isn't necessarily that highly recommended but may find his way to the preferential list that you use to dovetail into the national list that is put in for the national draft.

Because money always comes up when discussing jobs in professional baseball, let's get it out of the way here. The salaries of scouts in no way compare to those of major league players. Not even close. Some of the higher ranking scouts may make between ninety and a hundred-fifteen thousand a year, but the average is far less. On the face of it, if you're a working man, you may say, "Wow, you could pay me to do nothing but see ballgames!"

Well, I wish it were that simple. My first thought on that is this: if all you did was "nothing but see ballgames," you would not have a job as a scout for more than a fast minute.

There is so much more to it that people fail to recognize or consider. First of all, would you like to be away from your home and family four to five months a year? Would you like to drive maybe fifty thousand miles a year? Would you like to travel by air maybe a hundred and fifty or two hundred thousand miles a year? I don't think so. In most cases that becomes old hat. Scouts have a difficult existence in terms of family life. The divorce rate is high among scouts. Why? Because they're away from home so much. There are a lot of difficult details involved that people around us who live and work at home without travel don't encounter. Quite often you're not there when your kids are growing up, or when you're needed. It's a difficult lifestyle.

In addition to such obvious things as travel and schedules, there are so many elements of play a scout must observe and evaluate. In my case, let's just start when the ballgame ends. I saw a college game the other night that started at approximately seven o'clock and ended at approximately ten-thirty. College games have a tendency to run very long because college coaches want to control every segment of the game. After the game you exit the ballpark and drive home. So you get home around midnight, and to a certain extent you're pretty much wide awake, so you may sit down in front of the TV and kick back, maybe get yourself a soft drink or a glass of beer or something, and probably doze off within an hour. And then you wake up about three-thirty and finally go to bed and get up at six or six-thirty. When I'm in Southern California where my home is, I usually stay up late and get up early.

At any rate, the day starts early in the morning with breakfast, and you may read the paper and then go over your notes from the previous night. I like to write my own reports without reading the report of the scout who has recommended this player because I don't want to be influenced either for or against the player. When I write the player up, I refer to my notes, use the computer, and rate the player. Let's say that at this time in a season I have about fifty players that I have written reports on. So this player rates someplace in between one and fifty.

It's not really complex. You put a grade on the player and then you look at maybe three other players that have the same type of grade. They could be pitchers, infielders, outfielders, or catchers. And then you say to yourself, "Okay. I have four fifties." And looking at your list you see one particular guy that has a fifty on him that is higher than the other fifty on that list. Then you would take the player you just wrote up and ask yourself how he stacks up with these four players that score fifty. Well, let's say I like him better than the other four guys. So then I would rate him there. Does that sound confusing? It's just like rounds in the draft with number one being the best in the scout's eyes, and the closer to number one the player is rated, the better that scout thinks he is.

It's a matter of likes and dislikes. But you write your reports anyway and hopefully can stay ahead of yourself because it's really terribly tough to keep writing reports, especially when you're on a heavy traveling schedule. I write a lot of reports in airports, a lot of them. I write a lot of reports when I'm home, of course. And I don't do them late at night. I like to be as fresh as possible when I do this because it is so important to the young player to get it right.

When I am home my wife generally asks me, "Gib, what's your schedule today?"

And I might say, "I'm going to Riverside and see a high school game, and from there I'm going to San Diego to see a college game at night." So that means I'll drive about an hour and fifteen minutes to Riverside for the high school game that starts at three o'clock and probably ends at five. Then I'll drive to San Diego, which is about a two-hour drive, where I might see a college game in San Diego, and by the time that game finishes, it's probably between ten and eleven at night. And then I'll get into the car and drive another two hours home.

Professional baseball is pretty liberal in terms of travel accommodations and if I want to, I could stay in a hotel. But if I'm two hours from home, since I travel so much in different parts of the country, I would rather drive home.

It becomes more complex when you're in a different part of the country. For example, it becomes terribly complex when pitching rotations are prevalent. Let's say, for the sake of argument, you get on an airplane in California and you fly to Dallas, which is in north Texas, and then you rent a car to drive from Dallas to Oklahoma, let's say Enid, Oklahoma, or up to the University of Oklahoma in Norman. Then you go to a small town like Broken Arrow and see a high school pitcher, and quite often those are day games. But at any rate, your day is really very much full.

Please note I have not mentioned stopping to get breakfast, lunch, or dinner. Eating on the road is never easy. Fast food becomes a staple in your diet. Eating on the run is just the nature of the beast.

Now, it isn't that I would rather have spent my adult life working in an office or a factory or whatever. But I have spent over forty years scouting. I started when I was thirty-eight and turned eighty-one in 2013. I had coached probably twelve or fourteen years prior to that. So I have been in the game for a long time. There is a satisfaction in coaching and there's an exceptional satisfaction in scouting. It does require a certain expertise regarding evaluating players and projecting their future development that most people, even lifetime baseball fans, do not often understand.

Like every profession, scouting does have a negative side because all too often the issue comes up about how well organized you and the people you work with are. The perfect scenario is to have all your scouts using the same terms in their reports. That's how Bob Zuk wanted to train us thirty-five years ago. Ideally, everybody uses the same terms and there's mutual understanding. Now that's not splitting hairs, but it is difficult to decipher what a scout means when he says, "Boy, can this guy run."

As I noted before, we're talking about many stages of running. Probably the best way to analyze this would be to snap your fingers. The difference between a below average and an average runner is the snap of your fingers. And the difference between an above average runner and a flyer is a snap of your fingers. That's it. So the pace of the game is all-important at the highest level it's played.

And scouts must always be aware of the myths that exist in baseball. The first myth is related to a term used often in professional baseball: "If you hit, you play." The other comments along those lines are, "He's a good hitter, so we'll find a place for him to play."

Now the reality is this. At the highest level the game is played, you don't look awfully hard for a place for him to play. If he is not a good defender, or not at least adequate, people could say Player A has power, has maybe a twenty to twenty-five home run potential per year, and he will hit somewhere in the .280 range. That would make him a pretty good offensive player. Player B hits .260 and may hit ten home runs.

On the face of it, offensively, you say Player A has got to play. Not necessarily, because you're using a simple grammar-school grading system. If the position we're talking about here is catcher and A is considered a "D," meaning he has a below average arm, and Player B is an above average receiver with a plus arm that can shut a running game down, Player B plays over Player A. So the term "If he hits, he plays" is terribly overused and quite often is used at the lower levels of amateur baseball, high school and college baseball, where you have a scout who is trying to do the best job he can to sell this player.

There are all types of levels of defensive play, for sure, as there are all types of levels of offensive play. So the mere fact that one player out-hits the other must be tied closely to the position that we're talking about. One of the old terms that has been used over the years that I think does hold up over time is this. If you're going to have a good contending team at the highest level the game is played, you had better have good catching and very good pitching. To take it a step further, pitching can be subdivided into four solid starters, probably five, a good set-up man in the bullpen, and a good closer in the bullpen, probably accompanied by a good situational left-hand pitcher who can come in and bother left-hand hitters.

In addition, good catching is tied closely to having a good shortstop and a good second baseman and a good centerfielder. More often than not, solid teams in the major leagues that are contending teams have those prerequisites. They're solid up the middle. Sure, there are examples where that does not become an absolute. But there are no absolutes in baseball. So the theory that Player A may be one of the better hitters at the level he's playing, and hopefully has defensive ability, runs true because if these things are lacking he's going to have a very tough time becoming a regular in the big leagues.

There have been many examples of power hitters who don't hit consistently enough to stay in the lineup. Dave Kingman was one. He was called "King Kong" because of his power at the plate. But he was an inconsistent hitter and a poor defensive player. Ironically, he was signed as a pitcher and converted to the outfield because of his bat. Despite his power (he hit a total of 442 home runs), he bounced through seven teams in his sixteen year big league career. It's too bad because he was a good athlete, and many felt he simply did not apply himself to the defensive part of his game.

Usually young players have a tendency to want to spend the lion's share of their time doing what they do best. If they're considered good young hitters, they want to spend all their time hitting and rarely work on the part of the game that they have trouble with. And the same thing applies to the guy that's a good defender. You see him walking around prior to the game with a glove on his hand all the time. He does not want to work on becoming better swinging the bat, learning how to improve that aspect of his game, maybe choking up on the bat, or learning how to be an opposite field hitter or using the whole field.

In professional baseball you do not have someone leading you around by the hand saying, "Now, this is the kind of player you are. This is what you should do." It happens occasionally, but very rarely. Young players are left to their own devices, and I've always tried to encourage them by saying, "Look, do a study on yourself. Judge what kind of player you are and then try to cultivate that. What you are is what got you here. It attracted this scout or that scout who works for us and that's what got you drafted, not the fact that you may want to become someone else after you're drafted."

The other quick item that I think is a myth is when you hear a scout say, and I've heard this all my professional baseball life, "This guy will hit in the major leagues. I guarantee it." That is a misconception from day one. Usually scouts who make those kinds of statements are people who have never received decent training as a scout. "I guarantee you this guy will hit" is a misconception. Even if you see all the prerequisites that are necessary to become a good hitter, to hit well, good mechanics are necessary. Speed of the bat is even more necessary. An idea of the strike zone is highly necessary. And hand-eye coordination is essential. You put all those things together and you should have a good hitter.

Realistically, scouting does not allow a scout to spend two weeks with each player. That would limit him to seeing only ten or twelve players during the course of the year, and subdivide that by thirty teams that are involved in the draft, and he wouldn't get anything done. A scout has to have a trained eye and know what he's looking for. Just the fact that the youngster hits a ball over a tree on the other side of the football field does not mean he is going to have usable power.

"He will hit, I guarantee it," is an asinine thing to say, but I've heard it for over forty years. Along the path to stardom in the major leagues are players too numerous to count who had marginal ability in every phase of the game except one. At the level they played as youngsters they hit better than the other kids. Throughout my career I have worked with some very knowledge-able scouts. One of them was Eddie Roebuck, who was also a good big league relief pitcher.

He used to quote Kenny Myers, a longtime minor league player who once hit two grand slams in the same inning for Las Vegas against Ontario in the old Sunset League in 1947, and later was an outstanding longtime scout for the Dodgers and Angels. Eddie really admired him. One of Kenny's favorite comments about a youngster who played above the lion's share of guys he was playing with was, "None of them can play, but a few play better than the others do." That's probably a stretch.

But for every youngster I have seen who looks like he's going to be an encouraging major league hitter, I would say probably sixty percent fail. And there are several factors that make them fail. As the pitching they face gets better in the minor leagues, they struggle, which quite often results in them changing the things that got them noticed in the first place. And that creates a bigger problem because they can become totally confused when they run into hitting coaches who want to change their method of attacking the base-ball. Though hitting coaches are very well meaning, some of them have an unhappy tendency to want to restructure a player's swing, to change his mechanics. And that can be very dangerous for the youngster.

I've always subscribed to a comment that I think fits in this situation:

"If it works, don't fix it." If you think a player is going to struggle with a certain phase of his hitting, let him run into the wall first before you start correcting him. So to me the biggest myth is the comment, "He will hit. I guarantee it." There are so many phases of the game. Change is important for players, but drastic change can circumvent his development. .

And the same holds true for pitchers, with such things as deliveries, arm actions, angles, and the basic stuff the pitcher throws. I've seen it happen more often than I'd like to admit, and it's usually the result of a well-meaning instructor trying to give him additional weapons to make a position player or a pitcher more complete.

Patience is the key for everyone involved with young players from instructors to scouts, to coaches, and even general managers. It's highly important. If you are not patient you're almost doomed to fail because building a strong organization is done from the ground up. It's not just done by sitting back and saying, "I'm smarter than the balance of the other twenty-nine teams so I'm going to take players off their hands that they think can't play and I'm going to turn them into all-stars." That's a superficial and ignorant attitude to have. Your best approach in scouting, instructing, managing, coaching, or whatever, is to have a respect for the people you compete against. If you respect your opponents you have a much better chance to compete against them.

The best, smartest people I've ever been around have a great confidence level about what they do, but they never underestimate their opponents. Never. They promote their own players through the press and that type of thing, but they have a great respect for good ballplayers and good front-office people, and so forth, even in other organizations. And that's a good attitude to take in terms of not only procuring players, but seeing them develop to their maximum potential.

One of our scouts told me recently that he was recommending a player who didn't really work very hard but had potential because he had good mechanics to hit. And his defense was questionable also. My first comment was, "Why are you recommending this guy if he doesn't work hard?" Indifference by the player is important to note. If you get a young player who may have some skills but he's an indifferent player, you are flirting with big problems, basically because you know the nature of the game is built on "who fails the least." All players encounter failure and it doesn't make sense that an indifferent player at the amateur level, when he's unsuccessful, will deal well with that as a professional player.

The same scout, a hard worker with some ability, had mentioned to me earlier that he had seen a player, an outfielder from out of this area, who did not hustle to get a ball in when it was hit down in the left field corner. And he thought it was terrible. He was recommending a player in his area who didn't work hard, but was a good hitter at that level.

Simply put, that is inconsistent. And inconsistency in terms of playing the game is not really what scouts are looking for. They're looking for consistency out of players. And I look for consistency out of scouts. As a cross checker I have to be the devil's advocate. You might say, "I would handle this player differently." But this same scout, when I asked him if he observed the indifference of this player when he saw him play said, "Well, yes, sort of."

I said, "Did anybody else tell you the kid is an indifferent player? Because, after all, you're not around him all that much."

He said one of the coaches told him that.

It's All Part of Scouting

Scouting can be a lonely existence. You spend a lot of driving time, and it varies depending upon your job and your territory. Scouts who do national cross checking like I do have a lot of travel time, flying and driving. That schedule is demanding and can be difficult. The idea of an eight-hour day or a forty-hour week doesn't exist for baseball scouts. There is so much to do every day, every week, and every month that the scout must have excellent time management skills.

When I began I was running around California looking at players and faced the realization that quite often scouts don't get to see our own kids play their games. My sons both played the game, and my daughter was an active cheerleader and involved in academic events and school activities and stuff like that. Scouts often miss a lot of that stuff and it can be difficult on marriages. To my wife's credit, she knew I loved doing what I was doing and it never created a problem for us. But you do find that marriages in scouting often become shaky and don't last. I don't know what the proportion is in the country. Somebody told me somewhere along the line that about half the marriages end up dissolving into divorce. In my case, we were married in 1953, and we were both young kids, nineteen years old.

Along the way, as the years passed and my responsibilities increased, I learned more and more about scouting and the importance of good scouts to the success of an organization. Like any profession there are both positives and negatives. Without being too negative about it, baseball is such a pure game, but occasionally greed in the game is manifested by some very greedy people in it. That's a shame, but it does exist.

I am a member of the Society of American Baseball Research (SABR), which is comprised of baseball fans and researchers who gather information on any and every facet of the game and its history you can imagine and make it available to its members. One of their projects is to keep records on which scouts signed which players, and those involved work hard to be thorough and accurate. But I must acknowledge that I've had experiences in the game where credit on players is essentially stolen from the scout who should get the credit.

An interesting circumstance happened regarding one of the players I signed named Al Wiggins. When I worked for the Angels, they had hired a young pitcher we will call "Jack," a guy who went to Seton Hall, and I think he had been drafted a few years earlier. But he encountered arm problems and was released. He was a bright guy and very much interested in making baseball his career, maybe in the front office.

So the Angels made him the assistant to Tom Sommers, who ran the entire minor league program for several years. I was very fond of Tom and admired his work ethic and his knowledge.

Alan Wiggins had been drafted as the Angels first pick (8th overall) in the 1977 January draft. We had some workouts this particular year, and Wiggins was one of the kids I brought in for them. However, we couldn't get a wood bat light enough for him to swing. He had come out of a junior college where aluminum bats were used. He was six-feet-two and weighed about 160, and I think that was soaking wet! Jerry Remy came to his rescue. But that's another story.

Anyway, Jack threw some batting practice to some of these kids. Now, he was not involved in scouting and didn't have anything to do with the drafting of any of the players at all. I worked there another year, then went to Kansas City and ultimately joined the Dodgers in 1979.

Somewhere in the 1990s I ran into Jack in Salt Lake City. I was watching a Pacific Coast League game, and Jack had become sort of an entrepreneur. He was part owner of the Salt Lake City Club and was involved in other ventures. I didn't see him again until 2000, at a night game in Tucson, where he was working for the Tucson ball club in some kind of executive capacity.

It was, "Hey, Gib, how are ya, blah-blah-blah." We had a nice conversation and he asked me if I wanted a cup of coffee. We went up to the snack bar and were shooting the breeze and he said to me something like, "It seems just like yesterday we were together with the Angels."

I agreed. "Yeah, I know. Really, when you think about it, in baseball, time really does fly. And after you've been in the game quite a while you say to yourself, 'Gee whiz, where did the last fifteen years go?'" We were in agreement there. And I said, "I can still remember the workout when we ran Brian Harper. He was a catcher and such a competitive kid, but he wasn't a good runner at all, and he fell and everything. But he was no quitter. He kept saying to me, 'Hey, Coach, let me run again. I know I can beat those guys.' You had to admire the kid for it, you know."

Brian Harper, a Larry Himes draft, was determined like that. He was drafted by the Angels in the 4th round in 1977 and ended up getting to the big leagues, where he played in 1,001 games over a sixteen-year period, mostly in Minnesota, and was on a World Series team. These days he is a minor league manager in the Chicago Cubs organization.

But anyway, Jack then said, "I'll never forget the time that I first laid eyes on Alan Wiggins."

I'm thinking, "Now wait a minute," and I'm listening to this since I'm the guy that drafted Wiggins and had done the legwork and background work on him and everything.

I thought he was going to relate something about that workout. But instead he said, "I was off scouting him on a day when things were slow in the office. I went to this game and noticed this kid and the way he ran I just fell in love with him, and that's when I decided to draft him."

And I looked at him for a minute and this guy was deadly serious. Obviously what had happened was that I was the guy that had done the paperwork and scouted Alan Wiggins. So I said, "Where did you see Wiggins play?"

And he said, "Aw, I can't really remember."

I said, "Well, what part of town did you see him?"

Then I think he sensed there was something wrong, and he said, "Well, no, he wasn't from Anaheim, and I really can't remember." And he sort of stammered, "I think I saw him when his team was on the road and he was playing over in Los Angeles."

"Really, I'm curious where you first saw him play."

When he didn't respond, I calmly said, "Hay, Jack, now look. Alan Wiggins is not going to the Hall of Fame." In fact, when we had this conversation I believe Wiggs had died maybe four or five years earlier. But the kid did play seven years in the big leagues. I continued, "Jack, let's not dress up the story. You didn't have anything to do with Alan Wiggins, either scouting or signing him."

And he looked at me, a little flustered, and he said, "I know I saw him play somewhere."

"You may have seen him play someplace but it seems to me you would remember where you saw him play or what school he played for. Can you give me a town here he went to school?"

"Uh, well, you know, that was a long, long time ago."

I said, "Hey, Jack. If you're going to play that game, be careful who you repeat a story to, will you?"

I must acknowledge by this point I was annoyed because it wasn't the first time a guy tried to take credit for someone else's player, and it wasn't the last time, either.

He stumbled on this one basically because he had forgotten that I was involved with the kid. When he couldn't tell me where he first saw Wiggins or essentially anything about him, the jig was up. I'm not unique in this area, but anybody that has scouted any length of time and has drafted a player can tell you exactly where he first saw this player. It's just part and parcel of what happens.

Jack was terribly embarrassed when I didn't continue to question him but did say to him, "Be careful who you tell the story to." It's simple. Scouts who did sign the players in question can refute phony stories.

It's unfortunate, but there are scouts who do have a tendency to exaggerate their part in scouting, drafting, and signing players. There are some who are known essentially for that. That they have reaped the efforts of other scouts and then have gone around and told people, after a period of time, "Oh, yes, I was the guy who discovered Lyman Bostock, or I was the guy who discovered Bert Blyleven," when everybody knows it was Jess Flores.

Some of the worst at doing it are guys who have had success in their careers signing guys on their own. I could never understand why a guy would want to take credit for something he had just minimal amount of input on when he had achieved a certain status in the business for guys he had legitimately scouted and signed. I could never figure that out. But that has been done and it's still being done.

The first time I ever laid eyes on Alan Wiggins, he was playing for Muir High School in a day game against Pasadena High School. Incidentally, Muir was the high school Jackie Robinson attended. Wiggs played first base and hit sixth in the order. And the one thing he proved at that point was that he couldn't run. He could fly! He was a terrific runner. He didn't have any power, and he was just an adequate defensive guy. He played first base but obviously he didn't profile as a first baseman. He was not an exceptional hitter. The best thing he did was run. I saw him play summer ball and kept my eye on him.

At that time I was working for Montreal. But I was enticed to go work for the Angels when Walter Shannon was the director of scouting. He talked to me in the off season and said they had a job opening. He said they had heard about me to some extent, that I was a good worker and a good evaluator of players, and wanted to know if I'd be interested in working for them. I jumped at that chance.

My first draft with the Angels was the winter draft for junior college players, and Alan Wiggins was our first selection. Being picked in that draft meant the Angels had rights to him until just prior to the June draft of that year.

We worked him out and Al had a less than impressive workout. Once I drafted him I worked with him on the weekends, actually almost always on a Sunday. I picked him up at his house in Pasadena and drove over to the Veterans Administration Field in Sawtelle, which is now where UCLA plays. It has since been renamed Jackie Robinson Stadium. We went over there and worked out regularly as I tried to make a switch hitter out of him early. That process was slow because he was not really comfortable hitting left handed. But, to his credit, he stayed at it and worked hard.

One Sunday, Bob Clear, one of the Angels' major league coaches, saw me working with him at the field and got involved. What he said resonated quite well with Alan, who was a very intelligent kid, but he didn't communicate well. I spent a lot of time trying to make conversation with Wiggs, but he didn't trust people easily. I think he eventually got to the point where he trusted me. From there he sensed that if I trusted Bob Clear as a fine instructor and a strait-up honest guy, then he could trust him.

I remember when we were having a little skull session one Sunday in the middle of a workout and Bob said to him, "Do you know what kind of player you are?"

And the kid said, "Well, I think so."

And Clear said, "Let me review it with you. You're a great runner. I've been in the game for many years and I've never seen a kid in terms of quick acceleration in running the bases any quicker than you are. But you're not a good hitter. You don't have power, so switch hitting is your ticket. If you do that and if you learn to bunt, push bunt and drag, I'm going to tell you what you'll be able to do. Are you interested in finding out?"

Wiggs, who had been listening intently and noticed that I was as well, said, "Yes."

Clear continued, "On the strength of what you're able to do with the bat, you should be able hit two hundred."

Wiggs made a funny face and just looked at him with a funny look as if to say, "That won't work."

Bob was finally drawing him out and went on with his little talk. "Yeah, you should be able to hit .200."

"Two hundred?" Wiggs shook his head.

Clear said, "That's right. But if you can hit .200 you can run the other eighty points. And if you can hit .280, you can lead off for anybody."

And I think that really tweaked Wiggs' psyche because from that point on he did everything we told him. I used to constantly be after him to choke up on the bat and we finally got him working, from the mechanical standpoint, where he used his hands more while hitting. Wiggins was about six-foot-two and weighed about a hundred sixty pounds. He was slender with long legs. He didn't have the ideal physique for an infielder because his legs were so long and guys built like that had difficulty getting low enough to field ground balls. But as a major leaguer he played mostly second base and some left field.

But anyway, that got him going. And once we got him going and got him to the point where he felt comfortable hitting left handed, we worked with him that entire year. But he was not yet signed. So just prior to the June draft I went to Alan's home and met his mother. I still remember that quite well. His home was very small. He had a brother and a sister and I'll bet that house was not seven hundred square feet. It was probably the cleanest home I've ever been in. You could have eaten dinner off the floor. Alan was very conscious of his attire and was very neat in his appearance.

He was a very interesting kid. Very tough to get to, and it became obvious when I was in his home trying to sign him. His mother had some bad experiences with people who may have misled her in one situation or another and she did not trust easily. It was a tough negotiation. I signed Alan for twenty-five hundred dollars. I always had a special appreciation for Walter Shannon in any dealings I had with him, but especially in this signing. I eventually took Wiggins to the ballpark and had him work out a day or two before I actually had him signed. But he didn't really have a good workout at all. I think he was somewhat intimidated.

There were some big league players around. It was early and the big league players started showing up about three in the afternoon, and we were there at maybe one-thirty or two o'clock. Walter was there. Tom Sommers, who ran the minor league department, was there. Bob Clear was there, and Larry Himes, a scout for us who later became the general manager for the White Sox and the Cubs, was there.

We were all there and we were all paying special attention to Wiggins. He wasn't a physical kid. The bats were too heavy for him. And I'll always be thankful to the Angels' second baseman Jerry Remy, a little left hand hitter who was also a base stealer. He noticed the bats Wiggins was picking up were all too big for him and said, "Here, take one of these. I use the smallest bat on the club. It's nice and light." He gave Wiggins two bats and said, "If you break those, I'll get you another one." I think Wiggs hit two ground balls and with the second swing he broke the bat. But he continued and eventually started putting some balls in play.

I remember Walter Shannon saying to me, "Gib, you know, I know the kid's a great runner but I just don't think he's strong enough."

Bob Clear butted in and said, "Walter, we don't have anybody in the organization that can run like this kid. If Gib and I can help him put the ball in play enough, the way he can run, and he's making good progress learning to bunt, who knows? He maybe could hit .260 or .270."

Walter said, "I don't see it. Bob, but I'm going to trust you guys on this. After all, we're not investing Fort Knox in him." When he didn't make it to the big leagues with the Angels, he was released and picked up by the Dodgers. He was later procured from us by Jack McKeon and the San Diego Padres in 1981 after he had stolen 120 bases for the Lodi Dodgers in the California League in 1980. He was twenty-three at that time. Although I more or less kept track of his career, I didn't see him again until the late eighties. He had been traded to Baltimore and encountered some off-field problems and was suspended by the Orioles.

The first time I ever laid eyes on Todd Hollandsworth it was a cold, rainy night in the Seattle area. Our scout up there, Hank Jones, had found him and wanted me to cross check him.

I always had a lot of respect for Todd because he was a hard-nosed player. He was Hank Jones' player and I cross checked him. Hank is our scout in the Pacific Northwest and one of the best scouts in the country. He followed Todd closely and wanted me to see him, so I went to see him. I always call players like Todd "blue collar players" because he was a hard nosed, hard working kid.

Hank was talking to the coach, trying to get him to let Todd take a few swings in the cage because I was there, but the coach said he couldn't allow it because it was a league rule. So Todd was standing off to the side leaning on his bat and Hank said he didn't know what else he could do.

Todd was not to be denied. He came over there with one of his buddies with a batting tee. He planted the batting tee right in front of me, right where I'm standing. I'm standing about two feet in front of a chain link fence. And he says to the guy, "Okay, start feeding me." He must've swung the bat at least fifty times, saying to me, "If you want to see me swing, I'm going to let you see me swing."

Hank and I talked about him when we were driving back after the game. I never did see him get a base hit but I did see enough good swings out of him to see the potential. Todd was such a strong kid. He was one of those kids that didn't leave anything to the organization's imagination in terms of effort. There's a common thread in kids like that. Pete Rose was that way. Steve Sax had that. And when you see that, it jumps out at you. David Wright with the Mets today is another one of those players.

After he had been in the big leagues awhile I reminded him of that day and he said, "Honestly, Gib, did I really do that?" He was embarrassed. But he had grown up and matured. Aggressive kids aren't acting. It's who they are.

In 1991 Terry Reynolds took over as director of scouting when Ben Wade retired. The amazing situation with Todd Hollandsworth was that we did not have a first- or second-round pick that year. The way that whole thing turned out, Holly was the first player picked by us as our first pick, which was actually in the third round, and after a couple of years in the minor leagues he became the National League Rookie of the Year in 1996. That was quite an accomplishment for Terry Reynolds. The first player he picked in the draft became Rookie of the Year. Reynolds was with the Dodgers in several ranking capacities for over twenty-five years, then moved to Cincinnati in 2004 as scouting director and still works for them.

With Eric Karros my dealings were very pleasant. I liked him and had seen him play several times, although the lion's share of the scouting of Eric was done by Bob Bishop. But Bob had some difficulty trying to sign him. Then I was sent to close the deal and signed him. That took no great skill on my part. Apparently the Karros family had taken somewhat of an exception to a comment made by Bishop which was probably very innocent. I've known and worked with Bishop for many years, even before he worked for the Dodgers when he worked for the Mets. He's a baseball lifer who had been around the business for a long time, a hard worker, and a very good evaluator of players.

It's a wonderful story about Karros becoming an All-American simply because he was not recruited out of high school. He wasn't drafted out of high school. He wasn't recruited by the colleges. His family paid his way to attend UCLA, and he went out for the baseball team as a walk-on and immediately they noticed he had some ability, and by the time he was a junior he became an All-American.

But the way the whole thing developed, the Karros family didn't appreciate the fact that the Dodgers were not more impressed by his All-American status. That was essentially the negative there. I think once I explained it properly to them they understood Bob's statement better and the deal was completed. Eric went on to a fine career with the Dodgers for a dozen seasons and then spent the last two years with the Cubs and Athletics.

Most of the scouts I've known over the years and had decent working relationships with, and some are close friends, did not attempt to take credit when undeserved. They were always honorable. Guys like Eddie Roebuck and Joe Stephenson. You really don't replace them. They were ethical and intelligent scouts. Unfortunately there are scouts and scouting directors who claim undeserved credit. It's a damn shame.

Those are some of the negatives that do take place, and that's why it's very difficult for people within the framework of SABR to accurately determine who should get credit for signing this player or that player.

Back to Al Wiggins. I embarrassed Jack without really trying. I don't know how many stories he told about his involvement with Al Wiggins, but I would bet you money that Al Wiggins wouldn't have known Jack if they both got jammed into the same phone booth!

I did not actually sign Mike Piazza, but I was very involved in his signing a contract with the Dodgers. The scout who actually signed him was a wonderful scout named Dick Teed. He's a friend of mine who lived in the Northeast. He had scouted Piazza as a high school player.

Piazza was later scouted by Dodger scouts, among others, when he attended the University of Miami and Miami-Dade, which is a junior college. Mike first went to the university and then to the junior college. None of our scouts felt Mike was a prospect at that time, and I had not yet seen him. I got involved in the Piazza situation because of Ben Wade and Tommy Lasorda. Mike was selected in the 1988 draft as the last player we picked, player number sixty-two. During that draft Tommy Lasorda periodically would come into the draft room and asked Ben Wade, "Have you drafted him yet? Have you drafted him yet?" At that time I had absolutely no idea who he was talking about.

But I soon learned he was talking about Mike Piazza. And eventually we drafted the guy and, to be very honest about it, Ben waited until the last possible second to draft him. After all, we had picked sixty-one players ahead of him and he was number 1,390 overall in that entire draft.

The way the whole thing developed as far as I was concerned was this. Maybe two weeks after the draft process and after I had signed Eric Karros, I was called by Ben Wade to come take a look at Piazza, and I asked him to repeat the name. Then it came back to me when he said, "If you're wondering, he is Tommy Lasorda's nephew."

Well, I later found out that wasn't accurate at all. Tommy and Mike's father Vince Piazza had been close friends since they were young kids growing up in the same area in Pennsylvania. It's been said that Tommy is Mike's godfather, but I think he is actually godfather to one of Vince's other sons. When I went into the ballpark to see Mike I was not very encouraged or very pleased about it, to be honest, simply because I had been with the Dodgers about ten years at that time and it seemed like every time one of our scouts or one of our front-office people had a son who was playing high school or college baseball, it was always dumped on me to go see the player. And more often than not, if you were being honest about it, you would say, "I don't think the player is a prospect."

However, I did mention to my wife, "I hope Mike can do something because Tommy has been such a good guy to scouts. I would hate to have to tell him that I don't think he is a prospect." As a result, I went in and saw the hitting exhibition the kid put on during his workout at the stadium that consisted largely of batting practice, and it was one of the most impressive workouts I have ever seen. As I recall, Tommy was there and introduced me to Mike. Dodger scout Bobby Darwin and coach Mark Cresse were there and Joe Ferguson threw batting practice to him. He hit long line drives into the blue seats easily, one after another. Powerful. It was some kind of hitting exhibition. Ben went upstairs early because it was a terribly hot July day.

After the workout concluded I asked Tommy, "What position does he play?" And Tommy said first base. So he took some ground balls at first base and he was adequate. He was never going to offer competition to Keith Hernandez or any other fancy Dan first baseman. But then Tommy said that he also catches. So he put the gear on and we put him behind the plate and had one of the ball shaggers stand at the plate on the left hand side, and Mike caught a couple of pitches and threw to second base. His arm was okay. It didn't make the world forget Johnny Bench, but it was an average arm. But the main attraction with Piazza was his bat.

I went upstairs and talked to Ben Wade and he said, "Well, we haven't seen him in a game, and even though we saw him hit some balls hard, I want to see more of him."

At that point I think Wade was somewhat exasperated with me, and he said, "Well, what kind of money would you give the kid?"

"Twenty-five thousand."

Wade laughed. We had just signed Eric Karros as a sixth-round selection maybe ten days earlier or so, and Eric only got something like thirty-five thousand. And here was Piazza, number sixty-two.

At that point Ben looked up from his desk, and Bobby Darwin, an old major league pitcher-outfielder, was standing off on the side. But I have seen Bobby take batting practice in his fifties and hit balls in the seats. So Bobby knew something about power. So Wade said to Bobby, "What would you give him?"

And Bobby said, "I'd give him forty thousand."

That didn't go over with Ben. Then Tommy came upstairs and they got into a conversation about how to handle the situation. Ben suggested he had not seen the kid play in a game and he wanted to go back to Pennsylvania to see Mike in a game situation, at which point Lasorda said, "Look. You had Gib come in to see this guy, and we all know Gib is going to tell you what he sees, and he liked the kid. And Bobby liked the kid. And why not just go ahead and sign him?" Well, when push came to shove, Ben finally agreed to sign Mike Piazza.

Mike went back to Pennsylvania. And when the signing bonus was agreed upon, Dick Teed was sent to sign him. Dick signed Mike in the airport in Philadelphia. I had never seen Mike play in a game, but I saw this hitting exhibition that he put on at the stadium. And I think I had enough influence within the framework of the organization to get it done.

Subsequent to the workout at Dodger Stadium, I had a conversation with one of the Dodgers scouts who was kind of kidding me. He said, "I heard that you approved Lasorda's nephew."

I answered, "That kid put on the best hitting exhibition of any I have seen in many years. He has every prerequisite to be a good hitter. He's got a lightning-quick bat, and the ball just jumped off his bat. Those things are not teachable. When you see it, it's there. You don't need a lot of mumbo-jumbo to see that. And I knew what I saw."

There was no question that scout was not pulling for the kid or the guy who recommended we sign him. "Well, that being the case," he said, "we'll see how he works out."

Mike struggled some in the minor leagues. He didn't get an opportunity to play as much as he thought he would. He even jumped a club at one point and went home because he was so disenchanted with the situation. Tommy had to call him up and get him back. He told him, "Look, when things get tough, you don't pout and go home."

But once he got on the field and got established, he became what he was, probably the best hitting catcher for power, and possibly for average, in the game. He was never considered a great defender, but adequate. It's a funny thing when you start analyzing situations and how this or that happened and so forth.

When you cross check, though, you're in a different realm, in a different venue than a regular area scout. Do you have more so-called juice? Yes. Why do you have more juice? Well, if you're a national guy like I am you supposedly see the best players in the country. Yet there are still players who got away. For example, one of those was when we failed to sign Chase Utley. And along those same lines, Phil Nevin, too.

But those are two guys that we drafted and offered a lot of money to them, but they didn't sign with us. In the case especially of Utley, we fumbled the ball there. When we drafted Chase, we took him as a high school player in round two and offered him plenty of money. He did agree to terms, and then instead of getting it done he made a determination he was going to go on a senior trip, a graduation situation, and when he came back he had changed his mind and went on to UCLA. He was later drafted in the first round by Philadelphia, and Nevin was the first round pick of Houston in

1992 out of Cal State Fullerton. Chase Utley is still playing and Phil Nevin is retired — both exceptional players.

The point to this is that if you don't get them, you don't get them. It's that simple. Somebody else gets them and you can't take credit for this guy or that guy if you didn't get him in the draft. You have to give credit where credit is due. But you can't help but say, "Gee, that's the guy that got away."

Frankly, you have to deal with the players you select, good, bad, or indifferent. If you make too many selections of indifferent players all the rhetoric and the braggadocio that you may develop about ordinary players, even if they make it to the big leagues, just doesn't get the job done. It's just that plain and simple.

Al Campanis, a wonderful baseball man and the Dodgers' general manager from 1968 to 1987, used the word "self-aggrandizement," and used to say, "Don't become a victim of patting yourself on the back. There's enough of that going around in the business as I see it. If you're going to be respected by people in the business, the best way is to get it done."

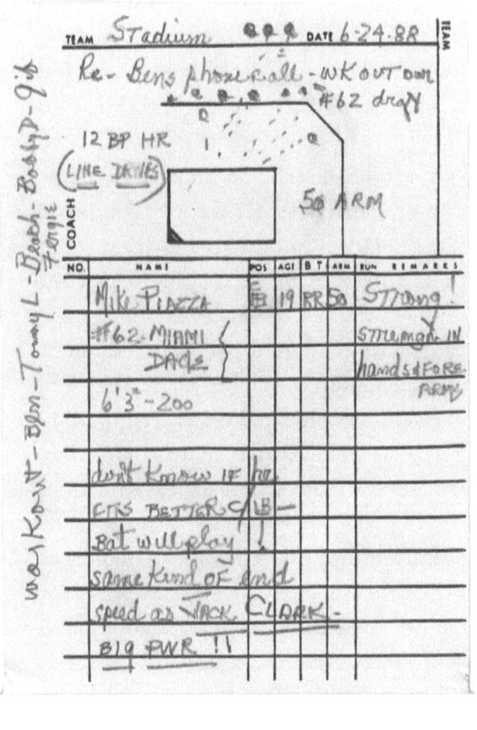

I've had the good fortune to work under some highly successful general managers. I worked for Harry Dalton at one point. I worked for John Schuerholz at Kansas City before John ever became a general manager. Obviously he's one of the best GMs that had come down the pike in terms of modern baseball. Look at John Schuerholz's record as a GM first at Kansas City and then with the Braves. It is without equal. During his tenure as GM they won fourteen consecutive division championships. That's terrific. They constantly replenished their players they lost for one reason and another, had a great farm system, and John was excellent.

As far as with the Dodgers,

Mike Piazza's scouting report I made the day I worked him out at Dodger Stadium in 1988 before we drafted him.

I would have to say Al Campanis was second to none. Terrific general manager and had a terrific wealth of knowledge about the entire game. There isn't any question about that. When I worked for the Angels, the scouting director was Walter Shannon. The scouting director with the Dodgers who hired me was Ben Wade. Ben was set in his ways, but he was very fair with me over the course of the years I worked for him, from 1979 until he retired in 1990 and was replaced by Terry Reynolds. But no matter who is the scouting director, scouts at every level go about their regimen of finding players and making reports.

You pick up bits and pieces in this business and knowledge from knowledgeable people who are in it. The best attitude to take is that you never stop learning. There are big responsibilities that go with it. All clubs want production. They don't want you to say "nobody can play." And from my experience the best scouts that I have worked with and competed with are very good evaluators. Secondly they are very logical guys. They don't complicate a simple issue. They have certain criteria they look for in players, true. But they do not go overboard in judging talent.

One example is when a scout says a player has great makeup. But how did he determine that? You ask, "Did you meet him? Did you talk with him?"

"Yeah."

"Now don't color the situation. How much time did you spend talking with him?"

"Well, two hours."

"Then why are you so convinced he's got great makeup?"

"Well, he's very polite and he has a good haircut, and I've seen him compete and he competes real well."

That's probably an oversimplification. Just because a kid says "sir" and is polite and maybe dominates the competition level he's in doesn't mean he's got great makeup. The makeup of the player is all-important and one of the most difficult elements to evaluate.

Most of the kids organizations deal with and draft are successful kid players at high school, junior college or college. But because they handle success okay at that level does not necessarily mean they are great competitors. You find out what kind of a competitor you're dealing with when he fails. When he struggles, that's when you find out. And of course when we're scouting them, they're far better than the people they're competing with.

I had an experience at a meeting where we had hired a guy who was going to work as a roving coach. He had been a coach at a small college and was asked by Al Campanis to give some background as to how he went about recruiting players for his program. His answer was interesting. He said, "Well,

I wait until the kid I'm interested in starts competing against prospects and then I go see him against the prospects."

Now that may sound good to a casual fan, but what if he never competes against a prospect? And quite often many of them never do as amateurs. Those of us in scouting who listened to his reply didn't buy it any more than Al Campanis bought it. And why didn't Campanis buy it? He had been a scout. He had been there before and he knew very well that you have to be able to scout players who play against non-prospects. Ideally, sure, it's wonderful if the best hitter in your area faces the best pitcher, but quite often they never do. And vice versa.

I don't have any animosity toward any of those guys who may have achieved some success because they're very good at promoting themselves. That's certainly not novel in the game of baseball. That can be the case in almost any walk of life. There are people who don't really get a lot done, but they take bits and pieces of what others have done and form a career based on taking credit. That's just part of things you learn in the game.

The key is to make as many good bets as you can make, and when you do that you do have success. But when you become scattered in your judgments or start making judgments on your gut feeling and so forth, you can encounter problems. Sure, gut feelings are important. But if you're going to spend hundreds of thousands of dollars or millions of dollars, you want to be able to tie into something tangible. What can he do? Can he play? The expression used many years ago by scouts, "Can he play?" is the all-encompassing question. This means can he throw? Can he run? Can he hit? Can he hit with power? Can he pitch? Does he have a good arm? Does he have good stuff? Does he have a good delivery? Does he compete? Is he a tough guy? Is he resilient? Is he a pouter? And you can go on and on and on with it to try to come up with a judgment.

This recently came up in a meeting. One of the veteran guys who had been around the game a long time and had a lot of success said he didn't understand the necessity for cross checking. He thought it was ridiculous. After all, he had signed a lot of good players over the years, and why should he have to have his players cross checked, scrutinized by another scout? "It's ridiculous," he said, "all anybody had to do was look at my record."

Well, on the face of it, that's fine and dandy to say that. But I don't want to eliminate a player who is recommended by a scout who doesn't have as long a list of signing frontline players. That in itself is defeating the purpose. So what that scout is implying is, "Everything is okay if you pick my players." But what about some guy across the country who has only been a scout for a few years and the player he writes up has better tools, size, strength, athleticism and so on than the veteran scout's player?

So what do you say about that? Do you stick with the veteran guy because he is a veteran? No. You have to go with what you see. Personalities enter into it, of course, and as long as the human condition exists, there are scouts that you like better than others but you don't want to short change your organization because maybe the player is recommended by a scout who is less than a hard worker. If he's less than a hard worker, you hope the organization doesn't keep him. More than likely he works just hard enough and is a premium exaggerator.

Good area scouts are critically important, and if you ignore that and do what we call "flash scouting," that's dangerous. There are people who have gotten into scouting over the years and will see a player not very favorably and just out him. "I don't like the way this guy does this or that." It's a negative business to a degree anyway because so few are capable of playing major league baseball. But there are those who act as if their judgment is absolutely infallible.

On another front, there were things that happened that still put a smile on my face. Some twenty years ago I was in Arizona watching some Fall League baseball and I was staying at a hotel where a lot of the instructors and coaches stayed. I was having breakfast with Johnny Keenan, one of the Dodgers' older scouts, a very fine scout who signed Davey Lopes and Billy Russell, to name just two of the many players he found and signed. So we were having breakfast and ran into a couple of the instructors that we knew. In those days the players would dress in uniform at the hotel rather than at the ballpark. Of course, today the park facilities have sufficient locker rooms.

A little bit later, in comes a guy in uniform, between thirty-five and forty, and he had his name on the back of his uniform. But I didn't recognize the name. I asked Johnny who he was, and he didn't know either.

Then we went to see an instructional league game. That year the Dodgers had drafted a young pitcher and given him a lot of money. But the young pitcher had really struggled with his command. His stuff was fine but he couldn't find the strike zone. As a result he was constantly behind in the count, walked a lot of people, and hitters started hitting him all over the ballpark.

We were out there watching a game and this kid was in the dugout when, lo and behold, in the third inning they sent him down to the bullpen to get loose. He was going to pitch. And sprinting after this pitcher was the guy we saw at breakfast. I thought he was a new pitching coach. A few minutes later I saw Johnny Podres, who's an old Dodger pitcher, and I said, "Hey, Johnny, did you guys hire a new minor league pitching coach?"

He says, "No, no. That guy is a shrink, Gib."

"Oh. Does he always run around like that?"

"He's down here for that kid and he doesn't let him out of his sight. He's going to psychoanalyze him and have him throwing strikes before we leave here. At least that's what he said at the meeting the other day."

So the kid runs out of the bullpen to the mound and throws the ball over the plate and actually gets some hitters out. But the hitters quickly adjusted and knocked him around before he left the game after just an inning and two-thirds. They sent him back to the bullpen to get some work on the side.

Across the diamond darts this guy that we've now determined is the psychologist. He darts down to the bullpen where Podres is working with the kid, and Johnny Keenan and I edged closer to the pen to get a better idea of what's going on. Podres is working with this kid's delivery a little bit to try to iron out a flaw that he saw. He did it once, and all of a sudden the psychologist is saying things like, "Think of your favorite color."

Johnny Podres contributed to the Dodgers and laughed at my jokes.

Geez, I still find this funny. The kid was looking at him thinking about colors, or not, and Podres was shaking his head. This went on for a few more minutes and Podres didn't say any more to him. The kid finally got his work in and went in to shower. Bingo! Off goes the psychologist chasing the kid again. I can't really recall the sequence of events, but the funny part of it was that I ran into Terry Reynolds was the assistant scouting director appointed right after Ben Wade retired in the early 1990s. At any rate I said to Terry, "Did you hire this psychologist?"

"No. that was a collective thing. He came highly recommended."

John Keenan wanted to know about the guy's background.

Reynolds said he was a highly sought-after psychologist in the west.

"I know the kid's struggling to throw strikes," I said, "but what is this thing about think of your favorite color? Is that supposed to help him throw strikes? And watching the way he darts all over the place, does he have any background in sports?"

A couple of days later I ran into Terry again and he told me the guy is the lead psychologist hired by Continental or American Airlines or one of those.

So I said, "Okay, one more question. When he works for the airlines, does he dress up like a pilot?"

It seemed funny to me. I could just see that guy and I could see Reynolds' face as he led me into that. And Johnny Keenan was drinking a cup of coffee during this and he laughed so hard he spilled his coffee all over his brand-new boots! We had a good laugh over it. Keenan went into the bullpen to tell Podres what happened, and I thought Podres was going to expire laughing in the bullpen.

We did have a lot of fun with that, and that story bounced around for a long time. We don't know if it got back to the psychologist or not. And we never heard whether or not he helped the young pitcher. But I know one thing. He was a very unusual fellow and he was in love with that Dodger uniform.

A similar thing happened with Atlanta's great pitcher, John Smoltz, who was drafted by Detroit in 1985. While still in the minor leagues he was traded to Atlanta for Doyle Alexander and went on to a Hall of Fame career with them. At any rate, I remember later when he was pitching a wonderful game in one of the playoffs, someone commented, "You know, John Smoltz had a terrible problem throwing strikes early in his career, which is why the Tigers gave up on him and traded him. But when he had trouble throwing strikes he had a sports psychologist who really helped him."

I'd never try to embarrass anybody. But there's a side to my sense of humor that some people don't get, and I always had some fun putting guys on. Terry Reynolds, a very nice guy and a loyal company man, was appointed director of scouting, but he had never scouted before. He was bright and he had been assistant general manager at Vero Beach. He was young and worked very hard. My attitude was, "I have to help the guy as much as I can," which I did. He knew of me because I had been there a long time, but he really didn't know me very well. But as time passed we laughed about that several times. He was a very pleasant guy and I had a good relationship with him.

Moneyball and Swiss Cheese
Both Full of Holes

With all the attention paid to the book and movie called *Moneyball*, as a longtime scout I feel compelled to respond, first to the so-called scouting theory it presents, and second to the way both the book and film fictionalized things to a great degree. Granted, some of it is based on facts, but only some.

The author, Michael Lewis, has not only insulted the scouting profession, but also many respected baseball people who were involved to one degree or another. The focus of all the hoopla was the Oakland Athletics and a new scouting concept they developed as their response to the high price of players and ever-increasing payrolls. They thought they found the answer to how a team could be competitive through the use of statistical data as a method of scouting and player recruitment.

And while the book was on the bestseller list there were almost no critics of it, except from the baseball world. The established scouting world said, "You know what? This book is a bunch of bullshit! It's a self-serving thing written by a guy who knows very little about the inner workings of an organization." And I was one of those people who said it.

I said it then and I say it now. If Lewis wanted to get a real cross-section of how an organization works, he should have gone to an organization that was terribly successful, like the Atlanta Braves. What did they do? They won 14 division championships in a row. They were terrific. Go talk to a guy like Paul Snyder, who was a marvelous director of scouting, or Johnny Schuerholz, who was the outstanding general manager over there who got his feet wet with the Kansas City Royals. I'm not saying anything more than that.

There was a piece in *The Sporting News* called something like "What Is Moneyball Anyway?" They go on to quote guys like former Dodgers and Expos GM Kevin Malone, who has not been in baseball in ten years. They quoted Bill James, a senior advisor of baseball operations, who is an author and a statistician. And then they quote a longtime National League scout, but they don't tell you who it is. I've always been hesitant about saying things, then adding, "But I don't want you to use my name." Maybe that's the advantage of writing a book, huh? It will definitely allow me to say what I see as truth and put my name right out there.

Frankly, I read the book out of curiosity. I had low expectations and was not disappointed. With that being said, I don't have a bit of objection, and I'm certainly not trying to set myself up as an expert who's going to evaluate the theories presented and tell you where they are weak and where they are not, or where they hold some substance and where they do not.

Moneyball was the catchy title Lewis selected for his work, but that word is not the name of the new scouting concept that appeared in Oakland in 2000 when they and Tampa Bay had the smallest payrolls in the game. Theoretically, Beane and his number-one assistant, Paul DePodesta, "invented" a statistical theory of scouting that they felt would get them the best lower-priced players rather than "overpay" for high-priced players. They had come up with a formula that was a combination of slugging average and on-base percentage, which they thought would determine the value of a player offensively.

They did not go into much detail at all about pitching, even though they had a very fine pitching staff which had not been assembled by Billy Beane, but largely by Sandy Alderson some two years earlier that included Mark Mulder, Barry Zito and Tim Hudson. It goes right to one of the first things I think I learned as a scout. Good pitching defeats good hitting. It doesn't matter whether you are in the 2012 playoffs or World Series, or whether you're talking about 1951 or 1931. That is a concept that holds up. Good pitching defeats good hitting. Mulder, Zito, and Hudson were among the finest in the game at that time.

I am compelled to give attention to the so-called scouting theory they espoused and point out how both book and film fictionalized things to a great degree. Lewis not only insulted the scouting profession, but also many respected baseball people.

If an organization goes by Beane's theory of statistical scouting, it would not need scouts to see players and evaluate their playing skills on the field in game situations. It makes no sense because good scouting has been around as long as baseball. It doesn't matter whether you are talking about the American or National League.

Essentially when you're talking about good scouting, you're talking about a very good scouting director, his very good cross checkers and, most importantly, good area scouts. If an organization doesn't have a combination of all three, or you just have one of the three, you are doomed to mediocrity. Over the years I've worked with good organizations, and I've been with the Dodgers since 1979. We've had good times, mediocre times, and bad times collectively during those years. We've won two world championships in the last thirty years and hopefully we may win another one before I retire.

In my opinion, what they said in *Moneyball* was, "This is how we can become terribly competitive because we know how to corral undervalued players and not pursue overvalued players."

I don't know Billy Beane, but I do know Paul DePodesta, who later became the general manager of the Dodgers. And I like Paul very much. He's a fine guy who strongly believes in his concept of evaluating players.

The bottom line in major league baseball is winning. The thrust of what you do in scouting and what you try to accomplish through the draft is to pick players who have a chance to get to the major leagues, prior to drafting them and redefining them while they are in the minor leagues. For players who have major league possibilities, scouts must be able to project the kind of player he is going to be up there. Is he going to be a fringe player? Is he going to be a mediocre player? Is he going to be an above average player? Is he going to be a star? There are very few stars, and there are quite a few average players.

Can a team that is generously peppered with average players win? Certainly. It's how they mesh together and whether the key players on a team are legitimate front line players. There have been many concepts espoused by managers and coaches over the years saying they knew exactly what to do and how to put a special team together.

But in this book, Billy Beane essentially defined about ninety percent of scouts as a bunch of middle aged mediocre guys who run around spitting tobacco juice in a cup, who are living in the past looking at players trying to discover the next Willie Mays or Mickey Mantle. And it amazed me later that they were sending emails out to scouts asking them to come down and try to get into the film. I couldn't get over it! I thought, "My God, here's a book with a basic premise that scouts are not very bright. In fact, that they are pretty dumb. And the people they work for are dumb. And the people that own the clubs are basically dumb." Isn't it a shame that they're not as smart as the people in Oakland?

The lion's share of competition that Oakland had during that period is portrayed as being a bunch of slow-thinking and not particularly bright guys. That hasn't been my experience at all. During my four-plus decades in baseball I have met some extremely smart individuals. I'm not representing myself as a spokesman for the scouting world. I'm just representing myself as a guy who has been in this business a long time, and peers of mine, whether they work in the Dodgers organization or elsewhere, are often smart individuals, not dense, as they are portrayed there.

The amateur scout is the guy who goes to see players and writes reports on players and recommends that they be drafted; the pro scout covers professional leagues and recommends whether players should be acquired in a deal or passed over. Obviously everybody in the business of scouting hopes that he can come up with players who will be good major leaguers.

The poster boy for Beane's new concept was a catcher from the University of Alabama by the name of Jeremy Brown, who was drafted as their number-one pick in 2002. But he didn't turn out to be a front-line major leaguer. This is in no way an attempt to defame or embarrass him. Instead, it's just an attempt to keep the record straight. After struggling at every level he played in the minor leagues, Brown was promoted to Oakland's big league club in 2006, where he appeared in just five major league games and that was it. His career came and went rapidly.

But in fairness to the Oakland people, there's nothing terribly negative about that. Every organization has been through that. You have great plans for the top player and he just never achieved what you projected. Apparently Oakland had looked at Brown's statistical data and they were convinced he was going to hit his way into the major leagues and ultimately become their everyday catcher.

I didn't cross check Brown, so that meant he was not one of the so-called "premier" kids in the eyes of Dodger scouts. Oakland took him and Michael Lewis was enamored with his selection: "What a great pick!" Brown became the so-called face of the entire draft for Oakland. He was the first guy they picked, and of course they tried to push him.

Our scouts at the time thought he was a fringe prospect, but did not feel that he had a chance to become an everyday player in the major leagues, at least not as a catcher. There was a place for him in the draft, and some of our scouts thought that he was a seventh- or eighth-round type pick. We would have tried to make a first baseman out of him. But that was the extent of it.

Now I certainly have no axe to grind or no animosity for Jeremy Brown. I've never pulled against a kid in my life in terms of his development. You like to see young players come along and do well. That's what the game is all about if you are a scout.

But it was simple. He couldn't catch. He couldn't throw. Now, it you can't catch and you can't throw and you are a catcher, you can't play in the major leagues. The concept of "if you hit, you play" goes out the window when you have to sit behind the plate and receive every pitch that quality pitchers throw. They don't want a catcher who can't "hold 'em," to use an old baseball expression. Can he hold good stuff? Well, Brown had lost a lot of pitches, had trouble framing pitches, and he just couldn't catch, couldn't throw, and couldn't play. But all that had not been determined when he was drafted by Oakland as a college player. The concept was that he would become a special player. Well, he never did.

The concept Billy Beane presented doesn't make a lot of sense because it presupposes that scouts are essentially so dumb that they don't look at statistics. Deep statistical analysis goes right by them. And as a result they are going to miss players.

The thought that scouts don't look at statistical data is a misconception. Any scout who covers junior college and college baseball is furnished with all kinds of statistical data from the sports information people at a given school, whether the player goes to Auburn, USC, Washington, or the University of Maine. All that stuff is available and we do look at it. But we do not rely solely on it. Simply put, there is no substitute for watching the actual playing of the game and observing first-hand how the player reacts in game situations. There's just no question about that.

Can scouts be wrong? You bet! But the cornerstone of any good organization is good scouting: how you go about it and what you do. And in my opinion the concepts in *Moneyball* are as flawed as scouting can be.

Statistical analysis at the amateur level, essentially high school and college baseball, should be and is reviewed to a certain extent, but certainly not to a great extent. If you're talking about a position player, there is no statistical formula which tells you whether the individual has instincts to play or whether he's really athletic. It does not do that. It just tells you his batting average, extra base total, his slugging average, and so forth. And it omits a very important element: who has he achieved these statistics against? In other words, ninety-nine percent of the kids he achieved these statistics against are not prospects. By that I mean, has he gotten a base hit off anybody who is a prospect yet? Or if he's a pitcher, has he faced a hitter who is a prospect?

I heard an individual one time trying to rationalize this. When asked the question, "When you were a college coach, how did you recruit?"

I'm reminded of this. Let's say Yovani Gallardo is going to pitch for Milwaukee against the Diamondbacks in a playoff game to determine who goes off and plays at the next level. I scouted Gallardo, who was recommended by a scout of ours named Mike Leuzinger, and this is the only time this has ever happened to me in the forty-plus years I've scouted. I saw Gallardo pitch and he struck out everybody he faced in the game.

Now was the competition level good? Not really. But what came out of his hand was exceptional. He had a good fastball, probably 90–93; a hard curve that had a hard, tight spin to it; he had a loose arm, he had a good delivery; he was athletic; he repeated his delivery. He competed well and was a very good looking prospect. I have absolutely no idea what his ERA was the year I went to see him, but more than likely wasn't high. But it had nothing to do with what he was. You did not have to look at any statistics to make a determination. He was a front line prospect. And that is what he has turned out to be.

Statistical data on young free agent high school and college players can be terribly misleading. To a lesser degree, it can be at the professional level as well. However, what happened is Michael Lewis became totally enamored with what had been discovered by Billy Beane and company: their new formula. In his mind it was right there neck-and-neck with Jonas Salk's discovery of the polio vaccine. This discovery had been made in baseball, which can be a terribly closed fraternity where you do not ever tell your competition what you're trying to do whether it's on the field or at the front office level in terms of scouting. You never do that.

One of the most distasteful parts of the film and book were the attacks on Art Howe, the manager of Oakland at the time, whom they portrayed as a somewhat dumb individual who had to be told where to stand in the dugout to give the impression that he had leadership qualities. My comments are not intended to attack the book or the movie because they were unkind to Art Howe. It's basically an attempt to keep the record straight. It takes a certain amount of arrogance to say you would have to take a baseball guy like Art Howe, who had played eleven major league seasons and had spent a dozen years as a major league manager to that point, and tell him where to stand in the dugout.

I did run into Art Howe long before *Moneyball* was ever heard of, probably twelve or fourteen years ago in Las Vegas after the death of Jim Muhe, who had known Art quite well when Art played in Pittsburgh and then Houston. I was in Vegas scouting the Albuquerque Isotopes, our AAA club in the Pacific Coast League, and apparently there was an off day or something at the major league level. Howe was managing Oakland at that time, and he was in Vegas with Sandy Alderson, possibly looking at a player. At any rate, there were quite a few scouts around. After a few innings this guy taps me on the shoulder and when I turned around I realized it was Art Howe. He said, "Are you Gib Bodet?"

I said, "Yeah," and we shook hands.

"I'm sorry to bother you, but a couple of scouts told me that you were friendly with a fellow that I understand we lost this past year, Jim Muhe. I just wanted you to know I feel terrible. I didn't find out about Jim's death until quite recently and I've sent my condolences to the family because I liked and admired Jim. He was such a nice guy. A real baseball lifer, and I just wanted to pass on that thought."

Of course I remembered Art Howe well as a player. We had some very fine teams in the late seventies and early eighties. He was quite a player for the Houston Astros during that time frame and he was always a thorn in our side. He was a very tough clutch hitter. A real gamer. He came from quite a sports background. I think Art had been a college football player, I believe at the University of Wyoming. He later graduated from there and had started a career as a computer programmer before he got into pro baseball.

Paul DePodesta became the Dodgers' general manager in February 2004 but was fired in October 2005. Following that, he had a big job with the Padres, then went to work with the Mets in a big upper-echelon position when Sandy Alderson became their GM. My experience with DePodesta was actually good. I liked him. But he and I do not scout the same way.

My background has been in what I call "dirt level scouting," and Paul's is different. He is very much a statistical-analysis guy, constantly searching for a remedy or a formula on how to come up with better players. With the Dodgers he was always a gentleman and very respectful of people who worked in scouting. I have nothing but good things to say about Paul.

Is it true that some organizations are better than others? Of course. And I would have to say the bottom line to all of this is how well you do. Are you contending? Are you a winner? Do you repeat? Are you constantly a winner?

Reality says Oakland has had some decent teams and they're okay. And at the time of this writing they are coming off a surprisingly successful 2012/2013 season. But are they a huge force in the game? I don't think so — not at this point, and certainly not as a result of their discovery of statistical data, which apparently nobody else was aware of, at least in their minds.

In baseball, one of the key excuses is, "It's not a level playing field. Other teams have a lot of money. They spend a lot of money. We don't have a lot of money." And that was theoretically Oakland's explanation. They said, "We were trying to see how we could do it more economically than the other organizations because we didn't have all that money." But having a ton of money does not always produce anything and may just result in a lot of overpaid players who were maybe overvalued.

Part of the equation that Oakland throws out is true. There are a lot of overvalued players, and there are undervalued players. And they have had a fair share of overvalued players. Again, from the free agent perspective, statistical analysis made Jeremy Brown the hero by saying he was this great discovery when it turned out he was overvalued. He was overvalued no matter how much money he got. And so the story goes.

I have heard the story about the so-called Moneyball draft which was dramatized in the book and film. Nothing is more unusual, nothing, than the incident that took place in the draft room when Oakland's General Manager Billy Beane allegedly became so incensed that he threw a chair against the wall because scouting director Grady Fuson supposedly had picked a player Beane did not want selected. The pecking order in any organization, from an operational standpoint, runs like this. The general manager is in charge. Below the general manager you have a farm director, a scouting director, and the manager on the field. Economics tell us that the manager on the field is probably going to be the highest paid individual of those I have just mentioned. General managers make considerably more money than scouting managers and farm directors. But let's get down to the reality of the whole thing.

If you are in this business and really believe that the general manager said, "I don't want you to pick so-and-so," and the scouting director picked him anyway, the way to unleash your frustration is to throw a chair? I don't believe it happened that way. Beane threw the chair for some reason, but I can't fathom that the scouting director would have defied him.

Their new theory didn't last very long. In the 2012 draft they drafted more high school players than they had done previously. They selected a high school shortstop, Addison Russell, as their number-one pick and signed him for $2.625 million, which is what's called "slot money" for an eleventh overall selection. And when the dust settled, nine of the forty-three players they picked were out of high school, or roughly twenty percent. So after a few years of relying so heavily on their "invention," Oakland's thought processes from that era have apparently changed.

I have a huge difference of opinion with their concept of giving the greatest value to hitters who hit with power and walked a lot, when they paid next to no attention to stolen bases. I believe one of the comments in the book is that the importance of stolen bases in a game is exaggerated. To me that conclusion is totally wrong and is perhaps the biggest hole in their theory.

What I never could quite catch onto was their "logic" that base stealing contributed very little and it wasn't one of the things they looked at. I'm not trying to equate any of this to quantum physics or the splitting of the atom, but what I'm trying to say is that when you use some kind of numerical formula, the key in baseball offensively, is to get on base. People on base score runs. Runs scored win ballgames. Period.

When they say the importance of stolen bases is greatly exaggerated, it puts a huge dent in the theory. For example, and I don't claim to be a mathematical wizard, but I do know one equation and it's this: $X + Y = Z$. It doesn't matter whether you're on earth or the moon. It doesn't matter whether it's football, baseball, basketball, or any major sport. $X + Y = Z$. More simply put, "X" represents getting on base via a hit, walk, hit by pitch, or error. "Y" represents getting into scoring position by stealing bases. And "Z" represents runs scored.

I'll explain in terms of real baseball activity. I actually did this once with Alan Wiggins. He hit 150 singles, which was a very good season for him. Add to that the seventy-five bases he stole. Basically, what that means is he reached second or third base as a result of those 150 singles half the time. I will still stand on that.

Any time a runner can advance to second or third base, he's in position to score a run. And runs are what win ballgames. Pete Rose was the kind of guy who kept all kinds of statistical data on himself, but one that he was very proud of was his runs scored statistic. If you have a singles hitter who doesn't hit the ball out of the park, but steals seventy-five bases alone and is on base 150 times because of his hits, not including his walks, he's potentially in a position to get to second or third base half the time. Most big league pitchers are considerably bothered by runners who can hurt their focus on the hitter. And that's never changed. You can play with all the equations you want and say you're only interested in power and walks. That's fine if the hitter is Babe Ruth.

In my judgment, good solid baseball does not need a formula like the one presented to make a determination whether a player fits into their offensive scheme of things. And I think that's what the preponderance of data that comes out of the situation attempts to do. A formula is not needed to determine whether Roberto Clemente or Tony Gwynn could play for the Oakland ballclub.

I have no problems with people who are constantly looking for something that will make their selection of players better. I have worked with certain people who believe that they have discovered something that may be revolutionary in terms of the game. That's okay. I think the more time you spend in the game, the more knowledge you acquire. And the more knowledge you acquire has got to be beneficial because you can look at exceptions to everything, whether it's hitting, pitching, or fielding, and say, "You know what? My thought about that doesn't apply."

Getting to the fall classic is what you get paid for if you're in player evaluation and player development in major league baseball. My concept has always been that you want to win the World Series, of course, though just getting to it is a terrific accomplishment.

To quote an article I read by writer Larry Stewart, "Longtime baseball beat writer Tracy Ringolsby, now with the *Rocky Mountain News,* said two things were apparent: 'Beane's ego has exploded, and author Michael Lewis has a limited knowledge of baseball and a total infatuation with Beane.'" I think that pretty well sums up the whole thing that has gotten blown way out of proportion in terms of its accuracy and value to the game of professional baseball.

Coverage of Amateur Players
Twelve Thousand Games,
Six Million Miles

I am always asked what's involved in finding players that scouts consider prospects and eventually decide to draft and attempt to sign. It's quite a process when you consider the millions of amateur players in the United States, not to mention those in the Latin American countries. It's a highly structured, year-round global business conducted by every organization that demands baseball expertise and patience.

When I was an area scout, I had a given area in southern California and Nevada. As I had a reasonable amount of success from year to year, my responsibilities have grown, and for the last twenty-plus years I have cross checked players recommended by area scouts. And I am always asked, "Do you see all the high schools in the country?" I don't, and actually our area scouts don't either.

Most area scouts cultivate a network of contact people who follow local schools and keep abreast of articles in the sports pages. You may have a former teammate living in your area that you can call and ask something like, "Hey, I've been reading about so-and-so in the paper. Is he a prospect? Should I go see him?"

If you scout long enough you establish relationships with coaches. But you have to be very careful doing that because my experience has been that some coaches who may be fairly successful as high school coaches do not have the first idea what it takes to play the game professionally. Of course, there are some who say, "Come and see my player," and you'd better go.

That was how I first heard of Jack Clark, who lived three or four miles from where I did in Covina, California. He played on the same American legion team as my oldest son Mike. But I first heard about him when he was probably fifteen or sixteen and I had read about a summer team that he was on that was winning a lot of games. They had a player whose last name was Thomas who had gotten a lot of publicity. I called a guy I knew in town, Jack Perticaro, who coached Little League and pony league and other kids' teams. "Jack, what about this guy Thomas I've been reading about? Is he a prospect?"

"I don't think he is. He's just more physically mature than the other kids. But there is a player on that team I think you should see. His name is Jack Clark." I went to see him play a night game and definitely put him down as a "strong follow." I suggested he play on a scout team I coached while he was still in high school.

As luck would have it, when he was drafted, we didn't get him. The Giants did, and they selected him as a pitcher, but signings of drafted players were slow that year and their rookie club needed outfielders. Jack had a big bat and was converted to outfielder, and he never toed the rubber again. He was such a good hitter. And he had other tools that were solid. Jack was actually a slightly above-average runner as a high school player, and he had an outstanding arm.

For the Dodgers, some scouts cover big geographic areas. Of course that depends on what area of the country they scout in. Hank Jones has covered the Northwest for many years and may drive forty to fifty thousand miles in just a few months. We have a scout in the Northeast, Rich Delucia, who lives in Pennsylvania. He is responsible for Pennsylvania, New York, New Jersey, and the New England states, including New York City, which is an interesting place to scout.

Let me review an area scout's responsibility. First of all, he has to line up his best prospects for national cross checkers or the scouting director to see. If you find a high school or college pitcher you have to find out his schedule. There isn't any question that in some of the bigger productive areas like California, Florida, Texas, they often pitch the same day and they pitch a thousand miles apart. On that rare occasion when the best pitcher plays the team with the best hitter presents itself, the area scout has to get that information to the people who cross check the players.

It is a process that involves much more than just the scout going out to see the kid play the game. It involves planning, and for that, communication is key. Lots of phone calls and email messages, because high school coaches have classes during the day and are difficult to reach more often than not.

Travel is extensive doing what I do, and ballclubs are very conscientious about saving money, especially when it comes to flying. You might assume you could take a direct flight from California to Boston, or to New York or Orlando, Florida. There are many direct flights, but very few clubs suggest to scouts with jobs like mine to take direct flights. They're much more expensive. To get to the Detroit area to see a player, I flew from California to Dallas, then from Dallas to Detroit. It's very rare that we just fly into a city and see a player. For instance, to see a player in Texas, you fly into Dallas and then drive to see the player in Lufkin, Texas, which is a hundred seventy-five miles away. So there is no question that scouts spend a lot of time on the road, a lot of time in hotels, most of the time the schedule is hectic, and often weather plays havoc with scouts' travel plans, for obvious reasons.

The Dodgers have a young lady who schedules flights, hotels, and car rentals for national cross checkers. But area scouts have to map their travels based on the most efficient way to get from place to place to see players. Of course all of that requires good time management skills.

I've seen twelve thousand games of one sort or another — high school, college, and professional, at every level from rookie ball up through the major league clubs — and have easily flown and driven six million miles in my forty-plus years out there beating those famous bushes.

Just so there's no confusion in terms of the thought process, a good scout will go anyplace to see a player. The theory that occasionally comes out is, "Well, they don't like to go into inner-city areas because there may be a crime element." Many years ago the inner city used to produce a lot more baseball players than today. There was a television show years ago about a white coach who coached an inner-city basketball team of predominantly African-American kids in an inner-city school and accomplished good things on and off the court with his boys.

That's a true story, except the sport was baseball, and that coach, Phil Pote, went on to become a longtime scout in the Los Angeles area. He coached a team of terrific ballplayers that included Bobby Tolan, who went on to play for the Cincinnati Reds, Bob Watson, who played for Houston and other teams for eighteen seasons, and others. These were great African-American kids, and I think at least six or seven of them played professionally.

As an attempt to assist kid players and their parents, the following is an overview of what scouts look for, position by position. A good scout begins by looking at tools. Can he run? Can he throw? Can he hit? Can he hit with power? Is he athletic? Is he determined? Does he work hard? Is he a smart player on the field? Does he interact well with his teammates? Is he a follower? Is he a leader? Is he a good competitor? All these ingredients go into making a player.

In an attempt to assist parents of kid players, the following is a brief overview of the things scouts and organizations want for each position. This is not a rule written in stone because situations and conditions are always fluid and subject to change. But I think it will prove helpful.

For parents of aspiring youngsters, let me review what we call "role profiles" for each position. A role profile is a prototype of what we're looking for at the different positions. In professional baseball it exists, but there have been many exceptions to whatever the position is, and that's hard for people to understand. When the player does not fit the profile it is conceivable that a scout will look at him and say, "Well, we don't care if he fits the profile. We think he is going to be an exceptional prospect and then an exceptional major league player." And that's where scouting comes into play.

Let's start with **catchers**. The catcher, of course, is the quarterback of the team. The first ingredient you want with a catcher is a strong arm. Would you want a quarterback on the football team who didn't have a strong arm? Of course not, but some obviously throw better than others. But when you start breaking the arm down to see if it's good enough, you must ask, "Is it an average arm?" Average doesn't sound very impressive, but we've had them in the big leagues. Mike Scioscia, a longtime catcher with us, never had an above average arm. But he had a quick release and good hands, and he could really block the plate. Offensively he was a good hitter; not a ton of power, but he was a good hitter, and was especially tough against good pitching.

Personally I have never liked real tall catchers because of the constant ups and downs. They have to set up low. They squat to give the signs and the target. Over time it becomes more difficult for taller catchers. But there have been many taller catchers who have done well. One guy I scouted by the name of Matt Wieters, who was Baltimore's first selection in the 2007 draft and got to the big leagues in 2009, is exceptionally tall at six-five. He's very flexible, sets up low and gives an excellent target. He has a good arm, very soft hands, and exceptionally quick feet. He's also a dangerous switch hitter with power from both sides of the plate.

You usually like sturdy builds behind the plate because the position is physically debilitating. The collisions at the plate, foul tips, and the up and down movement with every pitch he calls is very trying on his body. The catcher is involved in one way or another in every play in the game. Defense at that position has always been considered more important than offense. A power-hitting catcher is a definite asset to a club.

Of course there are exceptions regarding body type. Buster Posey is an example. He was originally a shortstop, but he didn't profile as a shortstop because he is a far below average runner. He was a shortstop as a high school player, and when he went to college at Florida State University they put him behind the plate. But scouts look for certain prerequisites a youngster who catches must have, such as a good arm, good hands, and a good bat.

Was Mike Piazza the equal of Johnny Bench? If you're a baseball purist and a scout, I think you would have to say you would take Bench over Piazza. Was Piazza a better hitter? Yes, he was. Some may not consider Piazza a premium defender, but he was certainly adequate, although he had some trouble throwing out runners. He played because he was an excellent hitter. But Bench was a premium defender, and a very dangerous hitter with power. There are two examples there.

First base: Here you're looking for guys with good hands and good feet. The left-handers are more popular at that position, basically because of angles. When a ground ball is hit, the left-handed first baseman does not have to turn his body to throw to the shortstop or second baseman covering second. A right-hander has to turn his body to make that throw. In essence, that's the real difference in right-hand or left-hand players at that position. And the exception here is one of the great defensive first basemen of all time, Gil Hodges, a right handed thrower. He was a big fellow, probably about six-three, a broad shouldered guy. At one point in time the Dodgers tried to make a catcher out of him.

I have to share this story about him which was told to me by Al Campanis. It does tell you something about courage. Eddie Roebuck was a teammate of Hodges. I never heard of anybody who played in that generation who didn't have great admiration for Gil Hodges, known by his teammates as "the Big Marine." He fought in a lot of terrible battles in the South Pacific in World War II and was considered brave beyond belief. And he was a peacemaker. I don't think he was ever kicked out of a major league ballgame in the days when they used to have a lot of scraps. But Gil Hodges always tried to break them up. After twenty years in the big leagues he managed the Mets and died much too young in 1972 at age 48.

When they made an attempt to put Hodges behind the plate, he had a bad habit of blinking or ducking every time a hitter swung at a pitch. He had a good arm and they wanted to leave him there, but it just didn't work. There are different kinds of fear, so to speak, when you're talking about position players. He had the habit of blinking and turning his head, yet he was terribly brave in war. I've seen kids on the football field hurl themselves into the bodies of much larger players to block or tackle them without showing fear, but they were fearful of a baseball being hit toward them.

Remember the old adage that the only absolute in baseball is that there are no absolutes? Two of the fine first basemen who played in the last twenty-five years, Mark Grace and Keith Hernandez, were both excellent defenders who won multiple Gold Gloves. Both were very good hitters and both did not hit with a lot of power. The perfect profile for a major league first baseman is a good hitter who hits for power and is a good defender. Remember, as I've noted, they didn't hit with a lot of power but they were very good hitters. It's an old cliché that if you have a great mix of power and a great hitter then you have something special. If you have a great hitter that doesn't hit with a lot of power, he is still a special player. Look at Mark Grace. He had more hits than Tony Gwynn in the decade of the 1990s.

But almost without fail, organizations want first basemen who are good defenders and also good hitters. Looking at major league players today, the perfect prerequisite for a first baseman would be a power hitter, somebody like Albert Pujols, or Prince Fielder.

Second base and shortstop: Almost all second basemen in major league baseball were shortstops as young players. Let's say you have two youngsters that you draft and both were shortstops. One was an All-American in college and the other was a highly drafted high school player. Who's going to play short?

If they both have exceptional arms, they're both going to stay at shortstop. But let's say they progress through the minor leagues at the same fairly rapid pace. One will become a second baseman, and it's always the player with the lesser arm. Remember again, there are no absolutes. Ozzie Smith did not have a great arm. His arm was borderline average, but he got rid of the baseball so quickly that it allowed him to play the position successfully. He had tremendous agility, what baseball calls "great feet."

Good infielders usually have good feet and how well their footwork works will usually determine how easily they get into position to field ground balls. But having great feet for an infielder has nothing to do with how fast a runner the guy is. But most clubs like their infielders who play in the middle of the diamond to be at least average runners with good quickness. There's a difference between raw speed and real quickness. Of course, there have been many fine shortstops other than Ozzie Smith, but he's a good example.

I scouted Ozzie Smith and I remember having a conversation at the time with Larry Himes, who was a sharp guy. We were both working for the Angels then. I scouted Ozzie as a high school kid at Locke High School in Los Angeles. But he made it clear to everybody that he had promised his mother he would go to college. He went to Cal-Poly San Luis Obispo and I had also seen him play there.

At that point we got into a difference of opinion about Ozzie Smith's ability to play shortstop. It sounds ridiculous now, but it wasn't ridiculous then because he didn't quite fit the profile. Why? He did not have an exceptionally strong arm, just borderline average. I remember Himes brought this up, and I'm not aiming this at Larry because he was a very sharp guy and a good scout who later became general manager for both the White Sox and the Cubs. Larry asked me, "When have you ever seen a shortstop in the big leagues that has just a borderline average arm?"

One that comes to mind is Phil Rizzuto, shortstop for the Yankees when I was a teenager and even before. He had a long run with the Yankees, thirteen seasons with time out for military service during World War II. Although he was a terrific shortstop and American League MVP, he didn't have a strong arm. He didn't play a deep shortstop but he had one great quality that Smith had. Both of them got rid of the ball with lightning quickness. The Yankees always had great double-play combinations when Rizzuto was the shortstop. There was Rizzuto and Joe Gordon, then Rizzuto and Jerry Coleman.

Did the Angels just accept my word on it? No. But we had an old time scout by the name of Ray Scarborough who pitched for Washington in the American League in the forties and fifties at that meeting. He had never seen Ozzie, but I remember him saying, "If Gib can say he gets rid of the ball like Rizzuto, then I'd have to say the guy can play shortstop. When a hitter hit a ground ball toward Rizzuto, he was out. And if this kid can do that as well as Rizzuto, then he can play shortstop." As things turned out, Ozzie was drafted by San Diego in the fourth round and went on to a wonderful career with the Padres and the St. Louis Cardinals before he went to the Hall of Fame.

There are no absolutes in baseball. Most shortstops have plus arms. Barry Larkin and Bill Russell had plus arms. Jeter has a plus arm. And there have been others.

Third base: The tools we look for in the hot corner are a good hitter with power, a premium defender, good hands, a plus arm, and good body control. Mike Schmidt had everything you look for at that position, and he not only hit with power, he hit with exceptional power. But he struggled early on and his career was the result of determination and a lot of hard work.

Development of players takes a while, and it is no different as a major leaguer than it is for the struggling little ten-year-old competing against twelve-year-olds in Little League baseball. The little ten-year-old does not become a force until he gets older.

Experience allowed Mike Schmidt to realize what his weaknesses were as a young player and to take advantage of his strengths. He was a terrific major league player who will probably go down as the greatest third baseman of all time.

Outfielders: left, center and right. It's pretty simple as to who major league scouts are looking for here. You're looking for hitters that play the outfield. They can be all combinations, all sizes and shapes. But you're looking for guys that can hit. Can they be different types? Sure.

Obviously your best outfielder will play centerfield. He's the guy who covers the most ground and hopefully has a strong arm. The right fielder should be the best thrower of the three outfielders because he has the long throw when a base runner tries to go from first to third. Left fielders do not worry about making the throw to first base, the longest throw they would have. Their throw to third, of course, is short.

Probably the best example of a power hitting outfielder would be Barry Bonds. While he played, he went down as a premium hitter in left field. Of course his body type changed. When he came out of high school in 1982, he was drafted in the second round by the Giants, did not sign, and went to Arizona State. In 1985 he was selected out of Arizona State in the first round by the Pirates and spent a good portion of his career with Pittsburgh until he was granted free agency and picked up by the Giants in 1992.

He was a better hitter than his father, Bobby Bonds, but his father had better tools. Initially Barry was a good runner and a base stealer when he weighed probably 190 pounds. However, during the lion's share of his career he weighed 240 if he weighed an ounce. We won't get into any discussion of steroids and just leave it at that. Bonds was the prototype of a guy who hit with power in left field, but he never was a particularly good outfielder and never had a strong arm.

You can take your pick here among centerfielders. In my life in baseball it's a difficult call to make, but I would have to say Mays, Mantle, and DiMaggio were the greatest centerfielders that I have ever seen. And they were different types. Mays was flashier. Mantle had great speed and may have been a better runner than Mays. DiMaggio wasn't as flashy, but he was a long loping runner who got great jumps in the outfield.

I'm told by the old-timers that he may have gotten the best jump of any outfielder they had ever seen. Mays could steal a base and may have led the league once or twice, and could hit the ball out of the park. So could Mantle. So could DiMaggio. And DiMaggio had a great arm in his younger days, Mays had a great arm, and Mantle had a good arm. All were premium players. Usually guys play center field because they get good jumps, they can run down and cut the gaps off, and they are usually timely hitters.

And there are exceptions. I saw Bob Dernier play center field. He wasn't a big-time hitter, but a good singles hitter and a great defender. Brett Butler was a singles hitter who had a career .290 batting average in the big leagues. He just lacked power. So there are all kinds of definitions of good centerfielders. Reggie Smith was a big-time right fielder for the Red Sox, Dodgers, Cardinals, and others, who had a great arm. He was a switch hitter with power.

An important prerequisite for an outfielder is, does he have a chance to hit? Does he have speed of the bat? Does he have good mechanics to hit? Does he recognize pitches? And you can see that there have been many in the big leagues over the years who have filled the bill in those categories. That's what scouts are looking for. Defense is equally important. If the player is a poor defender you don't want to see runs given up that his bat may have produced.

Before we get to **pitching** I want to offer a general suggestion for young kids. You have seen that "good feet" is listed as part of the profile for each position, both offensively and defensively. One of the things Al Campanis of the Dodgers used to always stress was improving footwork. How do you do that? He suggested you jump rope repeatedly. He said the best-trained athletes back in his era were fighters who all jumped rope. It's something a youngster can do by himself on his own schedule and monitor his own progress as his footwork, legs, and stamina improve.

I have saved the discussion of pitching for last because pitchers are a different ball of wax. Some scouts go overboard with speed gun readings, but good scouts love to see the ball kind of jump out of a kid's hand when he pitches, right hander or left hander. Is his arm action easy? Does he have a breaking pitch? Does he have a changeup? We like durable youngsters. If you look back at some of the old baseball photos as far back as seventy-five or a hundred years, you'll see that pitchers are quite often in the back row of major league photos. Pitchers have always been looked at as tall, bigger-framed guys. But there are exceptions.

The greatest pitcher I saw when I was a teenager and one of the greatest of all time was Bob Feller. I think he was probably six feet tall on his tiptoes. He had a great arm and a high three-quarter delivery with a big high leg kick. Many years later, Nolan Ryan had the same kind of stuff. Feller's career was interrupted by nearly four years during World War II during the prime of his career when he joined the Navy. He could have played for Great Lakes Naval Training Base, where they had some wonderful service teams, but he wanted to get into combat. He told navy brass he had joined the Navy to fight, not to play baseball. Despite that, he still accrued a 266–162 career record, and it's said he would have won close to 360 games without the loss of the years in the military. While with Cleveland he got into the 1948 World Series, when Cleveland defeated Boston. When the Indians got in it again in 1954 and lost to the Giants, his skills had started to slip.

Remember, clubs are limited within the framework of their system. Obviously everybody would love to have a great pitcher on his team, but great players don't necessarily create the backbone of a great team. There have been many players over the years that were considered exceptional, but their

The 1942 Service All-Stars, managed by Mickey Cochrane. Front row, from left: Vincent Smith, Don Padgett, Ernest Andres, Herman Fishman, Frank Pytlak, Fred Schaffer, and Russ Meers. Center row: J. Russell Cook (in service uniform), Don Dunker, O.V. Mulkey, Cecil Travis, Fred Hutchinson, Sam Chapman, Bob Feller, George Earnshaw, Cochrane, Hank Gowdy, Joe Grace, Mickey Harris, and Johnny Rigney. Back row: Ken Silvestri, Pat Mullin, Chet Hajduk, Johnny Sturm, Sam Harshaney, Johnny Lucadello, Johnny Grodzicki, Benny McCoy, Heinie Mueller, and Morrie Arnovich.

teams never got into the World Series. Ernie Banks of the Chicago Cubs quickly comes to mind. Was he an exceptional player? You bet he was! And many may not know that he played more games at first base (1,259) than he played at shortstop (1,125), even though he is usually remembered as a shortstop. And he was always a very dangerous hitter.

Frank Robinson from McClymonds High School in Oakland had a great career as an outfielder, but he was primarily known as a hitter. And during the course of his long career as both player and manager, he earned a boatload of major awards that resulted in his induction into the Hall of Fame.

Let's go back to pitching and look at some specifics about pitching and hitting. The speed gun has become prevalent because it tells you about velocity. Of course it can be deceptive. Over the years I've had some good conversations with old timers, and they agree velocity is highly important to a power pitcher. Would we call Greg Maddux, who is a cinch Hall of Famer, a power pitcher? No. He had great command of his pitches but he didn't fit into the mold of what scouts look for with pitchers. He was small, and by that I mean a narrow kid, but approximately six feet. When I scouted him as a junior at Valley High School in Las Vegas, Nevada, the winter league coach Ralph Meeder called him to my attention and said, "This little guy can really pitch."

He threw an inning or so — this was like in January when the schools prepared for their seasons — and it was a clear, cold day in Vegas. I saw him and said, "Well, he's got a pretty simple delivery, and his fast ball is certainly average." Remember when scouts say "average" we mean an average major league fastball of 88–90 miles per hour, not an average fastball for Valley High School.

The grades used by scouts are all based on major league grades. It's a numerical system. So if you said, "A guy had an eight fastball," it meant he would throw between 95 and 100 miles an hour. If he had a seven fastball, he would throw between 91 and 95. They have current grades and then projected grades. And there is a projection figure you have to use to estimate how much better he will get. In other words, is it reasonable to assume that a college pitcher that has an average fastball at 21 is going to end up with an above average fastball at 24 or 25? No, it is not.

Chances are a college player, if he has an average fastball, will have an average fastball with maturity. Then the question is, what can improve? Well, his breaking stuff and command of his pitches can improve. Maddux became a terribly interesting guy, not because of his stuff, and his stuff was good, but I've seen others who never achieved his status with very similar stuff. None of them that I've ever scouted have ever had the command of their pitches that Maddux had. For a long period of time he had as good a command or better than anybody who's ever pitched. And he was very hard for the hitter to guess with.

Scouts generally look for pitchers who are taller guys. If you think about it, there is a reason for it that goes back a long time. When I was a kid there were a lot of diamonds around that were not in good condition, but we played on them anyway, and we had a lot of playground teams. Prior to going to high school I had a pretty good arm and occasionally pitched a little. But there was no elevated mound, which gives the hitter a great chance against a pitcher. It doesn't matter who the guy is. That's why we have mounds, and that's what helps establish a down-flight of the pitched ball to the hitter.

And that's why scouts a hundred years ago were interested in taller pitchers. That is the reason for it. If you're tall, that doesn't necessarily make you durable. Obviously scouts like strength in the legs in a pitcher. Normally when a pitcher's career starts to wane, the legs are the first thing that will go. That's why a lot of organizations have pitchers run a lot, to keep their legs strong. An example is Bob Welch. I remember that once he had some problems late in the game where he got wild high, not left or right of the plate, high. The fastball rode up and out of the strike zone. And that's when he would get tired. Bob was a power pitcher, a great big-game pitcher, and wonderful competitor his entire career.

This may sound more complicated than it is. Theoretically he's pitching from a mound which is elevated from where the hitter stands. And of course, a tall pitcher would be throwing downhill, which creates an angle that makes it somewhat tougher for the hitter to square up a pitch.

Let's get into the reality of the game. In my era a great pitcher was Bob Feller, who was pretty much average sized. He was probably five-eleven or six feet. The great Nolan Ryan, who came along in the next generation of power pitchers, was slightly taller. They both had great arms and great stuff. Feller was a magnificent pitcher in the late thirties, forties, and fifties. Of course, Ryan's career was amazing, with 324 victories in three decades, 1966–1993. I saw Ryan pitch in the early, middle, and late phases of his career. And another great right-handed pitcher who was well respected by the opposition was Bob Gibson.

But the reality of the game is that being tall is no guarantee of anything. Pitchers must also have a loose arm, a good delivery, and a good fastball. Does the ball move? With a certain amount of coaching they can get the baseball to move to some extent. That, in essence, is the role profile for a right hand pitcher. Are there exceptions? Of course. Has this quality existed for a short time or for a long time?

Left-handed pitchers have somewhat of an advantage simply because of how often hitters face them, right-handed hitters or not. Basically the key there is that the ratio of right-handed to left-handed batters is so much greater. Left-handed pitchers that scouts are apt to pursue don't necessarily have to throw that hard. But hopefully they have a good breaking pitch and a good changeup and good command of their stuff. A good example of that is Jamie Moyer, who pitched forever in the big leagues since 1988, and is still out there with the Colorado Rockies in 2012 at age forty-nine.

Does a prerequisite exist for left-hand pitching? Not necessarily. Why? Well, first of all, I think the ratio of right-handed to left-handed people is ten to one. So of course the prerequisites are a little bit different because there are far fewer left-handed people. When you think about great left-handed pitchers, the first one you should think of is Sandy Koufax, who was six-two. He pitched for the Dodgers for a dozen years, 1955–1966, and absolutely dominated the National League. He retired with a 165–87 won-loss record and a 2.76 ERA. What pre-requisites did he have? He had an absolutely outstanding power arm. He had a great fastball and a great curveball.

And how can anybody forget Hall of Famer Whitey Ford, a little guy with big stuff and an even bigger heart?

Whatever generation you're from, you can think of a good left-handed pitcher that you have seen and say, "Boy, he dominated our era." I remember one in particular when I was a high school kid growing up and succeeding years was Bobby Shantz, who was a little left handed pitcher for the Philadelphia Athletics. If you look at Bobby Shantz in team pictures, he looked like the bat boy. He was no more than five-seven or five-eight and had good command of his stuff. He's a guy on a fourth-place team in 1952 who led the league with twenty-four wins. And this was an era when the Yankees were just totally dominant in the American League and quite dominant in the World Series. And all Shantz did was go out there and put it to them almost every time he pitched.

Johnny Podres was around five-ten. He was a great left-hand pitcher for the Dodgers, and a hero of the 1955 World Series when Brooklyn defeated the Yankees in seven games. Podres won Game Three and Game Seven, and then had succeeding years where he was very good.

Claude Osteen, who also originally signed with Cincinnati and spent nine seasons with the Dodgers during his eighteen years in the major leagues, was a teammate of Tommy Acker's for a very short time. I remember Tommy telling me way back, "We have a kid who just joined the club, a left-handed pitcher, and he is such a good hitter I wonder if they will make an outfielder out of him." He got to the big leagues at age seventeen and was a very effective left-hand pitcher for eighteen seasons. He was five-eleven, not a big physical guy, but a hell of a pitcher.

So you can see that prerequisites and role profiles are fine. But there's another quality at every level that scouts look at and can't help but be affected by it. "Can he play?" That was the general term used by scouts years ago. Let's say, for example, when I started scouting I was with Boston and worked for Joe Stephenson, I would tell Joe, "Boy, this kid can run and this kid can throw and play centerfield."

Joe listened very patiently and then said, "Can he play?" In other words, is he considerably above the competition he plays with? You can take all the qualities in a role profile, but if the player is not better than the people he's

Dodgers minor league and player development personnel at Dodger Stadium.

playing with or not somewhat dominant, then you start looking at the question of how he is going to dominate or be the equal to players as he develops and goes through a professional program. And that's really the key to what you're looking at.

Scouts often use the term "projecting" and asking if this player is *the* player. You usually get the feeling the player is a special player when he performs above and beyond the competition level, where he's playing. You're looking for athletic ability, of course, in all these positions. But generally speaking, I would say a pitcher can be effective, even at the major league level being the least athletic of any other positions. That's a generality. Quite often pitchers are athletic, but some are not, and yet they are very effective.

I don't think there was ever a more athletic pitcher or very few who were equal to the great Bob Gibson of the St. Louis Cardinals. An individual does not have to be a great athlete to be a pitcher. It is helpful if he is athletic, of course. If he is athletic he can repeat more often than not.

With all of the above in mind, those are the prerequisites I look for at given positions, and I'm probably no different from anyone else in scouting. The bottom line isn't just picking players, it's picking the right players. And that's really what we're trying to do. That in itself is what makes or breaks scouts who are considered good in their field.

Is He Having Fun?
Tips for Developing Young Players

One of the negatives, I suppose, in trying to do a book concerning instruction to young players and experiences that you've had over the years in dealing with coaches of young players and training methods for young kids is that there's the possibility of a perception of the reader that those of us in professional baseball for a long time may be living in the past. Today there are all kinds of devices, electronic and otherwise, that scouts didn't have fifty or sixty years ago. One good example of this is computer programs that allow youngsters to face different pitches to help them develop.

I've often said it's best to keep things simple in dealing with young players. You don't want to clutter a young baseball player's mind with too many things to think about. Trying to do too much in terms of instruction is dangerous. I really believe in keeping it simple and fun for young players.

A key word in dealing with youngsters eight to twelve years old is repetition. Practices that are fun and utilize constant repetition, repeating basics constantly, are the best instruction for young players. When dealing with kids maybe eight to twelve years old, as I did for years when my sons were growing up, try to make your practices simple. Try to make them fun. Work on things like how to advance the runner, how to bunt, and so forth.

If you teach a youngster the wrong way, he's liable to develop a habit that will be very difficult for him to break. It's the same thing with developing skills on how to be quicker with the bat. I would never suggest young kids get on a weight training program or anything like that. It makes no sense for players this young. I've had pretty good results in dealing with disparities between, say, fifteen-year-old players and seventeen- or eighteen-year-old players. The seventeen- and eighteen-year-old pitchers are bigger, stronger,

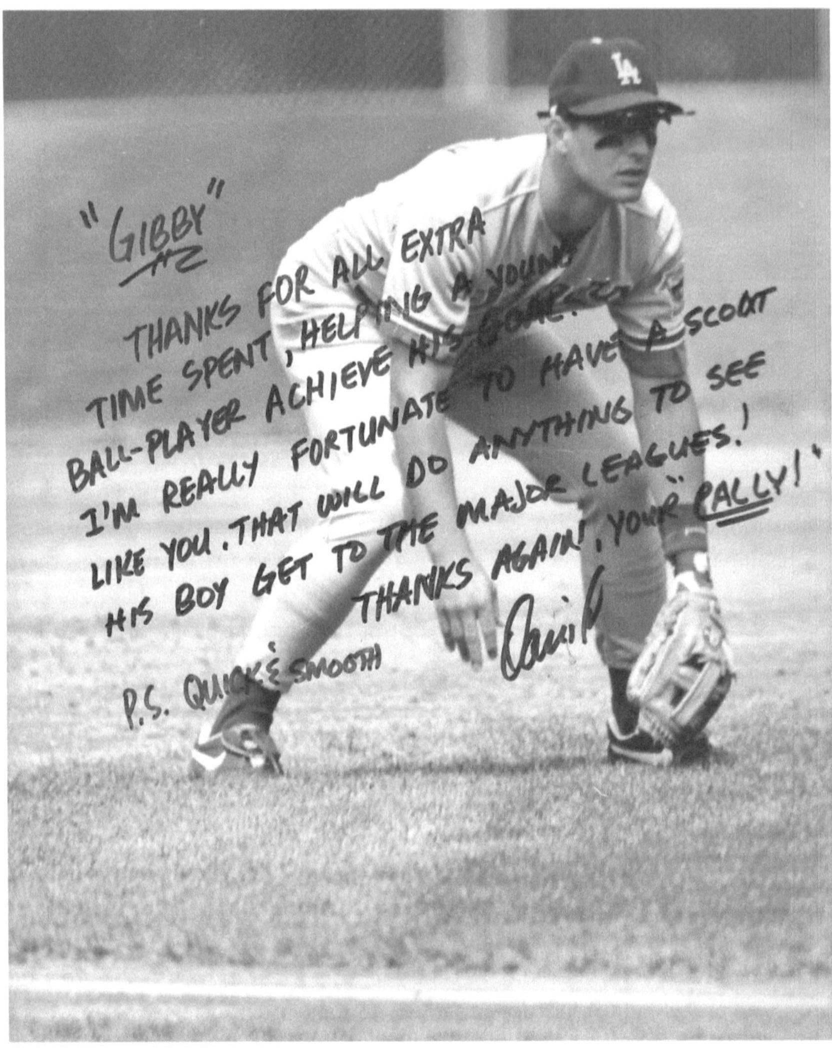

David Hansen is one of my all-time favorites. He always worked very hard and did all that was asked of him. After his big league career he was a hitting coach for the Dodgers for several years.

throw harder. A way to counterbalance that for a young hitter is to swing a weighted bat.

This helps provided the youngster has good swing mechanics because good swing mechanics are prerequisites to being a good hitter. A youngster can have good swing mechanics, but if he's not physical enough to grip the bat head through the hitting zone, then he can't grip the bat head position to hit a pitch if it's thrown hard. This is one way to counterbalance that. For years I worked with a very fine scout, Ron King, who signed a lot of very good players. He did that with Steve Sax. Sax did it for years.

You see a lot of young kids take practice swings, and they simulate a practice swing like hitting a pitch right in the middle of the plate. I see this even in high schools and colleges. They take pitches in the middle of the plate, then a pitch on the inside part of the plate, then the outside part of the plate, a pitch knee-high, belt-high. Moving the angle of the bat develops hand strength. I remember a player I signed who played fifteen years in the big leagues, Dave Hansen, did this for years. It is a great developer of hand strength because you do find that almost all the hitters in the major leagues, especially the real good hitters, have exceptional hand strength. They don't get the bat in too far into the palm of the hand. They grip it more in their fingers. The same thing applies when throwing a baseball. If you grip a baseball too far into the palm of your hand, that's called "choking the ball," and that will not allow you to throw the ball as hard. So those are just a few general tips that can be used with advanced players.

With younger kids, little league age, you have to play games during the course of a practice. That way you can teach them how to move a runner along. Do you bunt him over? Do you try to play hit and run? And you can arrange lots of different contests to do that. That way practice has an element of a game.

I can't emphasize this enough. *Instincts are developed by imagination.* If practices are terribly regimented, it does not give a young player a chance to use his imagination. That's really the main point I'm trying to make here. A guy with exceptional ability, natural ability, was allowed to develop on his own. He didn't have somebody telling him, "No, you can't do that."

If you talk with parents, they may tell you he's having a great time. But when he strikes out three times, well, that's not a lot of fun for a kid. It's not an awful lot of fun striking out and walking back to the dugout. So that's one observation, I suppose, that's important to develop with young players. Keep in mind that the great athlete is not always the best player and discuss it with him.

One of the greatest athletes to come down the pike in the last half century or longer is Michael Jordan. After his first retirement from basketball in 1994 he decided to give professional baseball a try. He played in the outfield with the Birmingham Barons in the AA Southern League for his only pro season. He batted .202. He struggled there and couldn't perform at a higher level and went back to pro basketball, where he was the greatest player in the game.

The outcome was predictable. Although Michael Jordan did play minor league baseball, he was not proficient at it. He was obviously a better athlete than a lot of the players he was playing with in the minor leagues, but he wasn't a better baseball player. There was one simple reason that he struggled. He never had a quick bat. In spite of all of his basketball skills, he never had a quick bat. Pitchers could overpower him and outsmart him.

So often the saying, "Well he's a great athlete," is pointed out. Athletic ability, of course, plays a part in a youngster developing, and non-athletes have a terrible time developing as baseball players. And occasionally pitchers are not terribly athletic. But, if God has given them a good arm and good stuff as a prospect, they then have a chance to later develop into a front-line pitcher. There are many pitchers who have athletic ability, but pure athleticism does not necessarily determine who is going to be a great pitcher.

I recall a conversation I had quite a few years ago with Ed Roebuck, who was a front line relief pitcher with the Dodgers for quite a few years. Eddie played eleven years in the big leagues, mostly with the Dodgers. He was always a first-rate reliever and a member of the 1955 Brooklyn Dodgers, who went on to win the World Championship and beat the Yankees. I worked with Ed for years and have known him over forty years. We were at Dodger Stadium quite a few years ago and we were chatting and watching batting practice. And then the game started. We were having a conversation, I don't even think it was about the game, but there was a very short passed ball that scooted away from catcher Steve Yeager. Eddie commented just off the top of his head, "Mays would have scored on that." Now he didn't play with Mays but he played against Willie.

I said, "Really? Is there anybody in the game today that would have taken the chance to try to score on a short passed ball like that?" And my question went a little bit further than that. I said, "Do you think Mays, who had all this natural ability and great instincts to play, do you think he would have developed as a player the same way if he came out of a highly structured program?

And Ed said, "I think it would depend largely on who he played for." You have to remember that Mays as a young kid played on the same team with his dad, a semipro team around Birmingham, Alabama, and most players were much older. Mays was obviously an instinctive kid and he was not discouraged from being a daring player. And Ed's comment to me was, "I'll never forget when I first laid eyes on Willie in a major league game. He had already been in the big leagues four years and was a star by the time I got there. But I'll never forget somebody getting a base hit for us with a guy on second and Willie was playing about medium depth in center field. This ball was not a slow hit ball, just kind of a hard-hit ground ball right up the middle. Willie charged that ball like he was an infielder playing a swinging bunt. He fielded it with his bare hand and threw it to the plate and threw that runner out when he tried to score from second. I'm telling you, Gib, by then I had been playing professional baseball seven or eight years and I had never seen a guy make a play like that. There was no thought in his mind about over-running that base hit. He just ran full ahead, scooped up that ball and threw it home all in one motion."

I knew what a great player Mays was, and having played against him, Eddie knew it, too. But that makes you wonder. Are great instincts to play natural or are they acquired?

Roberto Clemente played like that, too. He would swing hard, hit it

My longtime friend Ed Roebuck warming up with the Dodgers circa 1956.

hard, use the whole field, steal a base, throw the base runner out. He was encouraged to play aggressively and became a Hell bent for leather type of player who threw caution to the wind.

One of my pet peeves is when coaches constantly call the pitches. In scouting reports on young catchers, after describing whether he could catch and throw, swing the bat, and the rest, we used to have a section on the report which would say, "Comment on the catcher's ability to call a game." And if you have a youngster who mixed pitches well and got in sync with the pitcher, you would say, "Called a good game. Smart. Smart beyond his years." Or the other type catcher who doesn't mix pitches well. That was prior to the era that started twenty-five or thirty years ago when coaches constantly called pitches. It started sporadically, but now you see it almost every place in amateur baseball. In my opinion that does not help a player at all. You really can't help a young player by taking the game away from him.

We can help him in terms of how we teach him and how you prepare him to become a better player, but don't try to take the game away from him on the field, because if you do, you will inhibit his confidence. Probably the best instinctive young player I think I ever saw, probably smart way beyond his years, was Alan Trammel, the fine shortstop for the Tigers who was a high school boy when I first saw him in San Diego.

I'd like to call attention to some relevant numbers and percentages against you that parents should know about. If roughly eight percent of the players who are drafted out of each draft get to the big leagues, then, obviously, ninety-two percent do not. Am I trying to discourage young players from playing the game? Obviously not. If your skills develop as you go up the ladder, there's no reason that you can't get to the big leagues. Sure, the percentages are great. But the point is, if it's not you, it's going to be somebody like you.

It depends on how badly a youngster wants to get better and improve. But a young player at the Little League level should not really be concerned about becoming a big league player. What he should be concentrating on is trying to become a better player and developing in that respect. But as far as setting your sights on becoming a major league player when you're eight years old, well, that doesn't make any more sense than telling a boy who weighs eighty-eight pounds in Pop Warner football that he's going to be an all-pro player for the Green Bay Packers.

When professional evaluators, meaning scouts, watch games, they kind of skim through and may make a lot of notes on the game, but they don't focus on one player. But if they've never seen a particular team before, they start eliminating this youngster or that. This guy can't hit. That kid can't run. This guy can't throw. This pitcher has bad arm action.

From a scouting perspective Johnny Jones is not as big as the other kids; he's got a wiry type build, should fill out; has a good arm; he's a good runner. He struck out on a pretty good curve ball on a previous at bat, but he's got speed of the bat. He's an athlete. He plays hard. He interacts well with teammates. When the scout reads a report like that, he will go back and see that player.

If he's fifteen years old and he's playing on a Colt League team or on an American Legion team, he could be a player we call "a follow." And once he becomes a follow, he is entered into a scout's record system. Those things are all ingredients, or part, of the kinds of things scouts look for. Again, too much instruction or constant filming of a young player can be counterproductive, even inhibiting. It becomes almost like you're trying to program your player to be someone else.

An individual I know quite well in professional baseball is very conscious of trying to make his youngster a better player. And he tries to have this boy emulate the setup of a major league outfielder, how he sets up to hit, his stride, his delivery of the bat head through the hitting zone. You're not starting out where the boy is comfortable hitting, and most good hitting instructors will start out with a youngster and say, "Okay, let's see your stance at the plate. Are you comfortable that way? Is that normally where you start the bat?" And they work from that point on. Don't put the kid in an uncomfortable position and say, "Well, this is how Albert Pujols held his hands, up above his head, and this is how he loaded the bat to hit." You want the kid to be as natural as possible in terms of developing an approach to hit.

I suppose most people assume that everybody who plays in the big leagues is brimming with confidence. A common question, at least in my mind, is this: what comes first, confidence or success? Let's think about this. For example, if you watched the 2010 playoffs and saw the Giants beat Atlanta in close games, you can't help but have some compassion for Atlanta's second baseman Brooks Conrad, who had 3 errors and was shaky all night.

Then the next night Atlanta manager Bobby Cox didn't start Conrad, but did use him as a pinch-hitter twice. Nobody mentioned that Conrad had only played second base nine times during the regular season. The kid felt terrible. The team, the Braves, as a group, seemed to rally behind him and say, "Well, he's a great guy. He's worked very hard and gotten a lot of big hits for us during the course of the year, and we want all the moral support we can give him." That, of course is a great support system. That's what you look for.

Back to what comes first, confidence or success? There isn't any question, if you're a fan of baseball or a participant in the game in any capacity, you are hoping that the ball did not find the second baseman after he struggled mightily trying to field it because he had made these errors. But this can happen to any kid at any level. And at the highest level the game is played, the young player was on center stage and he just did not have it. To a certain extent, from a scouting viewpoint, Conrad had always been a shaky defender. But he was a pretty good hitter and that's why he was there.

But almost all big leaguers, whether they're position players or pitchers, have some weaknesses. They're not all complete players. That's why, when the scouts refer to five-tool players, you're talking about very few individuals who ever played the game. DiMaggio was a five-tool player. Mantle was. Mays was. Clemente was. When you start looking at some of the other names in the Hall of Fame and ask, "Was he a five tool player?" Not necessarily. Ted Williams was not a five tool player, but he's in the Hall of Fame because he was such a great hitter. He was a very mediocre defender, but his hitting skills more than overcame whatever deficiencies he had as a defensive outfielder. Ozzie Smith is in the Hall of Fame because he was a great defender but a mediocre hitter. Ozzie was kind of a pesky type hitter, a contact hitter with no power, and he became a better hitter the longer he played in the big leagues.

Now, the reason I'm drawing this comparison is that there is a tendency to want to play up what the young player does well and just pay lip service to things he doesn't. But what you find with exceptional players is they work quite often on the things they don't do that well. Eddie Mathews was a former player I got to know when he scouted. Of course I admired him greatly as a player. But he told me at one point in time that he had terrible problems defensively and that Billy Jurges, who was a coach in the Braves organization at the time when Eddie played in the minor leagues, used to hit Eddie two hundred ground balls a day. And he said, "I don't know what really drove me to work at it other than Jurges."

Jurges used to say, "You're going to get to the big leagues because you can hit, Eddie, but you don't want to be a guy that gets to the big leagues, then taken out in the late innings because you can't catch a ground ball and you can't make an accurate throw to first base."

So he said, "I worked hard at it and I think it has paid dividends." Of course he was being modest. Mathews became an all-around premier player both defensively and offensively. He went from being a below average defensive player to an average defensive player. And then he went from average to above average to being a gold glover. Those things happen, no question about it, and it depends largely on the youngster and his ability to absorb what he was being taught and applying it.

Those things are worth explaining to younger players because becoming a well-rounded player is a key to the whole issue. As a well-rounded player you can do more things, and the more things you can do well, the greater your chances are to have success. And some of these trite comments you hear from people in and out of pro baseball, especially the overused, "Well, if you hit, you play," always misleads the pupil.

There isn't any question about it, no matter how you view baseball, either as a parent or a coach or a scout, your interest in the player is for different reasons. If he's your youngster you want him to do well. There's nothing wrong with that, and that's actually a good approach to take. But when he doesn't do well, how do you treat him? Do you run right to the batting cage and have him take a thousand swings? Of course not.

Don't overdo the situation. Try to give him a good foundation to play, and explain to him when he doesn't do well that the greatest players that ever played don't always do well no matter who they are. The greatest hitters, you name them, don't always have success. Even the best hitters have lifetime averages in the three hundreds. It's a given that they are among the greatest, but they all strike out and they all make errors. Remember, the game is built upon a premise of who fails the least. The most successful players are those who fail the least.

Good coaching at a young level is really a huge advantage for youngsters and they get a lot of value from that. It occurs when coaches have a good general knowledge of the game, know how to teach, and above all relate to players in a way that makes the game fun.

Slumps, Streaks, Sliding,
Stealing and
Other "S" Words

How do slumps and streaks develop? Well, slumps and streaks are not really applicable at every level of play, including high school. The better high school hitter doesn't go into slumps. If he does, he's not one of the better hitters. It's that plain and simple. The slumps and streaks per se are probably almost entirely directed at professional baseball, and, for that matter, major league baseball.

Who encounters slumps and who experiences streaks? You can oversimplify it, but in general terms, the best hitters usually do not have much interaction with slumps. Do they have interactions with streaks? Quite often they do. In my scouting experience, and even when I played in the service, I never paid too much attention to a lot of statistical data. But some of it you do encounter along the way, and you pay more attention to it at the higher levels. By that I mean the major league level.

In my judgment, the toughest offensive record to break would be DiMaggio's fifty-six game hitting streak, which is almost mind-boggling to think that could be done. The only streak even close to his record was forty-four games by Pete Rose in 1978. And keep this in mind. Before that streak with the Yankees, when he played in the Pacific Coast League with the San Francisco Seals, DiMaggio hit in sixty-one straight games in 1933 when he was just nineteen years old, and set a record that is still unbroken. Today the name DiMaggio may not mean that much. Youngsters probably heard he was an old-timer who played with the Yankees and went to the Hall of Fame. Or you may have heard he was married to Marilyn Monroe, the famous movie star of the late forties and fifties. But that's it.

But digging into his career a little bit more tells you something about streaks and slumps. Just to clarify, when DiMaggio hit in fifty-six straight games in 1941, people may ask, "Were there that many guys who threw hard?" Yes, there were. Without breaking this into a numerical hodgepodge of minutiae, Cleveland Indian pitcher Bob Feller threw over a hundred miles an hour with a great curve. Virgil Trucks with Detroit, according to some, threw even harder than Feller. Yankees teammate Atlee Donald, some claim, threw harder than Virgil Trucks, and Tommy Bridges, also with the Tigers, was another good pitcher of that era. There were some great pitchers around. And while integration had not taken place in baseball yet, still, there were only sixteen teams. So the talent level was very similar to what you have now.

All of that being said, the fifty-six-game hitting streak is unbelievable. What makes it even more amazing is this little aside. I really don't remember all the details of this story but I know it's true. Somewhere on the road in 1941 while the streak was still going, I believe the Yankees were playing in Washington or Philadelphia on a Sunday. In those days they played doubleheaders on Sunday, and groundskeepers prepared the field for game two in between games. While that was being done, the players went into the dugout or the clubhouse to freshen up a little bit on those hot summer days when there were no night games being played. They changed undershirts.

At that point he had hit in thirty-some straight games. When DiMaggio came out for the game, he noticed his favorite bat was not there. He became almost panicky. As a result he asked Tommy Henrich if he had picked up the wrong bat, and Henrich said he had not and offered him his bat. DiMaggio was really upset and he didn't get a base hit until quite late in the game, I believe the seventh inning, using Henrich's bat. Then the streak continued for a couple more days, at which point it was discovered that his bat had been swiped right out of the bat rack by a youngster, and somehow or another the bat was recovered. There are all kinds of stories about that. And yes, his bat was recovered.

But think of this. If you watch major league baseball now, and being in the business for all these years, I'm thinking, "What an amazing statistic. The guy had used that bat for approximately thirty-four or thirty-five games and not broken it. It's amazing!" And then he recovered it, and I believe he used that bat until his streak was stopped at fifty-six games by pitchers Jim Bagby and Al Smith, only because the Cleveland third baseman Ken Keltner made two great stops on smashes that DiMaggio hit.

If you watch the World Series and so forth on television and you appreciate the fact that these guys' bats are shattered constantly, you may say, "I wonder, was the game played that differently back in 1941 when DiMaggio batted .357?" He won the Most Valuable Player award, hit with power, and hit many of his thirty home runs in Yankee Stadium, which was a huge ball-park. And amazingly, he struck out only thirteen times that entire season. Incidentally, that's the same year Ted Williams batted .406 and struck out twenty-seven times.

Okay, we're talking roughly seventy years ago, and you're saying, "Well, surely the game must have been appreciably different than it is now." But it really wasn't, in terms of how it was played. You had to hit the ball. You had to catch it. You had to throw it. The pitchers had to pitch it. The strike zone was probably even more liberal than it is now. And as a result, DiMaggio, Williams, and almost any great hitter in any era didn't experience a lot of slumps.

Now there are two types of hitters. You may have heard the saying, "Speed never goes into a slump." And there have been some great hitters who were great runners, too. And the best example of that is Ty Cobb. And progressing forward to some of the exceptional runners over the years, Willie McGee led the National League in hitting and he was a switch hitter with great speed. Speed never goes into a slump. It doesn't necessarily have to be speed in terms of stealing bases or covering ground in the outfield or the infield, but it is speed to first base. Now DiMaggio did not bunt. Williams did not bunt. But DiMaggio was a long striding runner and he could hit balls in the hole at shortstop and beat the throw to first base. And incidentally, Mickey Mantle may have been the fastest runner to first base than anybody who ever played. He was a straight-away runner. Mantle was unbelievable.

What I'm really trying to say is that slumps and streaks are interesting for this reason. When you start talking about people who have had exceptional streaks, Pete Rose at the height of his career, when he was chasing DiMaggio's record in 1978, is one. He was a switch-hitter and was at the top of his game at that time. Those special hitters don't encounter the same type of slumps that let's say the average major league hitter or those who are below average do. Although I've referred to DiMaggio and Williams here, you could also mention the name Rod Carew. Did he go into elongated slumps? No. Did Tony Gwynn? No. Did George Brett? No. Did Wade Boggs? No. And you can go on and on and on.

It's a fair question to ask, "Are you saying there are below average hitters in the major leagues? How do they get there?" The answer to that question is this: They usually get there because they are special defenders. They are aggressive defenders who prevent runs from being scored against their teams. While they contribute occasionally with the bat, they have more problems with slumps than the great hitters. Some of the theories about this are interesting because they become manifested at the time of the year when people watch playoffs and World Series games.

Gee whiz, in 2010 Josh Hamilton hit .356 with the Rangers in the regular season, and yet the Giants' pitching staff did a real number on him and he went two for twenty in the Series. Of course, it was a short five-game set and in which the Giants won four and the Rangers took one. Everything becomes more focused in a World Series because the number of games you play is diminished. You're not playing a team twelve or fifteen times like you do during the course of a year when a hitter may say, "This is how they're pitching me and they're getting me out. When I face Lincecum I'm going to have to spit on that high fast ball. I can't chase his high fast ball. If he throws me a changeup, unless it's right in the sweet zone over the middle of the plate, I'll take it."

In the course of an elongated season, when they play a team in twelve or fourteen games, hitters can make some adjustments. But in the playoffs or World Series they can try to make adjustments, and major leaguers are marvelous in how they adjust to hitting. However, for the most part, great hitters can adjust with almost every at bat. Occasionally, almost with every pitch. You'll see a great hitter, let's say he's a left-hand hitter, facing a very hard thrower and he'll foul a pitch off to the left, and foul another one off to the left. And the color guy in the booth may say, "Oh, gee. He's late. He's late." And the next thing you know the pitcher gets a little more of the plate than he intended and the batter hits it into no-man's-land.

Getting back to DiMaggio, he didn't bust a lot of bats because he hit the ball on the sweet part of the bat. It's that plain and simple. And as a result he did not go into extended slumps. And I have no problem with players who don't want to retire in today's game. Why should they retire? They're making a handsome living, and as long as the people they work for are willing to pay them, why not stay with the game?

Slumps and streaks are interesting on the flip side. I'll allude here to the 2010 Playoffs and World Series between the Texas Rangers and San Francisco Giants. Let's take Cody Ross. Unless you're a very interested fan in San Francisco or follow baseball closely, you would not know who Cody Ross was. He's an outfielder who has been in the big leagues since 2003 and is what we call in baseball "a backwards player," meaning he bats right-handed and throws left. The ratio of right-hand hitters and left-hand throwers to their opposite number, which is left-hand hitters and right-hand throwers, is probably two hundred to one. But that's another topic. Cody Ross has been called in scouting and in the game "a fourth outfielder." After he was drafted by Detroit in 1999, he's bounced around among six big league teams since 2003.

It's a great story because Cody Ross outhit everybody as far as I'm concerned. In terms of consistency in the playoffs, they couldn't figure out how to get him out. He's short in stature, listed at five-ten, but is more likely five-eight. He's strong. And his strike zone is about the size of an 8½" by 11" piece of paper. If you get the baseball to him in that zone he's got a chance to hit it hard, and he did. He did a terrific job for the Giants. You've got to give him credit. The Giants picked him from the Marlins on a waiver deal, late in the year. I know people say they were lucky. Well, there was luck involved, but I don't think they realized what they had. But you know what? Nobody else went after him. The Giants claimed him. On a waiver deal, the lowest teams in the standings get first crack at the player. The Giants were near the top at the time, but nobody else put a claim in on him. And he did a great job. It's a great story for a guy who was just absolutely on fire!

Now, is it fair to use Cody Ross if you're going to compare people? That's what scouts do all the time. Is Cody Ross the equal of Hamilton of Texas? Of course not. But during the course of that World Series he was the equal of anybody who was playing. He was not only equal, he was superior to the rest swinging the bat. Each time he was at the plate was basically a tough at bat for the pitcher, no matter who the pitcher was.

And, to continue reviewing that World Series, the same thing applies to the pitching. The pitching by the Giants was terrific. Texas' pitching was pretty good until they ran into the Giants, and then it was spotty in spite of Cliff Lee, who is a very fine pitcher. There's no question about that.

I went through a period one time a couple of years ago crossing the country, and I think I was in twenty-one airports in twenty-four days. Of course there was also a lot of driving involved everyplace I went to see players. But everyplace I would go I'd turn on the rental car radio and they had talk radio shows where these guys "know everything." If you want to know who should start at halfback for the Dallas Cowboys, they know it. If you want to know who the point guard should be for the Celtics, they know it. If you want to know who should start Game Four in the World Series, they know that, too. They know what the batting order is. They know everything, these guys. Since they work in almost every city and you hear them on almost every outlet. So, you say to yourself, "As long as they're talking about baseball (or whatever the given sport is), I guess that's good because, after all, interest in the game is what pays the bills." I think that's the only reason I listen to them aside from trying to pick up a late score or something.

I know I'm straying away here from slumps and streaks, but I got on the topic of Cody Ross, and it's amazing how many of these so-called experts who covered the World Series finally recognized what a great hitter Ross was by the time the Giants had won. Common sense tells you he is not the equal of Hamilton of Texas. He wouldn't be over the course of a full season. But he was on fire at that time. Whether I think he's a fourth outfielder or not, he wasn't an extra outfielder in the playoffs and World Series. He was a very special player in those games.

I hope Cody Ross continues with it because he defies everything professional baseball says they do not like. They do not like left-hand throwers who hit right-handed. They don't like them now. They didn't like them thirty years ago. They didn't like them sixty years ago, and they didn't like them when baseball started. It's a goofy analogy. It doesn't make a lot of sense that it should matter one way or another which way the guy hits. But I suppose the point is that since the guy threw left-handed, teams were limited where they could move him defensively.

One of the guys who had a terrible time during the playoffs was the Yankees' right fielder Nick Swisher, who was Oakland's first selection in the 2002 draft. He was a great contributor for them all year long and this is not to demean his contributions during the course of the season. Although Swisher was a solid performer for the Yankees that season, he is not a premium player in my judgment.

But remember, when you get into the postseason games, there's a reason these teams are in those games. Again, it can be an overriding issue, but more often than not, the teams who get to that point are better balanced clubs than the teams that don't get there. They are better balanced usually because their pitching is solid. And their hitting, if it doesn't overwhelm you, is clutch hitting. They're usually good defensive clubs. They find more ways to beat you than you face during the course of the season.

But getting back to streaks and slumps, you are much more apt to see a premium offensive player have an exceptional hitting streak. You are much less likely to see him go into a protracted slump. It has happened, but the two generally don't run hand in hand. It's the same with pitching. When you have a genuine premium pitcher and you talk about him going into a protracted slump, it means he is having trouble getting hitters out. That's usually the result of one of two things. He's either had some physical problem where he's gone from being a premium pitcher to becoming an ordinary guy in the big leagues. Or he lost some of his basic stuff and his command is no longer plus. That happens to almost all pitchers, usually with age.

The only pitcher that I can think of in modern times who retired with overpowering stuff, which is what he brought to the dance initially, was Sandy Koufax, who retired in 1966 after a dozen years in the big leagues because he had a circulation problem. He retired at the top of his game when he was winning twenty-five or twenty-six games. Nolan Ryan pitched forever and a day, twenty-seven years to be exact, 1966–1993, and was one of the all-time greats. But Nolan Ryan's stuff when he was forty-four years old was not equal to his stuff at twenty-four years old. Let's not kid ourselves about that. But he was still a tough customer.

Parallel to the career of Koufax there were "Lefty" Steve Carlton (24 years in the majors) and Bob Gibson (17 years in the majors), and others just off the top of my head. When they lose their stuff they didn't go from being a premium guy to a guy who gets battered from pillar to post. But their skills diminish and it's usually reflected in their ERA.

And then there's the other pitcher. We see more of them. Let's use Greg Maddux, who is a sure Hall of Fame pitcher as soon as he becomes eligible. He had good stuff. It wasn't great stuff. But he had good stuff with exceptional command of his pitches. And as a result he could carve up any lineup, when he was cooking, which was most of the time. Again, when his basic stuff diminished a little bit and his command was not quite as precise at it had been earlier, we started to see that reflected in his wins-losses and other statistics.

Common sense tells you this. You will see very few slumps out of exceptional hitters and exceptional pitchers. More often than not, any streak that you see is usually the result of a superior player who performs constantly. And when you think about the all-time hitting streaks you see names that you're familiar with whether you ever saw them play or not.

I want to touch on one more player, outfielder Kenny Landreaux. When I was with the Angels years ago they took him as their first pick in the 1976 draft. He had a great hitting stroke and was a good hitter. He could throw out a twenty- to twenty-five-game hitting streak for you. But one of the things he had a tendency to do was this. During the course of his streak when he was seeing the ball well, which was most of the time, he'd be going along and he'd hit one out of the park. When that happened his streak didn't stop immediately, but occasionally his swing would get a little bit longer after he hit the ball out of the park, and then he'd have a couple of "o'fors." Those are just some of the bumps in the road that even good hitters can experience.

This isn't my original thought, and I don't even know who came up with it, but I like it because it makes a lot of good sense. What do all good hitters or great hitters have in common? It's not a trick question either. What do they have in common? It's very simple. Good hitters hit. And that's it.

I can tell you a good lesson I learned when I was in my second year of scouting. I was not getting paid very much at that time, and that required me to have a second job in order to support my family. I had another job. But I was under the auspices of my mentor and supervisor (we didn't have all these fancy titles they have now in terms of scouting), a man by the name of Joe Stephenson, who was a wonderful scout for the Red Sox for many, many years. He signed MVP's, Rookies of the Year, and I believe at one time Joe had five players in the All-Star game. He signed players like Fred Lynn, Rick Burleson, Dwight Evans, and Bill Lee. Years earlier he had signed a little outfielder by the name of Albie Pearson, who the Red Sox ultimately traded to Washington. But Albie was the 1958 Rookie of the Year in the American League. Joe signed a player named Brady Anderson, who hit fifty home runs for Baltimore after the Red Sox traded him because he didn't hit enough, and he had a terrific career at Baltimore.

Joe was an old catcher who played in the big leagues in 1943 (Giants), 1944 (Cubs), and 1947 (White Sox), when he appeared in a total of twenty-nine games. He wasn't a big talker or a big bragger, although bragging does exist in scouting. But I suppose it's that way in almost any business. Joe was a very sharp baseball guy. As a matter of fact, I have worked with three generations of Stephensons: Joe, his son Jerry, and his grandson Brian. Both Joe and Jerry have passed away, but Brian is still out there representing the family name. I'll never forget the tremendous impact Joe has had on my career. He was a wonderful guy, a very logical guy. I worked with some terrific scouts over the years, but Joe probably had the best approach and best logical answers that made sense to me.

Anyway, in 1970 Baltimore and Cincinnati were squaring off in the World Series and I was expounding about my theory of why I thought Cincinnati would beat Baltimore. Joe and I used to meet occasionally during the season or late in the year at a bowling alley that wasn't too far from his house. We had a couple of beers and discussed what was going on in baseball. At any rate, he said, "Who do you like in this World Series, Gib?"

"Oh, Cincinnati. They're going to beat the Orioles. They have Bench and Rose, Concepción and Tony Perez, first baseman Lee May," and blah-blah-blah. He just listened to me for a little bit and I felt pretty good. Here was a guy who had been in baseball his whole life, and at that point I was in my second season as a scout. And here he was asking my opinion about who was going to win the World Series. I remember Joe, at that time in his life, smoked cigars. Now you can't see anybody smoke a cigar in a bowling alley or anyplace else, really. They have to go outside to do it. But he hemmed and hawed and took a big drag on his El Producto.

"Well," he said, "just remember, Gib, good pitching will always defeat good hitting."

It didn't shock me at the time that he said it, but the more I've thought about it over the last forty years, it does make good sense. Good pitching will almost always defeat good hitting. If you think closely about it and review the two teams that played in the 2010 World Series, there isn't any question in my mind that Texas had a more potent offense than the Giants had. But still, the Giants had enough clutch hitting and enough contributors to get to the World Series, number one. And number two, the Giants had superior starting pitching.

When you talk about it during the course of a season or in a World Series, it almost always prevails. You can look at this World Series or that World Series. I recall the 1966 Series, a couple of years before I started scouting, when the Dodgers were swept by Baltimore. The Dodgers had wonderful pitching and good clutch hitting at that point, but the equalizer there was that Baltimore had outstanding pitching also, and probably a slightly better hitting club. In fact, as I recall, the Dodgers scored two runs in Game One and were then shut out in the final three games. That four-game World Series sticks with me to this day.

Joe Stephenson didn't go on comparing the two teams player by player. You hear people do that constantly in the press after the event. The question was always, "How does your lineup match up with their pitching?" It was not a question of was your first baseman better than theirs.

An interesting development I've seen in recent years, probably in the last twenty years anyway, are the radar guns, speed guns that measure the speed of the pitch to the plate. It's become a standard instrument used in professional scouting and even, for that matter, in amateur scouting. And what's even worse, I believe, is that I've seen fathers of kids go to ballgames and have their own speed guns. The theory being that if they see a ninety-mile-an-hour fastball thrown by a sixteen- or seventeen-year-old boy, then that kid is ready for the major leagues. They think this because they were watching the World Series and the starting pitcher or somebody who pitched in the course of one of the games happened to be throwing eighty-eight miles per hour at given times. In a lot of instances the speed gun is a detriment to the development of the young pitcher.

I think this is important to keep in mind. The idea that a high school player who throws ninety on the speed gun is ready for professional baseball is as illogical as saying that if your youngster were to pass his driving test at age sixteen he would be ready to drive in the Indianapolis 500! The speed gun is a device that is used. Some organizations lean on it much more heavily than others.

But in the art of pitching, and pitching really is an art, great pitchers or good pitchers, however you classify them, will all tell you the same thing. Unless your stuff is unreasonably great and unhittable, which happens maybe in one out of every five thousand big leaguers, the fact that you can throw ninety miles an hour is simply a shortcut to saying that you have acceptable velocity. Remember this. Pitchers in the big leagues are trying to locate their pitches, and that means they don't throw them right down Main Street, right through the middle of the plate belt-high to hitters. Big league hitters hit that pitch. That's called a mistake. It's called being wild in the strike zone.

The object with a fastball is movement. Power pitchers get their fastball to rise usually. It has a sailing effect. They may throw what appears to the hitter to be about belt-high in the strike zone, but it rides up maybe the last ten feet, and that pitch is particularly difficult for a hitter to handle simply because he has trouble getting his arms extended. It's sort of a double edged sword there because he sees that pitch better than he does the so-called sinking fastball which is thrown knee high, because batters can get their arms extended much easier on a pitch that is down. So, that being said, I wanted to mention that because this is just one example of why the use of a speed gun by a parent is really of no consequence to a scout at all.

You go to games. You see scouts with speed guns. I've had conversations with pitchers over the years. One of my best friends is Red Adams, who pitched for seventeen years in professional baseball and was a Dodger major league pitching coach, and he says the same thing. Essentially the gun doesn't tell you anything. If you watch the game through a trained eye, you will see hitters at times have a very tough time getting their arms extended and getting the bat head through the hitting zone against a pitcher who's throwing maybe ninety, ninety-one, or ninety-two.

Tim Lincecum in San Francisco is a great young pitcher who has already earned two Cy Young awards. He pitched a terrific game in the 2010 World Series against the Texas Rangers. He can throw his ninety-two-mile-an-hour fastball by hitters, especially up in the zone. He's not trying to sink the ball. He has three pitches, the fastball, slider, and the changeup, which are all excellent pitches for him. He has great command and he's very durable, but he's not a physical guy at all. He's kind of a contradiction. He's a slender kid, maybe five-ten or eleven and 165 pounds soaking wet. He's not a big strong guy as major league pitchers are considered to be. Despite breaking down a bit during the 2012 season, he fought his way back and managed to be a big contributor out of the bullpen in the World Series against the Tigers.

I would caution every parent to save your money. Don't fall in love with a speed gun and follow your youngster around trying to get a reading from it. And I've had this same conversation with professional pitchers. I remember being sent to Albuquerque a long time ago, 1989, I think, to see William Brennan pitch. He was considered to be a good young pitcher in our organization. John Wetteland was on that same pitching staff. But anyway, Brennan pitched and he was really hit hard. He had seen me behind the plate with a speed gun and when I talked with him the next night he wanted to know how hard he was throwing.

And I said, "Going or coming?" When hitters hit the ball it might come in at ninety and go out about a hundred and five or more. I wasn't trying to be smart with him. William was a nice guy. But he was still worried about what his speed gun readings were. And the hitters normally will tell you how well they see the baseball.

I remember having a conversation with a former left-hand major league pitcher in our organization by the name of Al Downing. Al was a power pitcher when he was with the Yankees. But time and some arm problems reduced the velocity on his fastball. By the time we got him he was still a very clever, good pitcher. In fact, in his first season with the Dodgers, 1971, he compiled a 20–7 record for us. At any rate, I remember him saying, "Pitching is the art of getting hitters to reach for pitches in the strike zone or out."

You can see some funny looking swings as a result of some pitchers being very clever working to a spot. That's the important thing. Your stuff is important in professional baseball, that's for sure. But being able to locate it is everything. Things become more equal when the young pitcher with a real good arm and maybe good stuff starts facing very good hitters who don't chase pitches out of the strike zone, be it in high school or college or the minor leagues. So those are ingredients to remember when looking to develop a young pitcher's so-called repertoire of pitches.

I listened to a very well-known writer who is

Red Adams, longtime pitching coach and instructor with the Dodgers and a good friend.

basically stationed in New York named Mike Lupica, who has written several successful books about baseball. I heard him on a talk show recently and he was on with another one of these genius guys who has an answer to every sports question there is. And again, you become somewhat skeptical when these people tell you that their background is essentially that they're longtime fans but have never played the game. I'm much more apt to listen to somebody who has played the game and can appreciate the difficulty that exists in trying to play any sport professionally. Since baseball is my game and it's the one I've been paid to give opinions on for the last four decades, I'll stick to that.

Being analytical is one thing, but just filling up air space on the radio or TV is something else. I heard this program during a period right after the 2010 season when the Yankees and Derek Jeter were negotiating. Would they give him another contract or let him go into the free agency market? Lupica made a comment when he was discussing Derek Jeter and the fact that Jeter had a great career, but he went on to say that in his judgment the Yankees would re-sign him. But he was getting older and the question is who would play short on the Yankee team? And he said, "Well, he'd probably have to play somebody else. But he's a shortstop by trade, and after all, if he doesn't play shortstop, where can he play?" And then he went on to say that if the Yankees tried to move him to second base, that wouldn't work because Cano is such an outstanding young player. Cano may be one of the greatest all-around second basemen who have ever played.

Now I certainly appreciate the skills of Cano and think he is a very special young player. But on the face of Lupica's statement, it's almost laughable. Remember, Jeter came up in 1995 and is an established player. If he does not get another base hit, he's a cinch Hall of Famer, probably a first ballot selection five years after he retires. I've never heard anybody make a remark asking where a guy that plays shortstop like he does is going to play, especially if he has Hall of Fame credentials. It's a given that Jeter is not as good a player as he was five years ago. Anyway, the Yankees did re-sign Jeter in December when they agreed on a fifty-one-million-dollar, three-year deal.

I'm reminded of a statement I made some years ago when I went to see Bob Horner play. At that time Horner was a second baseman at Arizona State and I was working for Kansas City. Horner was one-dimensional. He had a short swing. He had plus power and he made good contact for a guy with power, but his defensive skills were very mediocre. He was a thickly built kid, stocky, strong, but he had the type of body where he may get heavy. So I came back after seeing him and I was working with one of the great old scouts with Kansas City, Rosey Gilhousen, who signed George Brett, among others. Rosey said, "What did you think of Horner?"

And I said, "I think he has a chance to hit and hit with power."

"Yeah, I agree with that," he said. "Do you have any negatives on him?"

"Yeah. Where's he going to play?"

Rosey just laughed and said, "Hey Gib, do you know where the eight hundred pound grizzly bear plays?"

"What?"

He repeated it, "Do you know where the eight-hundred-pound grizzly bear plays?"

I knew something was afoot, so I said, "Where does he play, Rosey?"

"Any place he wants to play."

That's oversimplifying it, for sure. But I got the point and had to agree.

This relates back to the Derek Jeter discussion by Lupica and others. They questioned where the Yankees would play him if he were re-signed because his double play partner at second base is an All-Star player and may be the greatest second baseman who ever played the game. Think about that. Does that cover some territory or what? As far as I'm concerned, it's typical of what we get with a lot of comments that come out of shows like that.

Earlier, I remember a program like that about one of our players, Andre Ethier. He's been a very fine acquisition for us. He is a very good player who started out this year on fire. He hit for power. He hit for average. And he hit in the clutch. When the season was about three weeks old, there were writers predicting that he would be a Triple Crown winner. Think of that. He made the All-Star team, and his average dropped off a little bit after an injury. He still has holes in his game. He struggles at times against good left-handed pitching. But beware of these big fancy comments that come out of the written and electronic press.

A guy I went to school with sent me an email this year that said, "I understand that you may retire shortly. I bet what brought that on was the Giants winning the National League pennant." Well, I don't have any intention of retiring at this point. And his comment is so far from the truth. When you're in professional baseball your chief hope is that you get into the post-season. And if you don't get in, you sort of follow the lead like everybody else does. You watch the games without being involved to the extent of charting pitches or trying to figure how to get this guy out or that guy out. I'm watching it just like the rest of the public. So I told my friend I really don't care who wins in the World Series. I have friends working on both clubs.

But I can't help commenting on the prognosticators about that World Series. Things like, Texas beat the Yankees. They outpitched them, which they did. They outhit them. They out-defended them. They're more athletic.

And there was a whole litany of observations about how good Texas was because they had beaten the Yankees.

Now, look. Let's be realistic. The Yankees did not win their division. Tampa Bay did. So let's accept that for what it was. Tampa Bay had a better club, by an eyelash, than the Yankees. But the Yankees are always tough. This was just not one of their great teams. This Yankee team is getting a little bit older, even though they had some very fine younger players. To be perfectly honest, I thought the Yankees would beat Texas. But the point is this. Texas beat the Yankees and the attitude simply was, "How could Texas not beat the Giants, the misfit Giants with a bunch of cast-off players?" The general attitude was the Giants had good pitching, but Texas had too many good position players. Look who they had. Josh Hamilton was later named the American League MVP. Vladimir Guerrero is still a terribly dangerous hitter. And Michael Young, the third baseman, well, here's a guy who usually pumps out two hundred hits a year. They were dangerous in a lot of different departments.

And they had former Cy Young Award winner Cliff Lee on the mound. But he couldn't pitch every game, and he is human, and was beaten. So the irony of the whole thing is this. When you listen to these prognosticators, many of whom come out of big league backgrounds, it tells you about the uncertainties that exist in big league baseball. And that simply is, "Who mentioned Cody Ross before Game One?" I don't know of anybody who did any color of any of the games, on radio or TV, who mentioned Cody Ross. And, again, if you're a student of who wins and who plays key roles in the World Series, then you say, "You know what? It may be somebody we're not even assuming is going to be an important player in the Series."

Realistically, and to Bruce Bochy's credit, Ross hit well down the stretch for the Giants, so they played him. You have to give Bochy a high mark for that. They paid Aaron Rowand a lot of money to sit on the bench. But Bochy went with the hot hand. And I believe in Game One, Ross hit in the eight hole. By the time they were playing in the fourth and fifth game, Cody Ross was hitting in the five hole behind Buster Posey in the cleanup spot.

That's the way he managed the team the entire way, and if I were to make an observation (and this isn't the way I make my living but you can't help saying it), there is no getting away from it. The Giants outpitched, outhit, outfielded and outplayed, and by far outmanaged Texas. With all due respect to Ron Washington, who I'm sure is a fine manager, he was far outmanaged in this World Series. It appeared as the Series went on that Bochy's decision-making was not spontaneous. It was well planned. He did a great job and the Giants got everything they deserved.

At this point I'd like to mention some subjects that are worth pursuing regarding young players from Little League age on, and some observations I've had over the years watching baseball at every level, amateur and professional.

One of the biggest gripes that I have in watching high school and college baseball now is tied to a certain extent to what youngsters see on television in terms of professional baseball. And that is, essentially, base running, base stealing, etcetera. Sliding is of particular interest to me because I see so often young players slide headfirst into all bases. It's prevalent now.

As a matter of fact, last night I saw a game, a scout day in Phoenix, and Arizona State had a scrimmage. In the course of the scrimmage when one team was playing against another but all were on the same roster, almost every base runner who would try to steal a base or go from first to third on a base hit slid headfirst. Now the question is, why do they do it? Does it get them there quicker? It really doesn't. Most who slide headfirst do so because they don't know how to slide feet first.

Teaching young players to slide feet first is very easy. It's almost a lost art, but it's very easy. And obviously they're not being taught to do this at a young age. Remember this. When you slide headfirst you risk breaking a finger, or a hand, or a wrist. Now the opposing argument would be that if you slide feet first you could catch your spikes in the dirt and break an ankle. That can happen if a player does not know how to slide feet first. But teaching him how to do it, the old standard pop-up slide where you go in feet first into the bag and then just pop up ready to run, that's another issue because that prepares you to take an additional base if there's an overthrow. But if you slide headfirst it's very difficult to get back on your feet.

The proper way to teach kids to slide is very simple. When they're eight or nine years old, take them out to a grassy area, have them take off their spikes so they're just there in their sox, and have them slide on the grass. Once they get the knack of it, which really is not difficult at all, they become proficient at it. In our generation everybody slid feet first and most of us were all taught the same way. We learned the pop-up slide, the hook slide. Of course, the hook slide is when you're sliding away from the tag. But sliding headfirst was heavily frowned on. I see it in the major leagues, even at home plate, and every time I see it, it looks to me like a collision waiting to happen. If the catcher has the ball, remember he has a chest protector, shin guards, a helmet and the glove. Now you slide headfirst into that and it can be real trouble where you could end up with a broken jaw.

But it is a lost art. If you think of the great base stealers, and I have seen quite a few, it's interesting. Maury Wills was a great base stealer. Rickey Henderson was a great base stealer. Lou Brock was a great stealer. Almost all of them predominantly slid feet first. But in this era I think it's been a neglected teaching mechanism when players are younger. When they get older, if they don't know how to do it and may be afraid of injury, they decide to go in there headfirst.

In my mind it makes no sense to see this skill not being taught. We've had many examples in recent years of position players sliding into bases headfirst breaking a finger, a hand. Sliding headfirst is an accident waiting to happen. And it's a foolish thing, really, because they're not learning to do it properly at a young age, so they do it the other way. A perfect example of that is Pete Guerrero, who had a great career with the Dodgers. He was not a base stealer but was a very good power hitter. Although Pete could really run, he was never, ever a good base runner. He was a good-sized guy, probably six feet, 190–200 pounds, a strong and well-built guy. He never ever knew how to slide feet first. He went in head first and he didn't do that very well either.

Most young players are taught that when you're running to first what you do is try to hit the front side of the bag as opposed to the middle of the bag. The front side, meaning the infield side as opposed to the outfield side, makes the run a foot shorter. That's what you should be shooting for. That's what the smart base runners, and the great base runners, though not necessarily the fastest base runners, all do. But Pete never did that. Instead, if he hit a grounder to the shortstop or whatever, he ran full speed to first, trying to beat the throw, and took a long stride at the end, landing in the middle of the bag. And more often than not he was out on a bang-bang play. The same thing applied when he was on second base.

When I first joined the Dodgers in 1979, the third base coach was Danny Ozark. He had started his career in the Dodger organization back in the forties. He played a long time in the minor leagues and even had a successful stint managing Philadelphia. But he was getting up in years, and once he left the Phillies he decided to retire. Instead, he was talked out of it, and he joined our club as our third base coach when Tommy Lasorda was the manager, early in his managing career.

I remember this particular circumstance. Pete Guerrero was on second base in the game we were watching and somebody got a base hit up the middle. The ball was hit pretty hard and there was no way in the world there should have been a play at the plate with Pete as the base runner. When that ball was hit he went hellbent for leather and tried to score on the play. Danny Ozark had been an excellent third base coach for many years and he was waving his arms in a circle for Pete to score. But he almost ran over Danny, who must have been thirty feet outside the base line between the third base bag and the plate. And Pete was out at the plate.

I knew Danny pretty well. He had been in the game since 1942 as a player, minor and major league manager with the Phillies, 1973–79, and was a very smart baseball man. Anyway, I ran into him a few days later and I remember him commenting on how good base runners would cut the inside part of the bag. He said, "Lopes could have scored easily on that play and been halfway to the dugout and yet Pete was out." Now, Guerrero was a guy who could really run straight away, but he did not have the instincts, and never developed them, on how to cut the inside of the bag. Danny said, "So there I was waving him around to score as I watched the play, the ball was coming back and there Pete was bearing down on *me*, and I was fifteen feet wide of the line!"

He took the long way around and he was out. Now you would think this would never happen at the major league level. But it does. When you see good base runners score, they are not all the fastest guys in the world, but the good ones all know how to cut the inside of the bag.

Years ago we used to pay attention to that. I remember playing ball in the service for a guy who was a very good coach named Al Espinoza. When you play service baseball, it's not like organized ball, even at the minor league level. I played with a lot of big leaguers and minor leaguers in the service. So these were not essentially high school kids. But you don't play in a series of games. It's not like organized ball. When Ogden plays Orem in the minor leagues in the lower level of rookie league baseball, you still play them six or eight times during the course of the year. In the big leagues, the Dodgers and Giants probably play each other twelve or fourteen times a season. At the organized baseball level you develop a feel and a visual experience watching guys play. So Espinoza always told us to watch the opposition, whom we may not have seen before, take infield, and pay particular attention to the infielders.

He was right. It's important to watch how the second baseman makes the pivot. If he goes to the inside part of the bag, the runner should go after him. Slide to the inside part of the bag because your job, if it's a double-play ball, is to take out the infielder.

Most infielders go to the inside part of the bag to turn a double play. Some infielders like to turn it on the outfield side of second base, let's say the left field side, where they keep the bag between themselves and the runner. And they're tougher guys to take out on a double play. There are a few second basemen who will approach the bag and punch the bag with their left foot and kick back to the right field side of the bag, so the runner should go to that side of the bag to take him out.

Watch one of these guys during infield because the way he does it during infield is the way he's going to do it in the game. Most of them do it as creatures of habit. Even in the big leagues they will pivot from their comfortable side at second base. And we were told constantly that if he crosses the bag, make sure you go to the inside because that's where he's going to be. If you watch him in infield and he punches that bag with his left foot and kicks back to the right field side of the bag, go to that side to take him out. You don't see that as much any more with the better base stealers, especially if a guy is a headfirst slider. The headfirst slider is not in a position to take anybody out. What's he going to do, lead with his head and hit him in the knee? Visualize that! It just doesn't make sense.

Now you don't see all of the above as much as you should in the major leagues because of the prevalence of the headfirst sliders. I'm not living in the past on this. I'm just saying an effective way to teach young players is to learn the pop-up slide, where you go in feet first and bounce right up if there's an overthrow. It's an important thing for a young player to learn.

When we were kids we played on all sorts of surfaces. It was not artificial grass for sure, but the infields were definitely not manicured. The first playground team I ever played on was Raymond Street Playground. It was about a block away from where I lived. We were just a bunch of bush league little kids playing on a surface that was almost like playing on the street. Yet, because we had learned to slide properly, we rarely got strawberries.

Another thing is this. When you look at good major league base stealers now, they're not stealing those bases because of headfirst slides. They have three key ingredients that enable them to be great base stealers. They have great speed, they get very good jumps, and they know how to read pitchers. The headfirst slide means nothing.

I'm going to draw a couple of numerical examples here. And these are used in scouting when you do what they call "advance work." When you do advance work, you use your stopwatch to time the pitcher from the second the ball leaves his hand until the catcher catches the ball. That's the first thing you do. Once you get the knack of it, it's actually pretty easy to do. If the pitcher can unload from the time he lets the ball go until the catcher catches the ball in anything from 1.2 seconds to 1 second flat or 1.1 seconds, he gives the catcher an excellent chance to throw out a prospective base stealer.

Now, there's another part to this equation. When the catcher catches the ball, how long does it take from the time the ball hits his glove until the throw gets to second base? And it doesn't matter whether the shortstop or second baseman covers second base. Average is 2.0 seconds. Guys like catcher Joe Mauer, who was the number-one pick in the country in 2001 by Minnesota, has a very quick catch-and-throw transfer, and he does it in about 1.95. When you total the two, let's say the pitcher's 1.2 and the catcher is 2.0, that's 3.2 seconds. The best base stealer in the world is going to be out unless he gets a rolling start on a good throw. And the throw doesn't have to be on the bag.

I would always tell young catchers, and you see a lot of this, make sure your throw to the covering fielder, the second baseman or the shortstop, is letter-high. Don't worry about throwing it on the bag because that quite often results in short-hopping the infielder, and then he has to try to field the short-hop throw and it's murder to try to do that with a guy sliding into the bag.

There's one important thing to remember about throwing the ball, whether you're a catcher trying to throw out a base stealer or an infielder starting a double play or whatever. When you get the baseball too far in your palm they call that "choking the ball." Youngsters want to have a good grip on the ball, but there is a tendency to grip it too tightly. When you grip it too tightly it inhibits your ability to throw it as hard. It's a sensation that has to be developed over the years because when little kids start playing, let's say at eight years old, their hands are small and they have to get their fingers all over the ball to hang on to it. Quite often they choke the ball. Hopefully this is a habit that will break itself as the youngster grows and his hand gets bigger.

Two catchers come to mind as the best examples of great throwing catchers in modern times: Johnny Bench on the Cincinnati Reds, and Steve Yeager for the Dodgers. Of course, Yeager was far below Bench in ability to swing the bat. But defensively he was probably Bench's equal. Bench is in the Hall of Fame and we know Yeager isn't. But he was known around both leagues for having a great arm. When you would watch them throw, their throws were constantly on the bag or caught letter high. They had great quick transfers and good arms. They threw about half the potential base stealers out, and that includes some of the best of them, like Lou Brock and Davey Lopes and a few others.

There are two big differences. Yeager and Bench had what they call 8.0 arms. The highest grade you can give a catcher in terms of his throwing is to give him an 8.0 arm. Both of them had that.

To draw a couple of comparisons, I recall one experience I had when I was covering the San Diego Padres doing some advance work. A good example there was an excellent right handed pitcher, Jake Peavy, who combined all the qualities you look for. He had good stuff, was a great competitor, very resilient, and simply outstanding on the mound. He has been with the White Sox since 2009 and may be on the downside of his career now. He's had a lot of arm problems recently. But when he was good, he was very, very good. A throw from Peavy to the plate was 1.1 and 1.0 flat with a runner on. That gives a chance to throw the runner out to even a mediocre throwing catcher, not Bench or Yeager, but a guy with let's say a 5.0 arm, which is considered an average major league arm. But Peavy still gives that catcher a chance to throw that runner out.

You can combine the two, let's say a pitcher at 1.0 or 1.1 and a catcher at 2.5, and that still totals 3.5 seconds. Unless the base runner gets a rolling start he will be out. All the catcher has to do is get the ball to the covering fielder.

But there's a kink in that armor, too, which is this. The pitcher still has to be able to hold the runner. You see this in pro ball quite often when there is a rabbit at first base. The pitcher will throw over there without intentions of picking him off, but to keep him honest. He doesn't want to take an additional three-foot lead to what he normally would take. And that's where the great base runners "cheat." An example of this is that their aggressive lead off first base allows them to peek in at the sign of the catcher. Davey Lopes was really good at this. The minute he saw the catcher put two fingers down, indicating a breaking pitch, he ran. Lopes rarely got the steal sign from Lasorda. He was allowed to steal on his own because he was so successful.

I remember an experience with speedster Davey Lopes. I had a very good kid who I signed who incidentally never played in the big leagues, and it's a shame because he was a hard worker and he had a solid chance to play major league ball. His name is Harold Perkins and he was a switch-hitter who could run. He stole ninety-four bases during his six years in the minor leagues; his best year was 1983 with Vero Beach, when he stole 32 bags. After that season his totals dropped steadily until he had only stolen four in his final season, 1989, when he was in the Baltimore system.

Now at that time I used to take young players I had signed from the L.A. area into Dodger Stadium in the offseason and use the batting machine and other equipment that's underneath the stands, and work with them. Davey Lopes had remained in California after the season and happened to be in the ballpark on this particular day chatting with Jim Muhe. I had Harold Perkins in there and I was working on his hitting stroke with the machine. When we had just about finished, I brought Harold to meet Davey. Now Davey was always a rather intense guy, all business, but he was really nice to the kid, and I think he gave him a glove and a pair of spikes. When a successful big leaguer treats a minor leaguer who really hasn't done anything at the major league level yet, it's a nice thing to see that they have not forgotten where they came from.

I mentioned the fact that Harold had stolen thirty-two bases in the

Harold Perkins listened to Davey Lopes about running.

Florida League that season and Davey said, "Gee, that's great, Harold. Do you have your sights set at stealing seventy-five or eighty bases this year?"

When Harold said he hadn't, Lopes said, "Always set goals for yourself and you'll do better." So we went out on the diamond and saw there was a catcher and a pitcher out there working, and Davey gave Harold some pointers on how to work his lead off first base. Davey said to him, "Most base stealers have a tendency to get very low as they take their lead. I never did that and the reason I didn't is because I'm only five-nine. Now this is the way I would take a lead," and he bent slightly at the knees. "Simulate the position you would take if you were playing basketball and somehow or another you would get caught under the basket and you may want to take a rebound. Flex your knees and keep the upper part of your body fairly erect. You don't want your weight leaning forward or backward. You want your weight evenly distributed."

They worked on that for a while and Harold caught on pretty well. Then Lopes went on to say this: "Always keep an eye on the catcher. Always do that. Your peripheral vision will allow you to see the pitcher, and the millisecond that his left shoulder twitches he's coming to first base, and you have to have the ability to get back repeatedly."

Because another excellent base stealer, Maury Wills, had preceded him, Lopes modeled a lot of his moves on what Maury Wills did. "But Maury was different than I was because he took exceptionally big leads to try and bother the pitcher, and he felt he'd accomplished this by drawing four or five throws to first. But I didn't do that because the ups and downs of sliding back to the bag could wear a guy down over the course of a season. What I did instead was to take a conventional lead like a guy who doesn't steal a lot of bases, but I would still get a good enough lead to pick signs from the catcher."

And, believe it or not, picking a sign off a catcher is a lot easier at the major league level than you might think. Catchers are not as careful as they should be about protecting their signs, and all signs are pretty conventional. If you sense it's going to be a breaking pitch, you can steal the bag. There's no question about it. A good major league fastball is 95, a let's-get-ahead-of-the-hitter fastball may be 90. We'll discuss that further down the line.

A breaking pitch, a slider, is roughly ten miles an hour slower than a fastball. So let's say the pitcher has an 85-mile-an-hour slider, and a 95-mile-an-hour fastball. If you can pick the sign being a breaking pitch, stealing the bag is going to be easier because it takes longer for the baseball to get to the catcher. If you're good at it and you can pick a sign where the guy's going to throw a changeup, that's even slower, meaning a changeup off a 95-mile-an-hour fastball may be 82.

Now there has developed in the major leagues in recent years what they call a slide-step pitch, which is basically not an exaggerated move by the pitcher's leg when he kicks to throw, but he more or less slides to first base. And that's worth mentioning here. Pitchers who have a tendency to be a little bit longer to the plate have learned to use the slide step, which makes them quicker to the plate with a base runner. If they don't have a base runner then they may be a high kicker.

As I'm organizing my thoughts on this, I'm thinking of some of the things that were explained by Davey Lopes. He said when he was first base coach for the Phillies guys could really run the bases but not all were base stealers. "If you watch their base runners on a potential double play ball, they sure go after the infielders." And another thing Lopes told me was that he had most of the catcher's signs that he'd been able to pick early in the year. He said he kept that to himself early in his career, never told anybody at all. "I had most of their signs except that damn Bench," he said. "I couldn't get his. He hid them very well. And the guy had a great arm."

From that, learn how to be aggressive, learn how to slide properly, and learn how to start. Lopes was a great starter. I mentioned Al Wiggins, whom I signed before I joined the Dodgers. He was a great base stealer. With the Dodgers' team in the California League, the Lodi Dodgers, he stole 120 bases in 1980. With the San Diego Padres in 1983 he stole 66 bases, and followed that with 70 in 1984. Al combined two great qualities. He had a great "burst," meaning a great start, and he was fast. He was extremely tough to throw out on a straight steal, even if there was a pitchout. Those two qualities helped him become a premier base stealer.

But, in terms of hitting, pitching, and throwing, this is an interesting quality. There was guy who came to the big leagues with the Chicago Cubs many years ago. I was not yet scouting or it might have been very early in my career. This fellow was an L.A. guy, went to UCLA and got a large bonus. His name was Chris Krug. He was considered one of the best prospects at the time he signed a contract. He was never a great hitter. But his defensive skills behind the plate allowed him to get to the big leagues. He was a fine catcher with a shotgun arm. So they tell the story, and I'm sure it's accurate, that the Cubs came in to play the Dodgers in Dodger Stadium, this was probably in the late sixties, and Krug took infield with the Cubs and really showed off his great throwing arm. He was going to show everybody that he could throw right up there with the best catchers in the game. And it was agreed that he had a great throw to second base. The saying was that you could hang the wash out on his throws, meaning he had a double plus arm. If a catcher did not exhibit a great throw they would say there's a hump in the floor when he throws to second.

So what happened on this particular day was Krug took this great infield. When the game started, Maury Wills went to the plate for the Dodgers in the bottom of the first and looked at Krug and said, "Hey, kid, you've got a great arm."

Krug said, "Thanks."

"If I get on," Wills kept talking, "I'm going on the first pitch."

Wills got on first, and you know what had to be going through Krug's mind. He knew he had a great arm and he must've thought something like, "If my pitcher gives me the chance, I'm going to throw that SOB out sure as God made apples."

The pitch came to the plate and Wills took off. Krug's throw almost hit the rubber on the pitcher's mound because he must have choked that baseball to death in his anxiety to get rid of it and throw a hundred-miles-an-hour-rocket to second base. Now to be fair, the pitcher's follow-through took him off to the first base side of the rubber. Of course, Wills was safe. Krug threw the ball so hard it was a skidder that went right through the infield and Wills made it to third base. I still get a kick out of that because those things can happen even when you have a great arm. But the great catchers have learned through experience that you never choke the ball.

Most catchers you get to know over the years have quite gnarled-up fingers from getting hit by foul tips. Now, I didn't know Johnny Bench, but I did meet him in the clubhouse one day when Cincinnati was in town. Our visitors' clubhouse man introduced me to Bench, and the first thing I remember about Bench in shaking hands with him was his grip. He had a grip like a steel vise. And his fingers were actually not as gnarled up as most catchers with his experience.

That leads me to another comment, which has to do with a scout that I knew quite well over the years who has passed away some years ago. I remember him when I was a young high school player back in the mid-forties. Bill Wight was a left-hand pitcher who was in the American League for quite some time and pitched for the Yankees. In those days he was known as a pitcher with great stuff who had control problems. Incidentally, his nickname was Whizzer after the football player who later became a Supreme Court Justice, Whizzer White. Anyway, I happened to be at a game probably thirty years ago and I bumped into Bill Wight. He scouted a long time for the Braves, and was the man who originally signed Joe Morgan, Dale Murphy, and many others. But the point is that we were sitting there watching a college game waiting to see a relief pitcher come in. It was kind of a dead game and we were passing the time of day and I asked him, "Who had the greatest arm that you ever saw behind the plate?"

And he said, "Well, when I joined the Yankees in the forties Bill Dickey had already retired but I've been told over the years by a lot of old-timers that Dickey had the best arm they'd ever seen. But I'll tell you, Gib, all the years I've been in the game I'd have to say the two best throwing catchers I've ever seen were Bench and Yeager." They were not contemporaries of Wight's but he had scouted them when they were kids and had seen them in the major leagues.

He said, "They had 'eight arms.'" But the key there was this. The very best catcher I ever saw was Jim Hegan, a catcher with Cleveland for many years, who caught more than four twenty-game winners. He caught the pitching staff of Feller, Lemon, Garcia, Early Wynn. And I think he caught three or four no-hitters. He was never much of a hitter for average but he did have power. He played in two World Series with Cleveland, in 1948 when they defeated the Boston Braves, and in 1954 when the Indians were swept by the New York Giants in four games.

At any rate, Whizzer Wight, a very modest guy, was telling the story and he said, "You know, with the Yankees I had a tendency to be wild and they traded me to Cleveland. Why, I was so wild I had hair all over me!" He was funny, too. "But I can remember this very well. I came in to pitch against the Yankees in relief and somehow I dodged the big bats for a few innings but had a high pitch count. These days they wouldn't have left me in there that long because of pitch counts. But I had pitched three or four innings and was not back in the bullpen the next night, but I was in the dugout. Feller was pitching. We were in the dugout sitting next to Jim Hegan while the Indians were batting. They got two quick outs on us and when Feller walked past us on his way to the water fountain, Hegan grabbed his sleeve and said, 'Hey, Bob, you crossed me up twice in the last inning, once to Keller and once to DiMaggio," and Feller apologized.

But the point is that Hegan not only caught those pitches but he didn't even go to the mound to say anything to Feller. "The thing I remember about Jim, was that he made catching look so easy it was almost unbelievable because he had the greatest hands I've ever seen. I can't remember him even dropping a baseball." He thought a minute and said, "I don't think they kept stats on percentage of runners who got thrown out back then, but I'll bet you Hegan threw out 75 to 80 percent of the base stealers. With a reputation of throwing them out, and they rarely tried to run against him. Think of the advantage that gave his pitcher!"

And there was a player by the name of George Case, who played with the Senators from 1937 to 1947 with the exception of 1946, when he played with the Indians. He was the premier base stealer of that era. He stole 349 bases and led the American League in that category six times and tied Ty Cobb's record at the time. He flew on the base paths. Wizzer Wight told me that one time Case told him that anytime his team faced Cleveland he hoped and prayed that Hegan would be resting and Joe Tipton would be catching because he couldn't steal a base off Hegan.

Here are some tips you can maybe pass along to young catchers. Do not try to be too quick. Catch it, throw it, hit the infielder in the letters with your throw. If your pitcher gives you a chance to throw him out, you will do it. But don't throw the ball on the bag. Try to hit the infielder at the letters.

Another thing you often hear from catchers is that the second baseman or the shortstop was late covering the bag. That's one of the things young catchers will say and one of the key things you have to tell them to do there is this. You don't care if they were on the bag or not, or close to the bag, the bag doesn't move. The bag is always where it's supposed to be. Throw the ball at the bag, air it out, throw it hard and make sure you get plenty on the throw. It's up to the infielder to get there. And that's very important. Young catchers have a tendency, if the infielder is late getting to the bag, to double pump. You never do that. The bag won't move. It's the job of the shortstop or second baseman to get there.

Another thing I think applies is this. I'm a strong believer in luck. And I find the harder I work the more luck I have. And another saying that rings true is that ability will never catch up with the demand for it. The reason I'm mentioning these things, what we're really saying is that working at it is the key to improving one's ability and one's so-called luck. These are keys to improving as a player. There is an adjunct to that, of course, which is simply that as a young player when you're having fun and making some progress, it doesn't seem like work.

Switch-hitting is another "S" word we should discuss here. I want to discuss when to branch out and see if a youngster is ready to pick up another phase of the game that can be helpful as he progresses. But who do you try to make switch-hitters? Who switch-hits? Who doesn't? Who can't? Who can?

There is no doubt about it. When youngsters are just starting to get introduced to baseball, mostly by their fathers or grandfathers or whoever, they will pick up the bat and hit either right-handed or left-handed. They don't do it both ways.

Let me just offer this thought. It is a great idea to start a youngster young, and by that I mean eight or nine years old, introducing him to hit both ways. Switch-hitting has been picked up over the years by certain players in the big leagues who almost all the time began switch-hitting when they were very young.

You can go back to Pete Rose, who was a switch-hitter as a high school kid. He was already a switch-hitter when he signed into professional baseball. Al Wiggins, whom I signed with the Angels, was not a switch-hitter. He was a right-hand hitter with no power to speak of, and possessed the quality of being a great base runner with great instincts to steal bases. We knew his lack of power would hurt him if he tried to be a power hitter. But the other facet of the game, the most important for Al, was his great speed. To take advantage of that I thought it may help in his case if we could teach him to switch hit, and that was polished up and worked on under the direction of Bob Clear with the Angels. Al Wiggins worked very hard at switch hitting and became very proficient at it. He never had much power at all. Al's career in the big league lasted seven years, 1981–87, and he only hit five home runs in all that time, but I think one of them was inside the park. But we were able to focus on his great speed and were able to bring it into play by having him hit left-handed. He didn't start switch-hitting at an ideal age. He didn't start until he had signed a professional contract. Now that's one example.

And others who became switch-hitters in order to enable them to use their best tool, their speed, include such former greats as Willie McGee with the Cardinals. And Willie McGee eventually led the National League in hitting twice. The second was Vince Coleman, who also started with the Cardinals and played there a few years before the Dodgers got him late in his career.

Years ago a great player development man with the Cardinals, George Kissell, developed young players with the philosophy that "if they can run but are not good hitters, teach them to switch-hit, get them on base, and let them win games for you with their feet." They all learned to switch-hit in pro ball. My point is that the younger the player learns this technique, the easier it will be for him.

A lot of youngsters have a terrible problem trying to learn this in pro ball because obviously the pitching in pro ball, even at the lowest level, is far better than they saw as high school or college players. When the pitching is better the hits become fewer. So the young player has to be very patient. Also the individual who works with them on this has to be patient also. Almost inevitably the young player says, "I don't know. It just doesn't feel right to me. I'm uncomfortable with it." The same thing is applicable at a lower level when kids are ten, twelve, fourteen years old. In fact, I would just say that is a great time to start youngsters switch-hitting.

Another well-known switch-hitter was Junior Gilliam, whom I met at a charitable golf tournament in the Los Angeles area when I worked for Kansas City, and got to know him a little bit. I was invited by my friend Ron Perranoski. who was by then a pitching coach with the Dodgers. Gilliam played his entire major league career with the Dodgers, fourteen years, after coming out of the Negro Leagues with, I believe, the Elite Giants team. He was National League Rookie of the Year in 1953 and was a very prominent player during the fifties and early sixties. I remember him as a player who didn't hit for power, had an average arm, was not a base stealer but a good base runner, and a switch-hitter. He played by his wits and the switch-hitting helped his club win ballgames.

After he retired as a player he remained with the Dodgers as a hitting coach and their major league third base coach. It was sad, really. He suffered from a brain hemorrhage the day after the team clinched the 1978 pennant and died a couple of days later. He was so beloved that the organization retired his number (19) just two days later.

I knew him a little bit and asked him one time, "How old were you when you started to switch hit?"

"I was about ten, I think. I was always encouraged to do it because I was always playing with older kids and wasn't expected to be a home run–hitting guy because I was younger and smaller. One of my brothers told me to switch-hit because he said I was a good runner. And at that time a lot wasn't expected of me and as I got bigger I got to be a better hitter as I picked it up. Actually, I got to be a better hitter left-handed than I was right-handed."

I will again say that if you start them young enough, be patient with their progress hitting left-handed. Throw a lot to them, tennis balls, whiffle balls, or whatever, so they get used to viewing balls coming at them from a different angle because they haven't hit from that side of the plate. Be patient with their failures. Encourage them with their successes. Really, a lot of it depends on how patient you are and how patient they are. If the issue comes up, which it does at times, about they are failing and they don't want to continue to do it, be a little bit rigid there. Say, "Hey, wait a minute. You'll never learn to do it if you don't try to do it now," I don't like to use the word "never" in the game, but it is a tremendous advantage for a youngster to learn to switch hit early. If you can emphasize this and encourage them to stick to it they will have a great chance to be better hitters.

Nobody ever suggested that Joe DiMaggio ought to be a switch-hitter. He was a great right-hand hitter with power. He hit left- and right-handed pitchers equally well. And nobody in his right mind would have said Ted Williams should have been a switch-hitter. But those are extreme cases. While we're on the subject, another great switch-hitter who had a tough year in 2010 with injuries, and he may be in the down side of his career now, but will be a cinch Hall of Famer five years after he retires, probably would be Chipper Jones. He learned to switch-hit as a young kid.

Naturally I'm not suggesting that every kid who comes down the pike that's a good young player at whatever level should switch-hit. But if he has exceptional ability, if he's playing against older kids, and he's a good player against guys who may be a little bit bigger and stronger, and let's say he's a pretty good right-hand hitter with good tools, then maybe he shouldn't be a switch[hitter. But learning to hit from either side of the plate gives the youngster a much better chance to become a special player in the long run.

And again, not to wear the point out, do not worry about the initial lack of success the youngster will experience from hitting on the new side of the plate. It is going to be a project and a process for him to get comfortable with that. If he really wants to do it, it is attainable. For the adults, start him with this as early as you can and don't let his initial lack of success bother him or you. Encourage him to give it a real try because it is attainable.

Almost all players who become switch-hitters that are right-hand dominant, almost all of them, Chipper Jones, Mickey Mantle, Pete Rose, all of them threw right-handed. All of them. Some of the rabbits who became switch-hitters, Willie McGee, Al Wiggins, and the rest, were all better hitters right-handed than they were left-handed. But ultimately, when they played the game at the highest level, they became better hitters left-handed.

When Junior Is a Prospect
Draft Guidelines

The draft is an interesting animal, so to speak. It is the culmination of an entire year's work of the scouting departments of every organization. And there's a lot of time and effort put into the draft. I joined the Dodgers in 1979 to begin my eleventh year as a scout. Although it would not be proved out for a few years, the 1968 draft had been a great one for the Dodgers. In fact, it might have been the greatest draft in the history of the draft!

Al Campanis was the scouting director in '68, and later became the general manager a short time after that. I hear people talk constantly about this great draft or that great draft. Some of our people have even talked about various drafts we've had over the years that we think have been pretty successful.

But none of them compare to '68 with the Dodgers and almost every other organization. The 1968 draft produced Davey Lopes, Bobby Valentine, Bill Buckner, Tom Paciorek, Joe Ferguson, Steve Garvey, Ron Cey, Jeff Zahn, Doyle Alexander, Sandy Vance, and there were a couple of others here. Many of them had long major league careers, some with the Dodgers and some with other clubs.

The essence of the draft, of course, is the recruitment of new players for the organizations. It's the finale, if you will, of the work and skills of their scouting departments. The scouts are the ones who put the teams and the talent in touch and they are, in most cases, the young player's first contact with professional baseball. This chapter is dedicated to imparting an understanding of the draft itself, the responsibility of the scouts in the process, and the responsibility of parents when Junior is a prospect.

So what's involved in that? There's more to drafting young players than scouts watching them in games. Much more. The scouting leading up to the actual draft is often a long and thorough process that involves so much more than a scout seeing a player in a game or two and deciding the youngster could be a prospect now or at some future date. And frequently a scout goes to see a game to get a look at one particular player and a different one catches his eye. The second player could be an underclassman and may be noted as a "follow" for a future draft. Of course, there are a number of other scenarios. And there are always a lot of questions concerning the whole process.

With that in mind, I think it's probably a good idea to touch on the guidelines of the draft and take a look at the interaction between the players, their parents, and the scouts that occurs before the actual days of the draft. Let me begin with some basics.

Who's eligible for the draft and who is not? High school seniors are eligible. College juniors and seniors are eligible. Junior college freshmen and sophomores are eligible. In addition to that, even though it's very unlikely, a youngster who is twenty-one years old at draft time and is a freshman. Maybe

he did a hitch in the service and was age twenty-one when he came out. He's eligible, too. So it doesn't matter what college he's in. If he is twenty-one within thirty days of the draft, he's eligible.

Once a player's eligibility is determined, then comes the question we hear so often: "All things being equal, would you rather draft a college player or a high school player?" That's a huge generality. The bottom line to most scouting is that all things are never equal. But in general terms, most of the organizations I have worked for, it's more desirable if you can get the player at seventeen or eighteen than it is if you get him at twenty-one.

The chain of events that occurs when parents

Al Campanis, "the Chief," was scouting director and then general manager with the Dodgers. It was a pleasure working with him.

learn that Junior actually is a prospect vary because, to a certain extent, each situation is unique. Quite often one of the more serious issues that comes up in scouting is the confusion that takes place on the part of the parents as to what decisions should be made on behalf of their youngsters. It's an interesting situation because each year the baseball draft is conducted in early June and quite often parents of youngsters who are prospects are not really prepared for it. They have maybe received home visits and phone calls from scouts, but they are really uncertain concerning what decision should be made concerning Junior. Of course, there is no question about it. I'm sure they talk in terms of their family with him, but it's a very difficult time for parents.

As you can see, scouts have a complex responsibility in a complex process. And the more parents know more about all of it, the better equipped they are to understand things when their son is deemed a prospect so they can guide him as he approaches his career in professional baseball.

This is an important point for parents to remember. If their son is considered a prospect by professional baseball, chances are very great that he is also going to be recruited by some college if he is academically qualified. And that process is an uncertain one. But let's just assume the youngster is recruited by a college where his grades will allow him to get in. The key to remember here is that college baseball follows closely along with professional baseball regarding who they want to recruit and whether they can paint a picture to the young player that his time would be better spent going to college first as opposed to signing a professional baseball contract. Before he gets drafted this is something for his parents to think about, but when he is drafted, it becomes reality that requires serious thought without a prolonged amount of time in which to do it.

Physically, maybe he is ready to go play professionally. If pro baseball drafts him in, let's say, the third round, they would offer him a considerable amount of money. The issue then becomes whether the kid is prepared to go out and play professionally, if he's prepared for it, or whether he should go to school first. I can't emphasize this enough.

The money is so large now in the high rounds that very rarely does a high school boy pass up the money offered for a first-round selection. And that's a key thing to remember. It's often in the millions of dollars. That's a huge amount of money to anybody, no matter what dad or mom make, if they both work. But that isn't the only reason you want to go. In addition, you want him to go if he is emotionally ready. If the youngster is a high-round player, if he turns the money down and goes to college and plays there and doesn't get hurt, he would be ready for the draft three years down the line as a junior. And these are things to consider.

That's where parents play such a key role. Let your ego go out the window and look at it realistically. "Is he ready?" That's the key to pass on to whatever organization drafts him. Don't try to play a game of saying privately you know he's ready and the youngster says he wants to go out and play and doesn't want to use the scholarship to USC or whatever. He wants to go out and play professionally.

The best attitude to take is, "Let's see where he's drafted." If he's drafted high enough, a major league club will not only give him a bonus, they will pay for his college when he does decide to go. But that's entirely dependent upon where he is selected in the draft. Don't take the attitude that you know he's ready, and if he's drafted high we're just going to sit around for the summer and pretend we can't make up our mind so we can make more money.

Professional baseball, at the level the game is played at the major leagues, is forgiving to a certain extent, but the youngsters' parents quite often don't face the realization that doors are not going to close at Dodgers Stadium or Yankee Stadium if the boy does not go out and play. No matter what kind of ability he has, polishing his ability until it's realized totally and he's ready to go play in the major leagues could take four years, or maybe five. So the club may pursue him, draft him, and have the draft rights to him through the summer before they must sign him. But if he wants to play and you're satisfied with where he's selected in the draft, don't impede the process by sitting back and saying, "Well, we hold all the cards here. We're the parents and we'll let him think it over during the summer playing Legion ball or whatever, and we'll make another hundred thousand dollars."

That is the worst possible way to start! It's been done and has worked out at times, but a good organization will go in and offer the youngster high round money for where he's picked. And if the parents do not select the organization in terms of having the kid sign, then that's where the process ends. It doesn't mean the organization is going to have a bitter experience and may not draft him again further down the line as a college player. That isn't the issue at all. Remember this. The selecting process has been in business a long time. Major league clubs select players, they develop good players, and they have had some players with average ability even exceed their God-given talent.

If a youngster really wants to play, don't try to play waiting games, essentially "liars' poker," with his development if he really wants to go. Now, if he's unsure about going, and you're not sure whether the process of professional baseball may be too advanced for him or he's never been away from home at all, or if you're not sure if you like it then I would suggest you don't sign. That doesn't mean there's anything wrong with the youngster. That's what sets high school players apart from college players.

In addition to putting a lot of responsibility on parents, it also puts a great deal of responsibility on the area scout. If you draft a seventeen- or eighteen-year-old youngster, he's going to go out to play in a program more than likely with about seventy or seventy-five percent college players, guys who are three and four years older than he is. Now, it is true if he goes to college and he's on the college baseball team he could be playing with players who are three and four years older than he is, too.

My experience is that if all things are equal I would rather have the high school player simply because he may be getting ready for the big leagues at twenty-two after progressing through rookie ball, A ball, AA ball, and maybe AAA ball by that age. This as opposed to the college player who starts his trek through the minor leagues at the same level the high school kid does.

Now this sometimes creates a lot of confusion. I'm talking about the advanced or special high school player who has a chance to get a lot of money because of the round he's selected in. There are all kinds of so-called tricks to the trade here, but the issue is simply that the higher the player is selected, the more money he gets.

My suggestion would be that if you're the parents of a high school player and he's going to be selected in the first few rounds, you would be wise to review what signing bonuses are. They're pretty much a matter of record, really, and you can get that information from *Baseball America*. And no doubt if your son is going to be a high draft, you're going to have four or five agents knocking at your door telling you that they're going to look out for your interests and you had better take one of them because a big bad major league baseball team is liable to cheat your son. It's crazy, but that's a whole industry now.

What I'm saying here is that if your youngster is an advanced high school player, and the scout recommends that he be selected high, the key for the parents is to make an accurate determination of how mature the youngster is. Remember, if he goes out and plays professionally, he's not going to have mom or dad there telling him to make sure he gets home on time, eats right, and so on. He's left, to a large extent, to his own devices. Is he going to know that he needs to keep his nose clean and not necessarily run around with some older players who might be old enough to go out and have a couple of beers, and so forth? You have to face the facts that some high school kids may not be prepared for that. Are they mature enough to look at it and say, "Nah, I'm not interested in doing that," and not worry whether an older player is going to call him a pussycat or whatever? Those are key things.

As a scout I'm looking at the overall ability of the player, which determines whether or not he can go out and compete with older players. Yes, I'd like to get the high school player because he's younger. And make no mistake about it. Instruction in professional baseball is far better than he's going to get at the amateur level. I don't care who he plays for or where he plays. There are some very fine coaches in collegiate baseball, no question about it. Still, a youngster is not going to get the same kind of training in college baseball that he gets professionally. It just doesn't happen.

On the flip side of it, if a high school player with ability is not sure about going out despite the money, then maybe he should go to college and his name will go back into the draft at the end of his junior year. When a player is drafted and does not sign, it doesn't hurt his chances for getting drafted again if his playing continues to develop as a college player.

I know that the bottom line issue becomes, "Well, if he goes to college he's going to get an education." Sometimes that's true. But quite often it isn't. The issue really is the maturity of the youngster. If anybody really knows that, it should be the parents. The scout has a chance to observe him. The scout may have the chance to get to know him. But who knows him the best? That's easy: his parents.

And that being the case, if his parents are comfortable letting him play professionally and he's a high draft selection, then I'd say let him go. But if you're uncomfortable, and I'm not suggesting there has to be anything sinister about his upbringing, but if he lacks maturity, and I'm not talking about physical maturity, my thought process is that it's in his best interest to go to school.

As a scout, my job is to say, "This is what he is now and this is what he has a chance to become." And all the people who will evaluate the player throughout his entire career will go through the same process.

Now the key there is this. Every college player who goes out and plays professionally is not necessarily a rocket scientist or a particularly mature player. That's a given. We're so preoccupied with the makeup of young players that we're hopeful every player we draft is a solid makeup youngster who is going to reach the pinnacle of what his skills will allow. But that's just whistling in the dark. That's not reality. And the kicker here, or the so-called fly in the ointment, is pretty evident.

In other words, scouts look for a high school player who not only has special skills, but is a special youngster. Frequently parents with a youngster who is considered a special prospect but is selected maybe lower in the draft than they expected take offense to that and say, "Well, my kid is better than so-and-so and he was drafted in the first round." Actually, we run into that quite often. That being said, there's one way to prove he's better than so-and-so, and that's to go out and play and prove it.

The key to the whole issue of dealing with parents comes down to when they ask the scout, "Do you think my son could play professionally?" When faced with that question I give a straightforward answer from a realistic standpoint and say, "Yes, there's no question about it. He has the ability, and I'm sure he's ready in terms of the physical skills that I see on the field. But is he a special youngster? Is he ready to take on the responsibility of playing pro ball?" I have to be upfront and discuss that because at that point I know very little about the player's makeup other than the scout has asked me to cross check him.

Scouts start separating players when we get into the makeup issue. Does he play hard? Is he a good practice player? Does he play hard against better competition? Is his body language negative when he struggles? Does he give you the impression that he doesn't give a damn if he doesn't have success?

Sometimes parents tell us or others in or out of the game, "Well, obviously I love him. He's my son. But I don't think he's quite ready to go." That doesn't mean he's not special. It's not a big time negative to say within the framework of a family situation that you don't think he's ready to go. If you have concerns that he may not be ready for professional baseball, are you concerned about him going away to college? He's not going to receive much supervision there, either. These are issues where the biggest responsibility falls on the parents to be truthful with themselves and the scouts for the good of their son.

All those things enter into it. But the problem you have making a judgment is that quite often parents, even those who are in professional baseball, get somewhat annoyed if you indicate you don't think their son is ready for pro ball. Sad to say, but that's the way it is. You can look at any number of your favorite players who have played in this generation or prior generations, and you will find that this one played in high school, and this one played in college.

The percentage slips off and falls away nowadays to some extent because the money is much greater than it was even twenty years ago. And as a result, my view is that college baseball, from a playing standpoint, is not as good as it was twenty years ago. That's a general term, but I believe it isn't, and here's why. The high-round kid nowadays can command a million or more dollars to sign, and twenty years ago it might have been a hundred thousand. The first-round player in this point in time is taking the money and not going on to school. So the advanced high school kid quite often does not go to college.

Now, baseball offers a program for the young player who had a choice between college and pro ball intended to make baseball more attractive to him. It's the college scholarship plan that can be part of the signing bonus in general terms and can be used by the player later in his life. It's because the seasons in college ball and pro ball do not mesh. But there have been players who took advantage of it and went to college in the offseason, or upon retirement from pro ball. To be more exact about it, once the player completes his baseball career, if he starts college within two years, the expenses for college are paid for by the team that signed him. And he can attend any college or university that accepts him academically. That policy is strictly adhered to. The commissioner's office keeps very good records on that and all clubs do as well.

But let's discuss the other player, the mediocre to poor student. It does come up occasionally, and more often than not there is some effort made to equate highly academic kids with nonacademic kids. That's an interesting subject in itself. People say, "How can a kid who is so uninterested in academics relate to all kinds of instruction he will get in pro ball?"

My experience is that I probably fell into that category as a high school kid myself. I was not terribly interested in school except for American history, I guess. I think a lot of the interest, or lack of it, is dependent upon what the situation is at home as well as other factors. But what about the young player who is not academic and as a result will have a very difficult time not only getting into a four-year school, but if he gets in, he will have a very difficult time staying eligible?

The key to that whole situation is this. Parents should be realistic. If the youngster is totally uninterested in academics, the scout will know it. The question that has come up in the past is, "Do major league clubs take advantage of that situation?" Realistically speaking, I don't want to say they take advantage of it, but let's look at two players as examples.

Player A is considered a very high-round player. It doesn't matter whether he's a position player or pitcher. Player B also is considered a very high-round player. Let's say both of them are essentially very much equal in their skills. Player A, however, is a 4.0 student. Player B will barely graduate in terms of his academic prowess.

So where do you stand there? Well, I don't want to say Player B has the same leverage because he really does not. In essence, major league baseball clubs know there's not going to be a college program in the future, or, if there is, there are all kinds of issues regarding if he goes to school, if he stays eligible, and what he has to do to exhibit that he really wants to be in the program. Player A, on the other hand, can easily get into almost any college in the country.

We do run into this occasionally. We will run into Player B, who we know is nonacademic. We're not suggesting that he's not a good kid, just that he is not a good student. He's never made it a secret that he does not like school. Player B's parents are not in the same spot as Player A's simply because Player A, while thinking about signing a professional contract, will want some or all of his college expenses satisfied by major league baseball. In other words, "Are you going to give me a college scholarship plan or will you give me a signing bonus of X number of dollars plus additional monies that I would pass up by not going to a major college?" Anybody who is in professional sports knows at this point you're talking far in excess of a hundred thousand dollars for four years of school in many of the colleges throughout the country.

So those are the issues. I'm not suggesting that we run into a lot of these youngsters, but we do run into some. I have never been opposed to nonacademic kids. I really haven't. But what I am opposed to is the youngster who is frequently ineligible in high school because of grades, and then you find the rules have been, shall we say, "specified to his situation" by his coach, maybe his principal, his academic counselor, or whatever. It's my job to tell him, "Look, you have to pass your courses without flunking any of them to stay eligible."

The kid who is unwilling to meet academic standards just from the standpoint of remaining eligible tells me quite a bit about what he is going to do athletically. But again I don't want to penalize the youngster who isn't interested in academics but does stay eligible. I've seen many kids who are not particularly academic at all who have wonderful instincts on the field, as opposed to the kid who is very academic but has a tendency to analyze and overanalyze every bit of baseball instruction that he gets.

Those are things to think about. Player A is academic and a very good player, and Player B is nonacademic and also a very good player.

If you're the parents of Player B, do not get into a negotiation and try to convince baseball people that your son, Player B, is not only an excellent prospect, but also wants a college education. I mean, the scout is in your home to get some idea of whether your demands will be reasonable or unreasonable if his club drafts him. If you want to incorporate in your thought process or in your demands that major league baseball should pay for him not to go to school and you want to use Stanford as an example, I would suggest that you not do that because baseball will know that he may have to struggle mightily to even graduate from high school, let alone think about Stanford. When parents do that, the result could be that the youngster is not selected and possibly cheated out of his chance at a professional baseball career.

To continue in that vein, I'll briefly touch on my role as cross checker, something I have done for over twenty years. It's checking players the area scouts feel are high-round prospects. They invite the cross checker to come see each one play and evaluate him. The cross checker must relate well to scouts, players, and occasionally agents. It's a tough job and some resent it to a point, but it's necessary.

And the reason it's necessary is this. Let's say Scout A has a player in California he really likes and wants you to come see him. More often than not we also like the players they recommend. The thought that we won't is a dream. But how do we compare this guy to a player in Florida who is a very similar type player? Let's say the player in Florida is a left-hand-hitting out-fielder, just like the guy in Southern California. He runs about the same, throws about the same, plays just as hard, loves to play the game and competes well.

How do we separate these two guys? There are issues that happen and we really have to be on our toes to do that. Just from a practical standpoint, let's say Player A in California has Scott Boras as his agent and the Florida player has the local insurance agent by the name of Joe Smith representing him. I don't want to get into a soap opera with the California player because the king of soap operas is Scott Boras. The kid in Florida wants to play and is not threatening to play in an independent league or whatever if the club doesn't give him the money Boras thinks he should get.

Getting back to the "game playing" about a player's potential to go to college, here is a perfect example of how that can evolve. I remember one particular situation quite well. The Dodgers had a meeting three or four weeks before the draft and a good portion of our scouts were there. If you're the scouting director or cross checker talking to a scout who may have seen the player and liked his ability, it's pretty standard that as you get closer to the draft there are many questions you want answered. Who is the agent? And once you know who the agent is, what college is interested in this player? Had he signed a letter of intent or is he being wooed by several schools? If he is a multisport youngster, what is his preference? Is he a legitimate big-time foot-ball player as opposed to a youngster who is considered a good high school football player but has negligible promise as a big-time college player?

We got into a conversation about a particular young player. He was a good left-hand-hitting outfielder and a good-looking high school player. The area scout had seen him and I had seen him. At any rate, this was the case. Agents were not a big part of the baseball draft at that point in time. It was very rare that a young player had an agent. So the first question posed was, "Can this guy go to college?"

And the scout said, "Oh yeah."

"Who is talking to him?"

And the scout said, "Stanford, who else?" And he also mentioned a junior college, at which point your common sense as a scout says, "Whoa! Wait a minute." For a youngster to get into Stanford, essentially, it's like getting into an Ivy League school like Harvard or Yale. But what we were really saying is that he could get into one of the top ten schools in the country. And they're saying if he doesn't sign professionally, he's either going to go to Stanford or a junior college. The comparison was hysterical! I couldn't believe it and couldn't believe the scout would repeat it.

We explained to the scout that those two comparisons don't quite fit, and they never did. So we drafted the youngster and we signed him. And we later found out he couldn't have gotten into Stanford if he tried to get in with a tank! Maybe the best he could have done was to go on a tour of the campus.

But why did the scout say it? Basically because that is what he had been told, either by the parents or by the kid. I have no idea which. Half of the info that he gave out was accurate. The youngster was being recruited to a certain extent by a local junior college, and the reason they were interested in him was they knew his academic background would not allow him to go to a major college. If he could have gotten into a four-year school, the kid was going to have to be totally occupied with a tutor and he would have had a miserable time trying to stay eligible.

My thought process in cases like that is more often than not the scout is going to know whether the player is an academic or not. Most of the time that type of information is really not difficult to procure. Whether you're talking to a college coach or a high school coach, the process is pretty simple. If a scout has interest in your youngster, somewhere along the line he is going to ask your son to fill out what is called a Player Information Card (PIC) that includes such information as height, weight, date of birth, mom and dad's names, address, etc.

Most scouts go through the coach to do this. The scout doesn't want it to be handled like he's on some secret spy mission. He'll go and watch a practice or watch a game and at the conclusion of the game he may ask the coach if it's okay if he chats with the youngster and leave a Player Information Card. Some coaches like to have cards run through them.

This is kind of a touchy situation. If the youngster is not a high visibility prospect or not well known, or maybe from an area that's not well scouted, the scout is somewhat apprehensive to run the PIC through the coach because that is liable to create the following scenario. The coach gets on the telephone that evening and talks to a friend of his who coaches in the next town or the next county or whatever, and says, "Guess what? The Dodgers are looking at a player of mine." And the next thing you know there may be ten people out there looking at the kid. There is some apprehension among scouts, especially in out-of-the-way places.

If a youngster is a high-visibility player then it becomes a different issue. I'm reminded, with the advent of the computers and the Internet, to show you the general attitude some people have. It is interesting. I got an email the other day that was sent to thirty clubs about a pitcher in a major college. This youngster has an absolutely outstanding arm. He was considered one of the better pitching prospects in the 2011 draft.

But at any rate the coach put this out as an email that said something like this: "This youngster, on the ninth and tenth of December, will make himself available to talk to scouts from the different organizations. But keep in mind your meeting with this player will be limited to fifteen minutes, at which point he will shake your hand and say, 'Next.'" This is a paraphrase, but you get the point.

It was a very unusual situation. And that's what can happen when people are totally unrealistic as to what clubs are looking for and are not looking for. This pitcher has exceptional ability. There isn't any question of that. But to set a limit for scouts to talk with him, and to do it within the framework of a college program, is not the best way to go. All I would say is whether the youngster is a high school or college player, it makes more sense to get some advice by dealing directly with parents, especially if the player is a high school player.

So the scout would hopefully arrange through the youngster for some evening when the scout could come by and talk with him and his parents prior to the draft. Now, the instance I just related involved a high-visibility college player who was saying that his time was very valuable and he could only give each scout fifteen minutes of it. That just doesn't sit right with me. I don't expect young players and/or parents of young players to be subservient to scouts, but just treat them like you would anyone else, which means in a halfway decent business manner. After all, the club is trying to find out whether you really want to play professional baseball at this point in time. That's all.

I suggest that parents can have an attitude that can rub people the wrong way. I'll give you an example. When this player was a high school player I saw him in a game and he was represented by an agent who is very difficult to do business with. He played for a big time athletic high school and I went to see him on a Friday night. The kids who go there are quite often very good. You name the sport and they always field good athletic teams. That night they were playing their toughest opponent.

This youngster was pitching, and of course was pitching very well because he has excellent stuff. The shortstop on this team was an underclassman, either a sophomore or a junior, and a pretty good little player. At any rate, he made an error in the course of the game. There were probably a thousand people at this night game. Of course, the kid who made the error felt terrible, and the result of it was that a runner scored and it ended up being the difference in the game.

I was actually standing down the third base line and the father of the pitcher went into an almost hysterical mode when the shortstop made the error. It was something like, "How can my son be expected to perform with that miserable type of support?"

And the first thing that ran to my head was, "I don't think I would want to get involved with this guy at any cost. The father sounds like a nutcase, and the kid prowled around the mound and started to yap at the shortstop who, obviously, felt terrible. And any guy who has ever played competitive athletics, whether he's the best or the worst you've ever seen, knows there is one common denominator. Errors are part of the game, even at the highest level. Nobody likes striking out with the bases loaded or making a fielding error at a critical point or any point in the course of the game.

But this pitcher continued mumbling and grumbling at the shortstop. The coach went out to the mound eventually to try and calm the pitcher down, but what the coach should have done, really, was to go out to the mound earlier and tell the pitcher to shut his mouth. He should have told him to concentrate on the hitter. That's what the coach should have done. But because the pitcher was the best-known player on the team and the coach was somewhat intimidated by the parents of the kid, he didn't. My reaction was total disenchantment with the actions of the father and the kid. Between the two of them, it just turned me off. And I thought at the time, "This kid had better grow up because even if he doesn't sign professionally, if he shows up a teammate in a college program, somebody is liable to take him behind the woodshed and turn him inside out."

That's what happens in competition. One of the most negative things is for one teammate to show up another teammate. It's one of the worst possible things you can do competitively. The only time I've ever seen it in the major leagues was when a player showed an extreme lack of hustle. I've seen guys in the dugout get on a player for that.

I can remember seeing a big league game where, on a double-play ball a well-known hitter, a power hitter who was never considered to be a bad guy, was the runner at first and he did not go after the shortstop or second baseman covering second. He veered off into right field, which gave the pivot man at second base a clear lane to throw to first base. When he got into the dugout there must have been three veteran players who got on him. The manager didn't have a chance to get on him. The players took care of it. Of course, that's an extreme case, and you don't see it on good clubs. But I don't care what level the game is, when a player makes a mistake, you want to encourage him rather than make him look bad. And there was this father shooting his mouth off while his son was making his teammate look bad.

Anyway, what happened to that pitcher? Two or three years later he was in college and eligible for the draft. He was the one who sent that ridiculous email offering fifteen minutes of his valuable time to any scout who wanted to talk to him. Unbelievable.

I remember another circumstance that happened before first baseman J.T. Snow was drafted by the Yankees in 1989. Snow was the first baseman at the University of Arizona. J.T. was the son of Jack Snow, a former Notre Dame wide receiver who played a long time in the NFL, mostly with the Rams. But at any rate, the coach at the University of Arizona was Jerry Kendall, a classy guy and a very fine coach.

He had the right idea about dealing with scouts. He let any of the scouts that covered his club know that any time they wanted to talk with the players, he would make the players available to them and the players could spend as much time as was practical for the young player. I mean, you're not going to go in there and spend an hour and a half with the kid. That doesn't make a lot of sense. But basically he was saying he would be as cooperative as possible and he set up a time frame according to his playing schedule. On a non-game day he said the scout could come in and use his office to talk with the kid and he would make himself scarce. "I'm not going to sit here and listen to what you want to ask him." And to me that's the way it should be done.

There is another issue that must be considered by all scouts, and it can be a sticky wicket. That is what we in baseball call "signability." In other words, if your team drafts him, will he sign? Does he really want to play? And I have some concerns there when some of them say, "Well, yeah, I'll play for this team or that team." I've had experiences where a kid has said, "Well, if I'm drafted by any of the following twenty-five teams, I will not sign. But I would consider these four or five." Maybe it's oversimplification, but I would rather be dealing with a young player who says, "Sure, I want to be a professional player. I have my favorite teams and everything, but the bottom line is that I want to play and I will play if I'm treated fairly." As a guy who has spent over four decades in the business, that's all I would be looking for.

All of that has to be understood by the parents, and hopefully the parental supervision is strong. But, unfortunately, it's often not that way. There are broken homes, no dad. Mom loves her son and knows he's a good player but she works and knows little about professional baseball.

I remember a situation we had about fifteen years ago. Dick Hanlon, a good scout of ours in Northern California, had found a high school first baseman that he really liked. We drafted the player but he had a tough time trying to sign him. I had cross checked the kid and went in to try to help Dickie sign him. Now, this youngster was selected down the line, I want to say tenth or twelfth round, but we made an offer to him, and for that time it was certainly very fair for the round he was selected in. He had a scholarship to Cal State Fullerton, which has a very good college baseball program, and it's a good academic school, too. But he could get in academically just by the skin of his teeth. He was probably going to require a tutor.

I went to the youngster's home with Dick. We met his mother, who was a very nice single mom who had raised him and a younger daughter. She worked very hard and was adamant about wanting him to go to college. When I asked her if she had gotten a degree, she said she didn't go to college. "I wish I had but I didn't," she said. So I explained to her that academically he may have a tough time staying eligible because he had no interest in study or academics. She said, "I'm well aware of that."

I asked, "Then why would you want to delay the process of him playing professionally if you're aware of the fact that he's really not a student?"

She said, "I really don't care about the academics that much, but I'd like him to have the college experience. I didn't have it as a young girl and want him to have it."

His contribution to that situation was minimal. He just let his mom speak for him.

So finally I asked him, "Do you want to play?"

"Yeah, but I'm not going to do what my mother doesn't want me to do."

As a result, we ran into a logjam there and we didn't sign him. Now, just prior to him entering Cal State Fullerton, I got a late phone call one night from Dick Hanlon and he said, "You know, they may be able to change their minds. The mother has just called me about it."

"What's the issue, what's the kicker?"

"Well, he said she told him if the Dodgers would double the signing bonus...."

I said, "Dickie, I don't want to do that. It really doesn't justify that. We're already offering him more money than his draft round calls for because we're allowing for the fact that he probably wouldn't fit into the college program academically and he'll probably have difficulty remaining eligible to play in college."

Dickie said he'd hate to lose the kid.

I said, "I hate to lose him, too, but we need some straight talk and I don't think we got it. I had never before talked with parents who said they didn't care about the academics, knowing that the youngster is a nonacademic, but because mom wanted him to have the college experience."

Well, we didn't go back to make a counteroffer, and he entered school. During his years at Cal State Fullerton he struggled just to be eligible. And more often than not it was because he didn't really apply himself in class. He didn't like school. He wasted his time, I think, because in terms of his ability he was ready to play, but he put this off because his mother wanted him to have the college experience she did not have. It was a shame.

Now, I have run into parents who say continually, "I didn't go to college. But you know what? I still wanted to get a college education, and if baseball is there when he's close to his degree, that's fine. But the education process is more important." I have total respect for that. But I have a huge amount of disrespect for what happened with that other kid, who put in his time in college but really didn't develop that much because every time the coach turned around, the kid wasn't eligible. He was not willing to treat the coach or the program properly simply because he vegetated instead of applying himself.

Don't forget, what scouts are really doing is trying to hire this youngster who wants to start his baseball career at seventeen or eighteen years old. We run into it with college kids who have been away from home and have seen better competition, or even got married. Occasionally, as a junior he may be selected in the third round and offered a considerable amount of money: $250,000 to $300,000. But he stalls and says, "I want at least a half a million. If I don't get that I'll come back to school next year."

In essence, this is a case of a guy with five dollars in his pocket playing a poker game against a multimillion dollar organization. You can't win that way, I don't care if you're the greatest poker player there is. There's a misconception in his thinking because professional baseball has singled this player out and told him, "Yeah, we think you're good and we're selecting you, which makes you one of the top kids in the whole country." But often Mom and Dad play hardball, thinking they'll win. But, actually, there's only one way they can win, and that's to have all their ducks in a row prior to the draft.

The flip side of that is the youngster who is not drafted out of high school but wants to play professional baseball. If he is at all academic, then collegiate baseball may possibly be the route to his goal. Eric Karros not only went undrafted out of high school, ,but he didn't get a scholarship offer from college. Not anybody. But he didn't let that stop him. He went to UCLA and made that team as a walk-on player, and then got a scholarship. Of course he was seen by many scouts and in 1988 was drafted by the Dodgers in the sixth round. He played over 1,700 games in his major league career.

Another player I can recall who went through a similar experience was Steve Kemp, who was also passed by the draft out of high school. He was a fine hitter as a high school player, but the attitude in general about his ability was, "Well, he can hit a little bit, but he's a below-average runner and his arm is below average and he's just a mediocre outfielder. He's not a big physical guy." As a result nobody chased after him.

Eric Karros was the first of five National League Rookie of the Year winners in a row with the Dodgers in the 1990s.

But his family paid for him to go to USC, at least for the first year, and he made the team as a walk-on and a scholarship followed. He became an All-American and was drafted by Detroit number one in the country in 1976 and had a good eleven-year major league career with the Tigers, Yankees, and White Sox.

Now, things I have just mentioned are examples of some of the conditions that can develop. But to give some advice to parents, be upfront with people, and if they're not upfront with you, you don't have to chase after them. If you have a youngster who is a player, chances are the good scouts will find him.

Also keep this in mind. Whether you have a fourteen year old son who is a good player or a twenty-one-year-old son who is an All-American in college, there exists in major league baseball people who have the job, the responsibility, to identify not so much what he is, because that's pretty easy to see to a trained eye. It's what he can become. And what he can become is based largely on what he is. That sounds very easy, but it certainly is not. And that's the toughest part about scouting.

Quite often we see this in the minor leagues before kids are really sure of their own ability. Sometimes they mask it and try to act indifferent because they think that's cool. They see big leaguers do things quite easily and the minor leaguer can get confused by that and think, "Well, he's not really playing that hard." But that player is playing hard and makes it look easy because he is so good.

This isn't to raise the question of how did you identify this player or that player, or how did you know this player or that player was going to be better. Is Player A better than Player B? I think you take all the information you can gather from your scouting department and you try to make good picks, good selections. And the parents need to know just how much time and care was involved in selecting their son for the draft.

The actual selection process is a distillation of all the information we were able to get on the player and then you factor in things like makeup. Makeup is a very interesting area to discuss. It's an interesting topic for scouts to kick around. What kind of makeup a player has very often is difficult to determine. The animated player is not necessarily a great makeup guy. You could have a quiet killer out there on the field, but still water runs deep. He may be a terribly competitive guy.

It's tough to determine what real makeup a young player has simply because you're seeing him at a level when he's probably better than the lion's share of the players he plays against. When he's better than the competition it really doesn't test how competitive he is. In pro ball that's not going to be the case. He's going to have to make adjustments to the competition in a million different facets of the game. That's a given. Some guys make those adjustments easily and some don't. Those who don't really struggle to play unless their God-given ability is so outstanding that it overcomes the fact that they don't adjust too well.

There are obviously certain tools all scouts look for in players. Of course one of them is hitting, particularly power or the potential for power. It's an interesting issue simply because power, at times, increases with the maturity of the player. And if you think about it reasonably, it should. Basically, if the player has speed of the bat and good mechanics to hit, and struggles hitting, why does he struggle hitting? More often than not he "gets himself out," as we say it. The pitcher doesn't have to make a great pitch to get him out. He goes far outside the strike zone. But there again, there are exceptions to that rule because you can look at every generation and find successful if not outstanding bad ball hitters.

Here's what I mean. Today major league hitters are taught to take plus high fast balls. The reason most hitters are taught to "spit" or take high-velocity fast balls, 95 or 100 miles per hour, is because they can't catch up to it.

Another reality is that fast balls above the belt are rarely called strikes, which is a break for hitters. The ratio of conventional hitters to bad ball hitters is roughly between seventy-five and a hundred to one. In other words, you have to hit when you go out of the zone, or if you don't, scouting reports just say, "This guy will chase — is an easy out."

There are all kinds of different situations when it comes to hitting. If the young hitter has exceptional mechanics to hit, speed of the bat and that type of thing, and his competition level is where the pitchers throw the ball all over the map and don't get the ball around the plate, that's one thing. That's a different issue. But if it's a competitive situation where this young hitter who is a prospect faces maybe a prospect or two in the league, or even if they're not quite there yet; if they have some ability and professional baseball feels they should go to school first and mature, but they do pitch to him, and have a tendency to try to work the corners; if he takes pitches that are off the corner of the plate by an inch or two, etcetera (and pitchers rarely crowd a hitter, which is to come in tight on a hitter, in amateur baseball; they work away constantly); if he has a tendency to take a lot of pitches, then I have a tendency to be turned off by him. In my judgment and the thought processes of many others, all good hitters have two things in common: all good hitters hit, and all good hitters are aggressive.

Personally, I have always been attracted to hitters who are highly aggressive. To point something out, let's assume the player has great mechanics. There isn't any question in my mind aggressiveness by itself does not get you by as you play at higher levels. It has to be controlled aggressiveness. Aggressiveness coupled with good mechanics is the key, and if a hitter forgets his mechanics as he becomes more aggressive, it can be self-defeating.

A good analogy here relates to the philosophy of Vince Lombardi. I have studied him because he was such an interesting guy. But even when he became coach of the Packers he didn't make the system more complicated than it was. He kept the system simple in terms of his teaching. And of course he was dealing with guys who had been stars in college who were then pro players. One aspect of it was how he looked at opponents on the teams they played each week. He drew some diagrams on the blackboard and said, "This guy is the most aggressive guy in the league on any team we've played. He's big. He's strong. He's fast. And he is hell on wheels. He's aggressive. And you know what we're going to do? We're going run right at this guy." When his assistant asked how they were going to do that, Lombardi said, "We're going to take the quality that he has and turn it against him." He told them the easiest guys to trap in pro football are the aggressive guys. And that's exactly how he approached the problem.

The comparison can be made to baseball insofar as the best pitchers and best hitters are concerned. The best pitchers are not intimidated by the opponent's best hitter; they go after him with their best stuff in order to keep that hitter from beating them. It becomes a one-on-one competition between the pitcher and hitter. But, for a hitter, even if he has good bat speed and good mechanics at the plate, it does not necessarily mean he'll be a good hitter. My contention is that without controlled aggressiveness at the plate, a hitter with a passive nature at the plate won't be a good hitter anyway. And to carry that one step further, defensively, if the pitcher does not want to attack the hitter and come right after him with his stuff, or if the first move of a defensive position player is not to the baseball, then they are not as aggressive or controlled as they should be for maximum success.

Don't misunderstand me on this. Good hitters almost without fail have very restricted strike zones. They don't go out of the strike zones to hit. If it's a borderline pitch and he has two strikes he'll fight it off and foul it off to stay alive for one he can hit. But when they get a cookie out over the plate, they don't foul it off, they drive it. They hit it hard.

Unfortunately youngsters get too far afield because of what I describe as over-coaching and under-teaching. You know, what you teach a young player, even when he's a Little League kid or whatever, chances are if you teach him well and show him the right way, he will have a chance to carry that with him all the way. The problems we see are habits that are learned in catching the ball, throwing it, or hitting it, and are quite difficult to break if the player has been doing this for six or seven years in his formative years as a youngster. We're creatures of habit, and as a result it's very hard to break a young player of a particular bad habit he may have.

Is it true that every player who gets to the major leagues has overcome all these bumps in the road and realized his potential? Absolutely not! There are guys who play in the big leagues who are considered pretty good players, but as a scout you look at them and say, "You know what? He should be better but he's never quite understood what kind of a player he is." And that's as old as the game is. His ability allows him to get there. His ability allows him to stay there. Maybe he's a good player. But as a professional scout you look at him and say, "You know what? He should be better."

What I want to emphasize is that kids who have taken an excessive amount of instruction have a tendency to be very choosy when they hit. And there's a reason why they take a lot of pitches. They become preoccupied with getting a pitch down the middle of the plate, number one, and number two, they can't hit the pitch that's off the plate by an inch or two. That's why they take it. Even the more experienced kids do it. And I repeat for emphasis: all good hitters hit, and all good hitters are aggressive.

Can the so-called bad ball hitters be good hitters? You bet. But the successful ones are few in number. In years gone by there was twenty-year big leaguer Ducky Medwick, remembered today as a member of the St. Louis Gas House Gang in the thirties before he moved to other teams in the forties; from the late forties through mid-sixties there was longtime Yankees catcher Yogi Berra; and Pirates outfielder Roberto Clemente was out there from the mid-fifties until 1972, when his career was cut short when he died in a plane crash. Today all three of them are in the Hall of Fame. That covers the period from the early thirtics up into the seventies. Other bad ball hitters who followed in the seventies and eighties included outfielder Al Oliver, who played for seven different clubs and logged a career .303 average; and infielder Bill Madlock, who was a .305 hitter with six clubs.

As I noted previously, all organizations would rather have the player at seventeen if he's a high-round draft than at twenty-one. It gives them three years more to develop the player at the professional level. Make no mistake about it. College is a way a lot of kids go, and it's the way a lot of them should go. But there are a lot of high school kids who are not ready, even if they have the physical ability. Makeup and maturity must go with ability.

I'm not trying to play the devil's advocate and say professional baseball has all the answers, because if a young player is not dedicated to becoming a professional player, but think he's going to go out and get away from home and be a hell-raiser, professional baseball won't put up with that, anyway. And as a direct result of all of that, all it does is impede his ability to develop as a player.

What happens at the draft reflects the way professional baseball views the players at the time of the draft. It does not mean that's the way the player is going to turn out. Remember, there were over thirteen hundred kids selected over Mike Piazza in 1988. He was seen by everybody as a young player and most all of them turned him down until we selected him only as a favor to Tommy Lasorda as the last player we picked in that draft. But he put a lot of hard work into it and went on to have a great career.

I got involved in that process when Mike had flown out and worked out with the Dodgers and there was hesitation on the part of my boss in terms of signing him. So he called me in to see him and I worked him out at Dodgers Stadium and when I did, I fell in love with his bat, and as a result we signed him. But we didn't pursue him hard. After all, we had drafted sixty-one players ahead of him and nobody else drafted him. But why didn't other scouts see what we saw in Mike Piazza?

That tells you about the flaw in the system. Nobody is trying to say the system is perfect. I'm certainly not trying to suggest that at all. The system is imperfect, yes, but it is still the best available system known to professional baseball. And this is the system applied in all professional sports. Simply put, it's the best system used because there is not a better one.

I'm reminded of a conversation I had with a coach by the name of John Stevenson, who coached at El Segundo High School in California and recently passed away. He was a very successful coach for fifty seasons and compiled more victories (1,059) than any other high school baseball coach in California. He told me a story at one point in time about an experience he had many years ago when he was a varsity coach and he had hired the junior varsity coach who was in his first or second year coaching.

At the conclusion of a practice session one day, the junior varsity coach came over and he said, "This is my list of kids I'll have to cut." They always had very good baseball teams in that school, so they had to cut kids. They just didn't have enough spots for all of them. So the cuts were made at the junior varsity level.

So Stevenson looked down the list of cuts and came across one particular youngster's name, and asked, "Why do you want to cut this kid?"

"Because he only weighs 95 pounds. He's a freshman and I don't really think he can play."

Stevenson said, "Well, he comes from a baseball family. You know he's got a pretty good swing. It's a given that he's not really developed and is one of the smaller kids, but I don't want you to cut this guy."

The younger coach said, "Okay, you're the boss. But if I keep a guy like this, he really doesn't have much of a future in the game."

Stevenson answered, "Well, I've been doing this a little bit longer than you have, and I don't want you to cut him."

"Okay," he said.

Well, this little freshman was George Brett, and he had an older brother named Ken Brett, who was four or five years older, and he had become a big bonus baby with the Red Sox. Actually, Ken was a two-way prospect. Many people thought he should have been drafted as a center fielder but he was a left-hand pitcher. So the Red Sox selected him in the first round of the 1966 draft and he went on to a fourteen-year pitching career in the big leagues.

That's an extreme situation, of course, but it does show you what can happen in kid baseball when early judgments are made about developing kids. And the same thing is applicable when you pass a judgment on a player too soon. Ninety-five pounds may turn into 195 pounds four years later. George was considered a good draft when he became eligible in the early 1970s, but still there were many scouts who thought there were too many negatives about George. He was not a great runner. He was a shortstop. And it was widely accepted by most in the scouting world at the time that he would have to change positions.

The first change was to second base, but he didn't have the quickness for that spot, and he was tried at third base. At that time the question became, "Well, he hits a lot of balls to the opposite field and he doesn't have a lot of power. Will that come?" So there again, the initial judgment was flawed. Evaluation skills for coaches and scouts are all-important because a career can hang on the balance.

As I have said, not everything falls as expected. Mike Piazza, who was not drafted out of high school, went to the University of Miami briefly. He did not play much there, but was primarily used in the DH role and didn't catch much or play first base. He then transferred to Miami Dade Junior College in Florida, where he thought he'd play more, but wasn't drafted from there either. Then he was finally drafted in the sixty-second round by the Dodgers, entirely as a favor to Tommy Lasorda, who was a good friend of Piazza's father. But when he came for a workout at Dodger Stadium, well, you had to see great bat potential there. And in his case, the rest is history.

When a scout turns a guy down and tells his organization that the guy can't play, that he's not a good prospect, there's a tendency to do what we call "chasing his report." If you brought a report and said, "No, the guy's not a prospect," there's a tendency to want to stick with that. And again, when I got involved in the Piazza situation, and went to the workout and saw him swing the bat, there wasn't any hesitancy on my part to say, "Hey, let's sign him. Forget about the draft. Let's just sign him." My attitude was that although I had never seen him before, I liked what I saw.

When we had instructional league in the fall and winter that year I had a conversation with one of our very good scouts in Florida. I didn't work *for* him but I did work *with* him, and he said to me, "I don't know what you saw in Piazza. He can't play, Gib."

I told him, "I didn't see him play. All I did was see him swing a bat. I probably saw a hundred swings and didn't need to see more than that. If I had it to do all over again, I'd take him and tell the club to sign him and give him the money." And of course that's what they did.

But this scout's attitude was, "Well, I didn't think he was a prospect."

And when Tommy asked us to scout him when he was a high school kid in the Northeast (he was originally from Pennsylvania), we had the scout from that region take a look at him and he didn't think Mike could play. It was a comfort story of, "Well, Gib, I didn't like him and that other scout didn't like him, so you're wrong."

I just said, "Look, I'll just stick to what I saw and what I said. And that was pretty damn good." And that's why I told my boss, scouting director Ben Wade, to sign him. It had nothing to do with Tommy recommending him. If the kid had not shown great speed of the bat and great power, I would have been forced to say, as I had done several times before with sons of former players in our organization, "I'm really sorry, but I don't think he's a prospect." I had been through that many times, but in this case there wasn't any question in my mind.

Now, the reason I'm relating this story is certainly not to show how smart I am. Nothing is more boring in my mind than to listen to a scout go on about players that he liked that his organization didn't select in the draft but maybe somebody else did, then the player shows up in the big leagues. On the face of that claim, per se, a casual listener to a conversation like that or somebody not in the professional game is liable to ask, "Why didn't he take him? Their scout liked him."

Quite often there is this all-important P.S. to the story. The issue may be that the scout had him on his list but he may have had twenty-five guys ahead of him on his list that he thought were better prospects. And in the final analysis, we come to find out the twenty-five guys he had ahead of this player all failed.

Off to the Races
An Inside Look at the Draft

In my career I have participated in at least fifty drafts, over forty with the Dodgers after I first started going to drafts when I worked for the Angels, 1976–1977. The first June Amateur Draft was held in 1965, four years before I began scouting in 1969. There used to be a January Draft for junior college players, but it was discontinued in 1986.

The days of the draft are the culmination of a year's work for the scouting departments, who know the future success at the major league level depends in large part on the success of each draft. It's an exciting time.

Every draft is the same and, at the same time, every draft is different. As a scout, when you're evaluating a major league team, your evaluation process is usually based on what the player can do. But inevitably what happens is, if your team has done reasonably well, you start comparing teams you have to beat. How does your team compare with the guys down the street? Down the block? On the other side of town? On the other side of the country? Are we better than the Angels? Are the Angels better than we (the Dodgers in my case) are? Are we better than the Yankees? Are the Yankees better than the White Sox?

Without getting into a lot of ridiculous comparisons, I would just like to offer this thought. There are several ingredients which make for a front-line major league team, a pennant contender, a pennant winner, a World Series team or a World Series winner. The items necessary to have a first-rate team are pitching, hitting, speed, power hitting, and defense. Now, if you're comparing the team that you work for or that you root for with the guys down the street, down the block, on the other side of town, on the other side of the country, there are necessary comparisons to be made and questions to be asked.

Is his pitching better? Let's say for the sake of argument, "No." Is his starting pitching better? Well, it's about even. Okay. How about his relief pitching? They're a little bit better. Okay. How about his offense? They're a lot better. Okay. How about their team speed? Well, they're better. Okay. How about their defense? Well, they're a little bit better.

Of course, you can overanalyze and look at all the statistical data you want. If you're comparing teams, and let's say for the sake of argument, you are basing your argument on your team, and you say, "They have a little bit better starting pitching, a lot better relief pitching. Offensively they have a better hitting club. Do they have more power? Yes. Do they have better team speed? Yes. Are they better defensively? Yes."

When you acknowledge all of those things, and you're talking about the opponents, when your comparisons are that slanted toward your opponents, you must face the inevitable. You must get some new players or you better basically acknowledge that you have as much chance as a hoot in hell of going anywhere in league competition. That's the acknowledgment you should make and that is basically what the story is.

Collectively, are your opponents better over the course of a season? They are. They must be. But you never know in a short series. I would say in 1988 the Dodgers were certainly were not the best team playing professional baseball in the major leagues, but we played the best in postseason games and we had two vital ingredients. We had very good pitching, and at that point the best pitcher in all of baseball, Orel Hershiser. And we had a very dominant key player by the name of Kirk Gibson.

Saying all of that, we not only beat the Mets, who on paper, were a very fine team and far superior to our team. Then we beat Oakland, who also had a very fine team, far superior to our team, at least on paper. We beat the Mets in a very tough league championship series. And we beat Oakland in a relatively easy World Series, four games to one.

As far as the draft is concerned, there is always anticipation about it. It doesn't matter how long you scout, I don't think you ever totally lose the interest in the draft. It's what you work for. My part in all of that as a national cross checker involves traveling. I go all over the continental United States, sometimes to Hawaii and Puerto Rico, when area scouts report so-called hot players there for me to see and evaluate.

The draft itself is an interesting period, one that's exciting and anxious for scouts. We used to say it was kind of like Christmas was when we were youngsters. There's great anticipation. There's a lot of hope that you will get the players that you want. And, of course, coupled with that hope, is the hope that your competition will not notice the players you want and like them as much as you like them.

It's a given that the draft process is flawed, but I've yet to hear of anybody who has a reasonable alternative to the draft. When the actual draft is complete and desired players are signed, the long process of player development begins.

I would like to point out that because the suggestion is made that these are the top players, it's sort of like looking at the morning odds at the race track. One horse is 3–1, another is 5–1 and another is 99–1. Who establishes that? Those are the handicappers who work for the race track. That being said, the race still has to be won. And the same thing applies with the draft.

Once a youngster is drafted, it doesn't ensure that he will become a major league player. He's just getting in the race. That's when the race starts; that's not where the race ends. From that point on he's going to be judged whether or not he has the ability — both physical and mental — to become a major league player. And that's the important part of it.

In 2012 the Dodgers' first turn to pick did not come until the eighteenth player in round one. We were eighteen. We selected as our first pick Corey Seager, a tall shortstop out of high school in the Charlotte, North Carolina, area. There isn't any question about it. We think he is the best prospect. Without going down the entire list of selections, I'll mention the first thirteen players we picked, just to give you an idea.

Jasmuel Valentin, a Puerto Rican shortstop, was taken next as a compensation player for the loss of catcher Rod Barajas to free agency. He happens to be the son of former major leaguer Jose Valentin.

These are two interesting kids. Seager is a tall, rangy guy who hits left-handed and Valentin is a short and kind of stocky switch-hitter. Both have very good hands, good arms, and good lateral quickness. I think Seager will probably end up playing third base and Valentin may end up at second. The point is that both have the makings of being very good major league players.

Steve "Paco" Rodriguez is a left-handed relief pitcher out of the University of Florida. As an aside here, he became the first member of the 2012 draft class to make it to the major leagues when he was called up from the AA team before the end of the 2012 season to replace injured LHP Scott Elbert. We'll see what the future holds for him.

Onelki Garcia, a tall left-handed pitcher, was actually a native of Cuba and had been showing his wares for the last year or so prior to the draft.

First baseman Justin Chigbogu is from Raytown, Missouri.

Ross Stripling is a right handed starting pitcher from Texas A&M University.

Joey Curletta is an outfielder-pitcher for Mountain Plain High School in Chandler, Arizona. Our scouting director lives there and our scouts had a chance to see him a lot. I saw him only at the pre-draft workout at Dodger Stadium.

Theo Alexander, an outfielder from Lake Washington High School up in the Seattle area, is a very good-looking left-hand hitter.

Scott Griggs is a relief pitcher from UCLA.

Zack Babitt is a second baseman I didn't see and I'm not very familiar with him.

Jeremy Rathjen, a right fielder from Rice University, was taken next. I've seen him a lot, probably since his second year of high school. I saw him during his entire career at Rice University. He was a fifth-year senior in 2012. He incurred a knee operation earlier and had to red-shirt for a season during his recovery.

James Campbell is a right hand pitcher out of Stoney Brook University in Long Island, New York. I saw him pitch against the University of Maine up in Bangor, Maine.

Darnell Sweeney is a switch hitting shortstop from the University of Central Florida.

That's basically the first thirteen and I don't want to go deeper than that on the list of players we selected. Of course, saying whether a draft is good or bad takes about five or six years.

Who made that happen? There were many very knowledgeable people sitting in the Dodgers draft room for the 2012 draft. Gary Nickles, our eastern regional supervisor, is a former director of scouting with Baltimore and a longtime scout with the Dodgers who has been scouting in one way or another for as long as I have. John Green is a national cross checker, just as I am. He has probably been around fifteen or twenty years. Logan White, the current director of scouting for the Dodgers, has been here for eleven years, so he has probably been scouting for close to twenty years. Another national cross checker, Paul Fryer, has been around scouting for twenty years or so. Our western national supervisor, Brian Stephenson, was there. Brian was a RHP for UCLA who was a second-round selection and played for both the Cubs and the Dodgers before he had Tommy John surgery and turned to scouting. He is a third-generation scout in his family. His grandfather was Joe Stephenson, my mentor at the beginning of my career, and his dad is longtime scout Jerry Stephenson, who recently passed away. Brian has been scouting close to ten years now.

Others present included Calvin Jones, who lives in Texas and has scouted with us probably eight or ten years; Orsino Hill, who has scouted with us a couple of years; and Dustin Yount, the rookie among the scouts with the Dodgers. This was his first year in scouting. And Tommy Lasorda was in and out, making sure we all had plenty of snacks. And I was there.

The idea of bringing scouts into the draft room, at least a few at a time, is based on the idea that it gives the scouts an idea of what the process is for those two days. It's a chance for scouts to see how we try to take every possible precaution to pick the right guy when our turn comes. That's the key: "when our turn comes." You can look at it any way you want. Collectively, as a scouting group, we often don't agree on where we should select a given player, and, like all organizations, we tell everybody who will listen that we were in total agreement on players we picked.

Sometimes there are discussions of players that you say you're not interested in when you know in fact that you can't get them. It's a form of sour grapes, I guess, and reminds me of something I experienced many years ago. I grew up with Johnny Stapert, who lived right in the middle of town in Fair Lawn, New Jersey. He was the second youngest in a big family. We had played a lot of basketball, baseball and football together as we grew up because we were from the same part of town and we hung out at the Fair Lawn Boys Club and played for Pop Milnes. When we got to high school we were on the same freshman basketball team, and we were on the same varsity basketball team. Johnny wasn't really a baseball person, but he ran track. We were close friends and when I finally got a car in my junior year, I paid a hundred bucks for it, and I quite often drove John to school. He was a very smart guy who didn't ever take a book home. He went into the Navy about the same time I went into the Army.

As kids growing up during the late forties and early fifties, we were very aware of who Marilyn Monroe was because of the famous calendar she posed for. And then we heard she was going to be in a movie. Wow! The movie was called *All About Eve*, and she had a very minor part in it. But this was the first time we had a chance to take a look at her on the screen. Johnny saw the movie before I did. On our way to school one morning when it was probably about ten degrees, and my little '38 Ford had a heater that sometimes worked and sometimes didn't, we had a very serious conversation about, of all things, Marilyn Monroe.

John brought it up. "Guess what, Gib, I went to the Highway," the only movie house in our town. "I saw a movie called "*All about Eve* and Marilyn Monroe was in it."

"No kidding?"

He said, "And you know what? I don't think she's so hot. I don't think she's as good looking as everybody says."

I had to laugh at both of us because at that time everybody knew her as the woman in the nude calendar pose. We didn't think of her as a movie actress.

I said something that probably didn't make much sense, I said, "Well, it really doesn't matter much whether you think she's good-looking or not, John, because you sure as hell are not going to get a date with her."

And I've always thought that same logic, or rationale, applies to scouting directors who, unhappily, instead of staying clear of commenting about draft selections made by other clubs, make comments like, "Ah, we didn't care for him anyway." That sounds like sour grapes, and to tell you the truth, it is. An experienced eye, a good scout, a good cross checker, a good supervisor, and certainly a good scouting director knows that if you're picking in the lower third of the draft you can pretty well tell who is going to be selected before your turn comes. In my judgment, though, sour-grapes comments like that don't happen with experienced people. They come from people who are trying to make some kind of reputation in the game and quite often tell somebody where it will get into print, "We didn't think much of that guy, and we weren't in the running to get him anyway."

Let's look at the actual selection process of drafts a little closer. Every organization keeps track of every player as he is selected and adjusts his own preferential draft accordingly. One question I am frequently asked after every draft is, "What about players you wish you had gotten?" You don't necessarily wish you had gotten them ahead of the kids that you did get, but there were players that you had seen during the course of the year that really impressed you.

There were two players in particular that we had a shot at that we didn't get and I really wish that we had selected both guys. Now, this is not excluding the kids that we got, because the first two players that we got in the last draft that I saw, I was very impressed with both of them. But that's the nature of scouting. You get one and you wish you had two. You get two and you wish you had four. It's just the nature of it.

I saw two particular players that during the course of the year who were very impressive to me. One was a centerfielder from Williston High School in Williston, Florida, which is in the panhandle section of Florida. I believe that little town has only twenty-five hundred people. It's a very small agricultural area. Incidentally, they had a very, very good baseball team that could have matched up with some very big high schools. They had a player by the name of Max White, the centerfielder. He was the third player selected by Colorado in the draft, the seventy-third player picked.

The other player who impressed me very much, but I didn't flash scout him because I saw a lot of him at the college tournament at the big league park in Houston, Texas, was a youngster by the name of Derek Barnes, who was also a centerfielder.

Max White was a left-left and Derek Barnes was a right-right. He attended Texas Tech University and was a junior when he was drafted. Max White was a high school boy. We had worked Barnes out in our workout that we conducted in Houston prior to the draft. He had a good workout and really impressed me. Both of them were what scouts call tool players. They could run, they could throw, they could hit, and they could hit with occasional power. And both were base stealers also. But all of that said, this does not take anything away from the players we selected

Those were two that we had a crack at who got away. Your guess is as good as mine about where we could have taken them. Our first pick was Corey Seager, and I really liked him, and Jasmuel Valentin, our second pick, was number 51. Let me clarify a little bit here. I assume the reader of this book knows more about the subject than most people might. But I think I should explain this. Earlier I said experienced guys could determine whether or not a player would be available for your selection if you were picking in the bottom third of the draft. What I meant by that is that there are thirty major league teams, and in the first round if you're picking from number twenty to thirty, you have certainly established pretty well which overall players would have been picked in the first fifteen rounds.

In the 2012 draft we were eighteenth to pick, and to clarify that, when you have been in this business for a long time you're very aware that there are a lot of "ifs" you're looking at ... if the agent has a reputation of having his players sign and is reasonable with what his player's demands will be, and if the kid is a highly skilled prospect, you can pretty well tell that if you are picking eighteen he will not be available by the time your turn rolls around. There would not be seventeen passes in terms of his selection.

And quite often the medical information we get about a player, which seems to ebb and flow, can be another "if." We went through a period about ten years ago when we got heavily involved with doctors who were talking about eye conditions. I don't want to get into that too deeply. We used as an example a player who had undergone laser surgery and seemed to be doing just fine and swore by it.

It's funny how many pieces of medical information we get that almost make us laugh. For example, we were assured by one doctor that players who had corrective eye surgery would hit until they reached the double–A level, but then they would struggle. How they arrived at the decision that these youngsters would hit the wall at the AA level is beyond reason, as far as I'm concerned. But the point is, that's what he contended. It was much easier many years ago before we had all these so-called specialists involved.

Every scout has his disappointments and he takes them in stride as being part of the whole thing. In my case, I didn't have a damn thing to do with the selection of Mike Trout, the high school youngster who was the first pick of the Angels in 2009. The only thing I did was that when I saw him I considered him the best player in the draft and I wrote a report to that effect. But, as luck would have it, the Angels selected him before we picked. Realistically, though, I think we would not have selected him. That's okay. That honestly doesn't bother me. I think I was dead right on Trout. And there have been times when I was probably dead wrong about a player I supported. I have seen Mike Trout play in high school. I have seen him play in the minor leagues. And I have seen him play in the major leagues. Remember, after being drafted in 2009, he broke into the big leagues in 2011 at age twenty. I think he is the best young player I have seen in probably twenty years.

Also, since you're dealing with the human element, the development of the individual players doesn't happen at the same rate. I'm sure any casual baseball fan knows who Matt Kemp is. He was drafted in the sixth round in 2003 and made his major league debut in 2006. But once there, it took him over five years to fulfill his potential and become the player he is today. His first few years of major league play was considered very mediocre both offensively and defensively. Yet today he's considered one of the premier players in major league baseball.

I suppose I should touch on the economics of the game here. Many years ago, 1986, I got the second player the Dodgers picked, David Hansen, and the third player the Dodgers picked, Mike Munoz. I want to say Michael signed for about $35,000 and David for, I think, $58,000.

The first player we selected that year was Mike White, a high school outfielder from a small town named Loudon, Tennessee, who had exceptional ability but never got to the big leagues. And so the story goes. Being a high draft pick just entitles you to get more money at that given time in terms of signing a contract. But it does not assure you that you are going to get to the big leagues first, or that you'll be the best player.

Obviously first-round picks enjoy something just from the business standpoint that others don't. It doesn't matter what era we're talking about. The club pays the most money to put them under contract and employ them. Conversely, they will get advantages lower-round players don't.

This reminds me of a happening that developed here some years ago. I had two players, Eddie Williams and Harold Perkins. They were both from Cal State–Los Angeles. Both were great kids. Both were lower-drafted guys. Harold was selected in the sixteenth round and I can't recall the round for Eddie. Both could run and throw, but they involved position changes. I

Mike Munoz (left) and David Hansen were great young players who always showed respect for the game.

selected Harold in 1981, and Eddie the following year. Both were great makeup kids. Played hard as hell all the time. Harold played eight minor league seasons and concluded his career at age thirty-one in the Mexican League which was good AAA-level baseball. Eddie did not play nearly as long.

Both were from Compton, California, and in the offseason I would go down to Compton on Sundays and work them out. I went down on one particular Saturday and I saw a youngster playing in what we call a beer league game. I watched him swing the bat and play the outfield and was kind of attracted to him. So I decided to check his background and I found out his eligibility had come and gone at Fresno State. So I asked him if he were interested in playing pro ball, and he said he would love to have a chance.

So I talked to Ben Wade, our scouting director at that time, and he said, "Yeah, if you want to sign him, go ahead." I signed him for $1,500. On Sundays, Jim Muhe and I took him to work out with Harold Perkins and Eddie Williams. We used to do these workouts pretty religiously. I hit fungos, threw batting practice to them, and I ran them constantly because running the sixty-yard dash was very important in the Dodger organization for many years. It's less important now (which I don't agree with) but it was important then. Dodger teams have always had players that were considered exceptional runners. Davey Lopes was a great runner and a base stealer. Billy Russell wasn't a base stealer, but he could actually beat Lopes in a sixty-yard dash. The Dodgers have a history of shortstops who could run, going back to Pee Wee Reese, who was succeeded basically by Maury Wills, and everybody knows how he could run.

We worked them out to try to help them get ready for spring training. I called the three of them together and I said, "Now listen. You've got to face reality. You guys were low-drafted players. Stay out of the training room." After a period of time, let's say three or four years down the line, if a low drafted kid looks like the best young player among the top players in the organization, people in player development do not give a hoot in hell if he was drafted low. They say, "He's the best kid. He's better than the guy who was drafted first and got a lot of money." But there isn't any question about it that early on in the development of young players you want players who were selected low to stay out of the training room.

So I asked the three of them, "Does everybody understand?"

"Oh yes," they said they understood.

It became a habit for Jim Muhe to keep a close eye on youngsters that I had signed. Quite often in those days I would get lower-drafted players, and Jim was good at getting major league players who may have an extra pair of spikes or glove, and somehow those spikes found their way into the locker of a player that I had signed. But it was agreed they would stay out of the training room.

Tommy Lasorda had a habit in spring training of playing minor league players in big league games. I remember getting a call from Jim when he said, "Tommy's going to give Harold Perkins some playing time tomorrow at second base." Of course, this was a big charge for the young players. Quite often they called home to tell the folks all about it and ask them to listen to tomorrow's ballgame. Tommy never let any of them down.

The third individual that I signed here is a guy I'll call "Jack" because he's still involved in baseball. Later that day or the next day I got a phone call from Muhe and he said, "Guess what? Jack will play today."

After the game I called Jim back and said, "How did he do, Beau?"

"He played two innings in right field. I saw him in the clubhouse after the game and he had an icepack on his shoulder."

So apparently Muhe asked him if his shoulder was bothering him and the kid said that it wasn't.

"Then what in the name of good sense are you wearing an ice pack on your shoulder for?"

The kid said, "Preventive ice."

What can I say at this point? In other words, the very first thing he was attracted to was to get some attention by putting an icepack on his shoulder. His arm didn't bother him, but he got some attention that way and made it into the training room. He never had any real success because when reality set in, it was his makeup. His makeup wouldn't allow him to be a grinder.

To explain that, I'll explain some of the terms I use in the draft room. One which is a total acknowledgement or emphasis of respect is when I see a kid who plays extra hard, I'll say, "This kid's a marine." Or I might say about a player like Steve Sax, "He has a big heart," or "He has a fire in his belly." Those are terms used to show respect for the player's efforts.

And the scouts use terms that are not so respectful. One that comes to mind is I'll say, "He's a cruiser," meaning he plays only as hard as he has to play. That terminology is used when we get into the area of makeup. Front-office people, quite often, are concerned about great makeup players. A question asked repeatedly by front-office people is, "What kind of makeup does this player have?" And honestly, makeup at the level at which we scout is very, very difficult to determine.

The reason it's tough to determine is because most of the players that all big league organizations are attracted to are young players who have a lot of success as players. For the most part they dominate their competition. It's very difficult to make a determination what kind of makeup a player has when he's totally dominant.

You find out about competitors when they're not having success. How do they react to that? It's a grand old good time, a Sunday walk in the park, when you hit the three-run homer to win the game or throw the shutout or strike out the last hitter with the winning run standing at second base and the tying run at third base. It's a different experience.

Yet makeup to a large extent governs how much a player will progress in the game. Quite often scouts are asked to make a determination. Rarely will you hear a scout say that the player he is recommending for draft has bad makeup. Yet, we find that when youngsters do get into organizations, for one reason or another they do not always play hard. And when that happens they have an exceptional amount of difficulty developing as players.

The ultimate compliment a player can pay to a teammate or former teammate is to say, "What a great competitor he was. I felt good just being on the same club with him."

I've heard players, and often they're the guys who have achieved success and in some cases even stardom, say things like, "A hangnail would keep this guy out of the lineup if you were facing a quality pitcher. He didn't always play hard. When he was having a good day he played hard. But if he was not having a good day and somebody else was, or he was not the center of attention, he was not a good teammate." And so scouts are asked continually, "Tell us what kind of makeup this player has."

I heard an interesting bit of dialogue the other day between one of our national guys and scouts. They were looking at a list of players who were further down the line in terms of the draft and trying to separate them. A scout I work with, Paul Fryer, a cross checker with the Dodgers, asked a scout, "What kind of a player is this guy?"

And the response of the scout was, "Oh, he's such a nice kid."

Fryer cut him off and said, "Wait a minute. I'll just remind you of something a former scouting director told me." And, incidentally, that former scouting director was in the room. He's now the East Coast supervisor for the Dodgers, and that's Gary Nickels. He said, "Gary Nickels told me when he was my boss some twenty years ago, "'Don't tell me about a kid that you would like to have date your daughter. I want to know about a player. Does he have sufficient skills to play the game professionally?'"

If it turns out he's a nice guy to go with it, and baseball has had its fair share of very nice guys, so much the better. One of them was Harmon Killebrew. He was signed by the Senators at age seventeen right out of high school and went directly to the major leagues.

Historically we can refer to people like Ty Cobb, who was considered by friend and foe alike as not a very nice guy. But baseball historians will tell you, whether we're talking about his character on or off the field, we have to regard him on the field as one of the all time great players. He was a .367 lifetime hitter in what was called the Deadball Era. That's probably when the league average as a group didn't hit .260.

I remember a player I knew well who was an exceptional player but who had a problem with alcohol. And I remember that he was very open about it. I asked him how he got started drinking, and he told me. "The first time I really got started drinking I got drunk with my father. I got drunk in the house and as a result I missed the high school basketball game, and I was a member of the team." Obviously his father had a problem, and as a result he had a problem.

Saying all of the above, the judgment of the scout often is accepted. How well does a scout make a determination about whether a guy can run, hit, field, throw, pitch, and whether his stuff is plus stuff, double-plus stuff, average stuff, a cut below average, or just below average. Scouts are pretty good at making those determinations.

What's projectable? How likely is it the kid will get better? That's where the makeup issue becomes critical because it's well known in most of professional baseball that the kids who have a terrific desire to get better quite often do. And when they do, it's because of their drive, their interest in improving. There's a term in scouting which I do not like at all, but it's there: "He'll figure it out."

That's the loosest term I think I've ever heard. Quite often it's used to describe a youngster who has a lot of physical ability but may have, let's say, a glitch in his development or problems with a particular phase of the game. The way some scouts approach that problem is to say, "Well, he'll figure it out once he becomes a pro player." That's a generality that would not have been accepted by Al Campanis or by any other good baseball front-office executive. I want to know what the problem is.

Again, alluding to the draft room, we're not talking about whether this youngster is coming to date your daughter. What we want to know is whether or not this player is a prospect. Can he run? Can he hit? Can he field? Can he throw? If he plays an infield position, is he agile? Does he compete well? There's a myriad of questions you can ask a scout. But when you hear the response, "He'll figure it out," I've never been an easy individual to accept that explanation.

I guess I could touch on a couple of expressions you hear in the draft room. I'm kidded about it quite often, I guess because I'm the oldest guy in the draft room and I've scouted longer than all the guys I work with.

One of the terms I use is, "The gun is his friend." Before speed guns became prevalent, your first reaction would be, "Does the curve ball have hard breaking action?" In other words, is it hard or is it a slow developing curve, a soft curve ball? Does the fastball sink? Or does it rise? Does a changeup have fade to it? Or is it straight? And along came the guns. And what happened when the guns came along?

The first comment out of a scout's mouth might be, "He's ninety to ninety-two, and he's only eighteen." I guess the next step would be that when he's twenty he's ninety-four to ninety-six, and when he's twenty-two he's a hundred. Frankly, I don't like it when the very first thing the scout utters is the reading on the radar guns. You'd better be careful. Is the fastball straight? If it's straight, hitters hit it. If it moves or has a tendency to bore up or sink down in the strike zone, that's what you look for. The guns don't measure that. You hear people say, "Well, I can teach him the sinker. I can teach him to ride the fastball." You better have something to start with.

That's always been my philosophy. My interest in the speed gun is secondary. I like to see a youngster versus a hitter. I like to see how a youngster who pitches reacts to getting out of a jam or in a jam. Does he compete harder or is he looking in the dugout hoping the manager or the coach will come out and get him? That's why we go to games. That's why I'm a lot more interested in what the scout says when he reports visually looking at a player as opposed to looking at videotape. Videotape doesn't tell me how he competes. It's that simple.

If you scout just videotape, you almost become a slave to technique. Quite often kids do look good on videotape, yet they can't play. They can't pitch. They can't field. Or they can't hit. But they still look pretty good on videotape.

Another common expression is, "The guy has a pretty swing." That doesn't tell you how quick the guy gets the bat head through the hitting zone. A squared-up delivery where the guy is nice and balanced tells you it looks good, but it tells you nothing else, like who he is competing against.

Scouting, the preparation for the draft, and the actual draft days are all very interesting. The process before draft takes as long as a couple of weeks when we carefully compare all information on every one of the players whose names we have and arrange them in the order in which we hope to draft them. Videotape helps, but will never replace scouting live action. Believe me, a lot of thought and a lot of discussion are involved in that.

I'll give you a couple of examples that we've run into in the draft. I was looking at some signing bonus figures as we approached the year 2012. Signing bonus figures are pretty well established and can be obtained fairly easily. We can spend as much as $1, 900,000 on the first player we draft, and $984,000 on the second player we draft. In 1985 the first player we drafted, outfielder Chris Gwynn, younger brother of Tony Gwynn, got somewhere around $150,000. He was the tenth pick overall in that draft. He had a productive career, but it was not as good as we thought he would have. We thought he would be a regular. Instead he became a platoon type player and never was an everyday player. He's a very nice guy who works for Seattle now as their director of player development.

Saying all of that, signing bonuses today are essentially ten to twenty times greater than what they were twenty-five years ago. With that I must add that salaries of the scouts have not increased anywhere near that level over the same period of time.

That is scouting. Quite often scouts in the field will tell us they have been checking with this player and his parents and his agent. Most players now have agents. The mere fact that a youngster gets an agent means absolutely nothing to an organization in terms of evaluating him as a player. And I certainly am not hesitant about saying, "I would love to get this guy. I think this guy is an exceptional player in every phase of the game. In addition to that, he plays the game like it's important to him. He's driven." I have no problem with that type of player. I have no problem if he becomes a first-rounder and the going rate is what I previously outlined. If I think he qualifies for that, I would say, "Take him first and give him the money."

And scouts also run into the player who says, "I'd better be taken in the first three rounds, and if I'm not, I'll go back to college and not sign." I'm really not interested in the kid who has marginal skills that you would take further down in the draft who comes up with, "If you don't give me what a first- or second-round players gets, I'll go to school."

"I'll go to school." It's that simple. Parents, agent, and players, even though they're young, I think that if a scout talks to them to get some background information, they may misinterpret some of the scout's questions. Do you want to play professional baseball? How interested are you? I think the general impression gleaned from that process is, "This organization really wants me badly."

And this is where the business aspect of all of this comes in. We get paid to evaluate the skills of that youngster. How badly we want him is a private situation that comes up when one player is played off against another. But the idea that Junior, who hit .320 in college and is sought by five or six teams, becomes an item that the organization is saying, "We have to have this guy," and scouts leap up on the table and say, "We've got to have him." Sorry. That doesn't happen.

Quite often the scout will say, "Yeah, I saw him. How do I feel about him? There are four or five guys that play the same position that I'd rather have." And they do not feel that the kid should be selected in the first or second round. Scouts' opinions change and quite often scouts' opinions differ. There was a player in the 2012 draft selected possibly late in the first round. I saw him and I didn't care for him at all as a high-round pick. In my opinion he was probably a fifth-round pick based on what he could do. Most of our people did not feel he was a high-round pick, but one of our scouts did and was not hesitant about saying he liked him so much. Time will tell.

My view on the player is this. I signed a player like this thirty-plus years ago. Of course, the draft was different then, and the guy I signed wasn't drafted. He could do everything this guy could do. This player is just a good player in a high school program but he doesn't have exceptional tools. The player I signed did get to the major leagues as a utility player. But clubs want first-round picks to become major league regulars if they are position players or front line major league pitchers.

There was a kid who came down this year and worked out during the draft who is an exceptional youngster. There are some questions about his skill level, and he's not artificial at all. He loves to play. He works his tail off. He works hard at getting stronger and getting better. But he lacks what I consider a necessary ingredient to be a front-line major league player. While the draft was going on I said to our scouts, "Let's face it. In terms of makeup this kid probably has the best makeup in the draft." When the draft came, he was picked very quickly in the very first round, and I said, "Good. I'm glad. He's a great kid and that means he's going to get a lot of money."

I'm happy about everything that has happened for him so far. And I'm double-happy that we don't have to give him the money, because I don't think his skill level is there. I'm not trying to be a wise guy about it. That's where your judgment has to supersede the fact that you think he's a great kid. I've seen many people get influenced by that, even in an organization where constant evaluations of a young player are made, they'll say, "Oh yeah, he's a great kid."

But that really becomes academic. Let's talk about big league players. Is he a front-line player in the big leagues? Is he capable of becoming a front-line player? I don't want to hear that he's a nice kid. That's all extra, the icing on the cake, when front line players are great guys. But baseball is no different from any other business in the world. Not every individual who is at the top of his game, whether it's sports or business, is a particular favorite that you would enjoy having into your home. Some of them are peculiar guys who are not very well centered in almost every aspect of life.

So when you get a premier player who is also an exceptional guy, you appreciate him, as I said about Harmon Killebrew. And most guys are appreciated for their ability on the field and not anything more.

Just in talking about previous drafts that I've been to and different conversations, one of the things that is interesting in the course of developing a player is how he interprets the interest a scout shows in him. Is the youngster convinced that you are really interested in him? And he reads the paper and says, "Well I read where so-and-so got a million bucks last year and I played against him and I think I'm better, so I'll ask for two million."

Being interested in a player does not mean we have to have him. Usually when a cross checker or a scout talks about this player as being ultra-special and the best he's ever seen, the first thing that crosses your mind is this. Who has he ever seen? I want to know that. If he's a new scout, let's not compare this player to George Brett, who was not seen by this scout because Brett retired before the scout making the comment was born.

I have to be careful when I refer to people like Mays, Mantle, DiMaggio, Feller, and players like that because I saw all of them play when I was a teenager. I try to deal more with contemporary players, but even there I can't call

Bob Gibson contemporary. Quite often you can't even refer to Steve Carlton as contemporary. So you have to be thinking of the Albert Pujols or the Matt Kemps of today's game when comparisons are made.

There isn't any question scouting is interesting for the same general reasons it's always been. It's your ability to project how good the player is going to become in future years. First of all, is he going to be a big leaguer? Secondly, is he going to become a premium player or is he going to become an ordinary player? Ordinarily, when you take a player in the first round, what you're shooting for is that he becomes an exceptional player. You're not looking for him to become an ordinary player. It's that simple.

If a lower-drafted player becomes an exceptional player, I never felt you had to be an apologist for it. We've heard that to some extent on a guy like Kemp. Well, you couldn't have thought he was that good. Why did you draft him in the sixth round? Well, we drafted Eric Karros in the sixth round and he became a front-line player. And we drafted Mike Piazza in the sixty-second round. I never want to apologize for any of that because, when you get down to it, we did draft them. Anybody else could have picked them. So why do the people who select the player have to apologize for *where* they picked him?

We're still dealing with human beings. When the day of the draft comes, that's the way you rate the players. And that is the last time you should rate the player that way. From that point on his development should depend on himself and how hard he works to get better. It doesn't matter what era you're talking about, front line players always work hard at becoming better. They work at it constantly and they never stop. They're always trying to maximize the ability that they have and become the best at what they do.

And no matter how you view it, judgment is still a part of what the player is and what he can possibly develop into. So much of it is dependent upon the player. The idea that a player is going to get preferential treatment throughout his career is a dream. He may get some at an early stage. There may be certain allowances if a first-round pick struggles. But it doesn't last. Sooner or later he has to produce on the field. And very often players who were selected further down in the draft end up being better players than those who were picked earlier. Maybe it's because they work harder. Maybe it's because they feel they have something to prove. Often young big leaguers feel that way and that's what drives their engine. That's okay.

But the idea that should really be accepted by parents and young players is this. Either you want to be a professional player or you don't. You want to be treated fairly, and you should be. I have no problem with that. But the idea that you can make comments like, "If I'm not picked in the first three

Peter O'Malley and me in one of the meeting rooms at Dodger Stadium in 1998.

rounds, I won't sign," or when a young player is asked what kind of money he thinks he should get, and he says, "I want life-changing money. If I don't get that I won't play baseball"— that doesn't cut it with me. Most of those kinds of comments are made by young players and/or families that just lack the knowledge to understand the draft.

Looking back on every draft I can simply say, "I wish we had gotten this player or that player." One player can make a terrific difference, whether you're evaluating his skills or just in the normal development situation. I go back to my experiences and say this: not all players who play in the major leagues are driven. They are not. That's just the way it is. More often than not, probably an exceptionally high amount of the time, the reason they are there is because they have exceptional ability. Whether they're trying to maximize that ability or not becomes another case.

Naturally my career as a scout does not cover baseball a hundred years ago. But it does cover more than forty years. Through all that you realize who wants to maximize his talents or who is just happy to be there wearing a big league uniform. Generally speaking, the former has the chance to become a special major league player while the latter may go on to have a nice major league career. And it's not unusual to have a large number who are just happy to be in the big leagues.

I guess you could sum this up like this. Baseball is a terrific game. It's almost perfect the way it's designed, and when it's played well it's an exceptional game to watch and enjoy. The imperfections in the game, however, are almost entirely created by people. What is less than perfect in baseball is the result of the people who run the game and play it.

Four Decades of
Baseball Observations

I started watching major league baseball as a young kid probably in the late 1930s. My dad told me I had seen Lou Gehrig play, but I really don't remember because I was probably only six or seven years old. I do remember well seeing Charlie Gehringer play around 1942, which was near the end of his career. And I saw Pepper Martin, the Wild Horse of the Osage, play when he was brought back to the major leagues during World War II, long after he had retired, because there was a shortage of premium players. I did see him get an extra base hit in the Polo Grounds and slide headfirst into third base.

These names probably don't mean a lot to the current group of executives in the game. Because of big corporate ownership of clubs, we are seeing fewer real baseball people in baseball getting the higher echelon jobs.

I'm not attempting to change it. It's a fact that we are seeing a lot of high-office executives get jobs with little experience in baseball. They may be intelligent people, knowledgeable in their own fields, but most of them are not far removed from college. There was a general manager in Boston that six or seven years ago was an intern with the San Diego ballclub. Think of that. He went from an intern to making probably close to a million dollars a year or maybe even more. Now, I suppose looking at it objectively you could ask if there was any jealousy on the part of baseball people. I don't think it's jealousy, but it's a matter of amazement more than anything. Common sense tells us that people ascending to that job level at a very young age with limited experience almost never happens in the corporate world. It rarely takes place in the military unless there's an extreme situation involving combat. You don't have somebody go into the military as a buck private and come out a general within a few years.

In baseball now, at least within the framework of four or five clubs, it's there, and I think it's a dangerous precedent. How does it happen? Basically it's because the corporate mentality that ends up purchasing the clubs and running them sees baseball people, so to speak, who have been in and around the game for many years as being out of touch with the electronic age.

Is experience of any value? I think it certainly should be. I know when I started in professional baseball at the scouting end of it, there were people like Hollis Thurston and Dutch Ruether around. Hollis "Sloppy" Thurston, so nicknamed because he was such a stylish dresser, was a former pitcher in the major leagues who had been a teammate of Babe Ruth when he had pitched for the Yankees, and later pitched against him. And the same was the case for Dutch Ruether. They were both in their late seventies and were quite a pair when I met them. They ran around together. They dressed up in nice sports jackets and fedoras and sat there in the stands and discussed how they pitched to Babe Ruth several decades earlier. And they were part of the characters who ran through the game at that time. It was not unusual to see people like that representing clubs as scouts.

There was Vinegar Bill Essick, who had pitched a few games for the Red Legs in 1906–07, before he became a longtime scout for the Yankees and signed Joe DiMaggio in 1934 after his sixty-one game hitting streak with the Seals in the Pacific Coast League. And later Hall of Fame pitching great Carl Hubbell was the GM of the farm system and scouting for the San Francisco Giants. I remember seeing Hubbell about thirty years ago when he came into a ballpark to see a young pitcher in Southern California and there was a great deal of presence about him. I had an opportunity to have a couple of general conversations with him.

Most of the old timers I got to know were scouts, men like Joe Stephenson, Gene Thompson, Spider Jorgensen, Gene Handley, and Al Kubski, among others. All of these guys had started playing baseball professionally in the 1930s and 1940s. These are guys who cut their teeth in the Depression era and played with and against some of the great players. And when they talked about players, you listened.

I remember Al DeRenne, a former minor league player. By the time I knew him he worked for the post office, and was a part time scout for San Diego. He was a very interesting guy who played six years of minor league baseball and was then drafted into the service in World War II and lost a leg in combat. He had an artificial leg by the time I met him and he got along just fine. He played golf and was a very enjoyable guy to be around. His father-in-law was an outstanding major league pitcher by the name of Wilbur Cooper who pitched fifteen years, mostly with the Pirates, and I believe he won over two hundred games. In that time the old workhorse pitched almost 3,500 innings, 327 each in 1920 and 1921. Imagine that. So Al had a lot of stories that had been passed on to him about Ty Cobb and Honus Wagner and others.

Baseball is history. I recall when I was a youngster hearing my dad and my uncles talk about seeing Joe Jackson and Wagner. I mean, those were players who started before Babe Ruth did. My Uncle Phillip saw Joe Jackson play for the New Orleans Pelicans in the Southern League somewhere around 1909. Imagine that ... over a hundred years ago.

If you're interested in baseball history, there are things you can learn from it that can apply to current players. I'm talking about Mickey Mantle, Willie Mays, and those players who were contemporaries of mine in terms of age. But when I talk to people I work for now who are maybe thirty or forty years younger than I am, I get the feeling that they're not very interested in the history of the game or those players.

You hear occasionally, "Well, Wagner couldn't have played now, he's a big fat guy that waddled around, and all the players he played against were little. Those players weren't physical. They were a bunch of clowns playing in the big leagues." There's a lot of ways to look at it, and most old timers look at it with a jaundiced eye. Most of the old-timers feel, "Well, there were only sixteen teams as opposed to thirty. There were many, many more minor leagues than exist now. It was a time when batters faced pitchers who did everything to the baseball and it was legal. They cut it. They spit all over it. They threw a shine ball, a palm ball, a coffee ball. And they didn't throw baseballs out of the game like they do today."

And the old-timers suggest the competition level was probably tougher. I don't necessarily agree with that, even though I can't prove it one way or the other. But I do believe this. The very good players and the great players of any era could play in any era. Think about that for a moment. Careers overlapped. Remember that when DiMaggio joined the New York Yankees in 1936, the star of the Yankees was not Babe Ruth. Ruth had just retired. But Iron Horse Lou Gehrig was there. Gehrig was *the* Yankee at that time. Of course, this was before illness had diminished Gehrig's skills. So, is there a question, really, that DiMaggio could have played with Mantle? Remember, DiMaggio owned center field before Mickey Mantle came to the big leagues in 1951, which was the season DiMaggio retired. And you can play games like that with many other stars. Ted Williams played with Jimmy Foxx and Jimmy Foxx played against Lou Gehrig.

I do know you gain a greater respect for the game if you accept that instead of looking down your nose at it and saying, "Well, the game is different than when those guys played." Jimmie Reese lived to be over ninety years old. I knew Jimmy. He loved to talk about the old-timers. But he was a contemporary of the modern player because he was a coach for the Angels for many years when Nolan Ryan was there. As a matter of fact, Nolan Ryan named one of his sons after Jimmie Reese: Reese Ryan. And so it went. Jimmie Reese roomed with Babe Ruth and played on the same team with him. He also got an opportunity to see the great Bob Feller and Nolan Ryan pitch, plus all the contemporary greats.

When I asked Jimmie who the greatest player he ever saw was, he said, "That's not hard for me to answer. Babe Ruth was the greatest player I ever saw. Pitchers? Well, I saw all of them and the greatest left-hander I ever saw was the great Lefty Grove. The two best right-hand pitchers, well, that would be a little bit tougher, but I would have to say you can take your choice between Bob Feller and Nolan Ryan." Now if you want to ignore Jimmie Reese, I suppose that's fine. I never ignored those guys because I felt they had something to say and what they said was worth listening to. I cut my scouting teeth around people like that.

Whatever the reason is behind it, there is a fascination not just from the general fans, but quite often from people who come from so-called high society. You can get into a social situation where you're standing around with a highball in your hand and you're in the middle of a group of doctors and researchers and somebody finds out that you're a baseball scout. Within a very short period of time you've got three or four people who want to know how you go about it, how you do it, and how fascinating the work must be. And that's a fact. That has been in existence for many years. And I don't think it will change as long as the general public per se has a fascination with the game.

The game, of course, is what people are so attracted to and what draws people together. The people who run the game are real, solid people, and are quite often fascinating individuals. At one time I worked with Frank Lane, who had been a general manager with the St. Louis Cardinals, the Chicago White Sox, and the Cleveland Indians. By the time I worked with Lane he was probably in his eighties and we were working for Gene Autry and the California Angels, where Harry Dalton was the general manager. He was a fascinating individual who had a million stories that all dealt with the good old days in the game.

When he was a general manager he was known as "Trader Lane" because he would trade anybody. During the 1960 season with Cleveland he traded manager Joe Gordon for Tigers manager Jimmie Dykes. I think that's the only time that ever happened. When I was with the Angels in 1978, I happened to be sitting next to him during the Yankee-Dodger World Series and watched the famous confrontation Bob Welch had with Reggie Jackson when Welch kept throwing his good fastball up there and Reggie kept fouling it off until he finally struck out. The Dodgers went on to win the game, but not that World Series, as the Yankees beat them when the games returned to New York.

Others that I've gotten to know over the years, well, probably my closest friend in baseball and out of it is Ed Roebuck, who was one of the original boys of summer that Roger Kahn wrote about in his great book. Getting to know Eddie got me acquainted with Sandy Koufax and Johnny Podres. Of course I knew pitching coach Ron Perranoski from high school in Fair Lawn, New Jersey. I was a few years ahead of Ron.

It was an interesting experience, especially when you get to know someone as well as I got to know Ed. I got to know quite a few people over the years with the Dodgers. A former pitcher with the Dodgers, Ben Wade, was the scouting director and my boss when I was hired. He always called Ed "Sears."

The Dodgers had never beaten the Yankees in the World Series but had come close a number of times, only to lose. The 1955 Dodgers were an exceptional team that included Roy Campanella, Jackie Robinson, Pee Wee Reese, Duke Snider, Junior Gilliam, and Carl Furillo. That particular season Johnny Podres beat the Yankees twice and closed them out in Game Seven in Yankee Stadium in the famous game where Sandy Amaros made a great catch in the left field corner.

It was a very interesting run I had working with all of those guys. I got to know Mike Scioscia very well. He's a classy guy, and a very sharp manager. It's a damn shame the Dodgers lost him because he had an awful lot to offer any organization and they just let him get away. It was a terrible mistake on our part. I got to work for Peter O'Malley, who was the best owner you could possibly think of. He was one of a kind in an era of hands-on, family-owned baseball organizations. Peter was always concerned about the welfare of all the employees.

In scouting young players, we're always looking for some advantage or nuance that will help us determine whether or not a kid will be successful. We're not referring to physical ability because raw, pure physical ability in baseball is not too difficult to determine by people who know what they're doing. But what is very difficult to determine is how big a heart a kid has and if he competes well. I mean, a kid can be competitive, but when there's a stress situation involved, does he have problems remembering what he should do or how he should go about it?

I had a coach years ago when I played baseball and basketball in the army. We got into a sort of a theoretical conversation about being creatures of habit. His contention was that if you don't believe it, just watch a basketball player. Often he'll go to a spot on the floor in the pregame where he knows he shoots very well. He likes to do that. Guys you see in spring training and around the ballpark who swing the bat well usually walk around with a bat in their hand. The guy who's a good defensive player is usually walking around with a glove in his hand. In other words, young players like to stick to what they do best because they are more comfortable in certain phases of the game.

Scouts quite often get into conversations with each other. I remember talking with a good scout on one occasion when he said to me, "You know, I think I have a pretty good idea of what to look for in a young player in terms of physical ability. But the other thing is that I like kids who are extroverts. To me the extrovert has a much greater chance for success."

And I told him I had thought about that at one time or another. The extrovert is not necessarily any more successful than the introvert. As a matter of fact, you can go a little further with that story without being a psychologist, which I am not. But why are people extroverts? Perhaps it is to draw attention to themselves. My experience in the game at the big league level, observing and talking to and knowing big league players over the years, taught me it can be just the opposite.

Can you equate being an extrovert with success as a baseball player? Maybe this little aside about Eddie Roebuck will make my point. Baseball made so much noise about Eric Gagne's eighty-four consecutive saves for a new major league record at that time, 2003, but how about this? Eddie Roebuck pitched in eighty ballgames and never got a loss. That's hard to do. I don't care if you're Lefty Grove, or Sandy Koufax, or Bob Feller or Roger Clemens. He was a reliever, and of course, the requirements for relievers in those days were a lot more stringent than they are now. At a banquet many years ago the speaker said, "Here's Ed Roebuck, member of the 1955 Brooklyn Dodgers World Championship team. Eddie, say a few words."

Eddie then stood up and said, "Thank you very much," and sat down. I've known him for many years. What a guy! He's very intelligent and a hell of a scout. Eddie is right at home on the golf course and he's right at home around scouts that he's friendly with or boys he played on the same team with, like Duke Snider, Carl Erskine, and Ron Perranoski.

Sandy Koufax was much the same way. A very bright, articulate guy who maybe goes one step past Ed. I like Sandy a lot. He's a very considerate and thoughtful person. He moved to Maine one time and didn't want to be around the crowds. That's just Sandy. Both Sandy and Eddie are introverts, and both had wonderful careers. Even though I did not know him, they tell me that Mickey Mantle was a very shy guy. We all know DiMaggio was terribly shy, but that may have waned as he got older.

Jimmie Reese told me a story that about some of the festivities before an All-Star Game in Anaheim when they brought back some of the great old-timers. Joe DiMaggio, then in his seventies, was one of them. Since Jimmie Reese was a former Yankee and still coached with the Angels, he sort of shepherded Joe around. Brian Downing was an avid baseball card collector who still had a lot of little boy in him, and he had brought a DiMaggio card and wanted Joe to sign it. But he was too intimidated to ask him. When Jimmie Reese brought DiMaggio into the dugout before the game, Downing asked him if he would get Joe to sign the card. DiMaggio did, and Jimmie said he also signed four or five baseballs and said to Jimmie, "Get me out of here. I don't like being confined like this."

Tommy Lasorda knew DiMaggio well and enjoyed the time they spent together. There were all kinds of stories, good and bad, about DiMaggio. But there is no question that DiMaggio's personality was terribly introverted.

To carry this a step further, let's look at our great infield with the Dodgers, the longest-running infield in the history of baseball, with Ron Cey at third, Bill Russell at short, Davey Lopes at second, and Steve Garvey at first. They played together over eight years, yet those guys are about as different as can be and came from extremely different backgrounds. Bill Russell was as quiet as Ed Roebuck. Ron Cey was sort of between, all business, very focused. They say he used to get pissed off at batting practice if the ball was not delivered right where he wanted it. Garvey could give you forty minutes on the Republican Party, probably thirty minutes on the Democratic Party, and probably twenty minutes on anything you wanted. He just loved to talk. He was an extrovert. Davey Lopes, another focused individual, a highly intelligent guy who liked very much to talk baseball, but you had to draw him out.

Paul Konerko, one of the players I cross checked who started with the Dodgers but has spent the bulk of his career with the White Sox, is extroverted. He was a very confident, self-assured youngster who was not intimidated by anybody or anything. Alan Wiggins was a highly intelligent kid who was very introverted. He hardly ever spoke. Jason Thompson, a power hitter who hit over two hundred major league home runs in his career, was shy and somewhat introverted. He would talk if you gave him an opportunity and he felt relaxed around you. He rarely volunteered anything. Eric Karros is another player who comes from the Garvey school. He was a very self assured, smart young player who went to UCLA and worked hard for everything he has ever gotten in the game. He is an extrovert. And Todd Hollandsworth, another intelligent player, was also kind of an extroverted kid. A great favorite of mine was Bobby Welch, very likeable and, like the others mentioned, he was a true competitor.

The reason I mentioned Roebuck is because I know him the best of all of these guys. When I asked him about pitching in front of sixty thousand World Series fans at Yankee Stadium, he said, "Gib, you have no idea. I loved every minute being on that stage. I know I'm shy but I never felt shy on the field."

One of the most self-assured guys I've ever met is a big league player I have seen over the years, Derrell Thomas. He was a utility player for the Dodgers. He has the best line of BS you ever heard. But if you walked into him in the right scenario and you weren't prepared for him, you'd walk away thinking, "Boy, what a great guy."

I recall one January I had some minor league players in Dodger Stadium. We used to work them out early prior to going to spring training. So I had four or five guys in there taking batting practice and fielding ground balls. During that juncture some big league guys would come in there and pitchers would stretch out and throw a little bit. If they were position players they would take a few hacks. But this was after Thomas had retired. I was in the corner of the dugout on the telephone talking to somebody upstairs and he came into the dugout and asked Jim Muhe, "Who's that guy down there?" meaning me. "He looks familiar."

I had not signed Thomas and had never interacted with him more than to exchange nods with him. So it certainly didn't bother me that he didn't know who I was. He had a beautiful husky puppy on a leash, and was all dressed up like he was going to a dance or something. He had an expensive-looking pair of slacks pressed to a razor sharp crease and a yellow sport shirt, and he was wearing a sort of tam-o'-shanter. Oh, God, what a beauty this guy was.

Jim told him my name and that I was one of our scouts. A couple of minutes later when I got off the phone, Thomas came down by me and says, in a thick Irish accent which was totally phony, "Gibby, me boy, how are you? It's great to see you. Damn, I haven't seen you in I can't remember when. I think it was about '81 or '82 when we won the whole thing and went to the big show."

So I said, "Hey, Derrell, how are you? What's going on?" and we passed a few casual remarks. I was a pretty good friend of his former coach when he was a high school player, Art Mazmanian, so I mentioned his name. "Do you ever see him?"

And he ran through a whole litany of "Oh, Art, blah-blah-blah." Then he said, "Hey, Gibby, I ran out of the house in a hurry this morning and realized I was without my wallet or my money."

"Geez, that's too bad," I said. "Sorry, but I can't help you out." That cut the conversation short.

Paul Konerko ready to hit one out of the park at Wrigley Field in 1999.

Derrell Thomas was drafted in the first round, secondary phase, by Houston in 1969 and played in 1,597 major league games in his fifteen-year career. He is known as a premium extrovert. As with every profession, the big leagues are full of all kinds of personalities, introverts and extroverts and many in between. It matters little when they get out on the field what the guy is because in baseball ability will manifest itself on the field.

And I have to mention Jack Clark, who was an introverted young kid on a scout team I coached when he was in high school. I couldn't get Jack to say much at all. I recall a situation before one of the games when we were watching a highly touted pitcher warming up. I was standing there talking to two of the other kids on my club, both of whom ended up in the big leagues, Kevin Bell and Mark Clear. Kevin was a red-headed kind of excitable but great kid and he said, "Boy, Gib, this guy looks tough. He throws hard."

Jack was standing there and didn't say a word. When Kevin and Mark went on their way, I said, "Hey, Jack, what do you think at this guy?"

He just looked at me with an expression that told me he thought it was a dumb question, and he said, "Oh, I want him. I want him bad." Then in his first at bat he hit a ball out of the ballpark. Then he repeated that trick two innings later. Jack also pitched for me. He pitched and played right field. On another occasion we went to play a five o'clock game in San Gabriel. I can remember this like yesterday. Worth Valentine, who had caught him in high school, was his catcher for that game. I flipped the ball to Jack and told him to go warm up with Worth. About three minutes later he came back and he flipped the ball back to me. "Not today, Coachie, not today." (He always called me "Coachie.")

I said, "What do you mean, 'not today?' What's the matter? Is your arm bothering you?"

"Nope."

Now I'm sensing this is coming from deep out in space because Jack could be sort of a spacey kid, and I asked him, "Well, then, what's the matter?"

He says, "No people."

There were no people in the stands and Jack didn't want to perform because there was nobody there to watch him. That's how he felt. He could have said his arm bothered him, but he simply told the truth. He was always a blatantly truthful kid and I respected him for that.

Thirty-five years later, Jack was a hitting coach for our major league club after he completed a great career as a power hitter in the big leagues, mostly with the Giants and the Cardinals. He was a hitting coach for the Dodgers until he got fired by then general manager Dan Evans. The club wasn't hitting better or scoring more runs because at that time it didn't have that many good hitters. That got him in trouble. But he still had the habit of being very truthful.

Getting back to the scout team, we had very good bench jockeys on that team. One was a kid named Jerry Waters, and Mark Clear was another one. When Mark wasn't in the bullpen he'd get on guys pretty good. Jack never really said much at all, but the one thing I do recall is this. There was a loud-mouth on one of the clubs we were playing against who was a big strong physical looking guy. At this time Jack was playing third base. He had a great throwing arm. Anyway, this big-mouth kid was making a lot of noise about what he was going to do with our pitcher when he hit against him.

Rick Hayes, who was ultimately drafted by the Braves, was our pitcher that day. He had a good live arm and struck that guy out the first time and he never swung the bat. Then he made a lot of noise on his way back to the dugout about how he was going to get the pitcher next time. The next time up, strike one was hit behind the first base dugout, and this guy was a right hand hitter. Now Jack liked to whistle. Just a short blast. So he whistled and said to the hitter, "Right on him, baby. Right on him." Now, that was an expression Jack used whenever a batter swung late at the pitch. If that hitter had been any more late, he would have swung at the ball going back from the catcher!

Jack Clark, originally drafted as a pitcher, was one of the better players on a scout team I managed when he was still in high school.

Several years later, our instructional league team was playing in Arizona and Jack was sitting out by the dugout. He had introduced me to his son earlier that day. The boy was not the ballplayer his dad was, and Jack told me on the side, "He's not really a prospect, Gib, but he likes to play and that's all I give a damn about. But I'll tell what he can do. He's a hell of a fly fisherman. He's a lot better than his dad at that."

So Jack was sitting in front of that dugout and our instructional league kids were getting beat up pretty badly by the opposition team. One of their guys was a loudmouth kid. We had a pretty good pitcher on the mound by the name of Jose Diaz. He was six-foot-six and weighted in around 260 pounds and was called Jumbo. Damn, that kid could throw hard! Anyway, he blew his best fastball up there and this guy swung at it and he was so late that the ball just missed Jack, who was sitting on a little stool by the first base dugout. Jack just whistled at it like he had done so many years before.

The hitter wore number 6 on his jersey. Jack said, "Hey, Six, you're right on him, baby. You're right on him." And he smiled at the kids on his team in the dugout when he said it. I got such a kick out of that. "Damn," I thought, "he's still got a lot of little kid in him." He's just a straight-up honest guy.

On the other hand, with a player like Barry Bonds, being introverted or extroverted was never a factor. With him it was all about confidence. Even as a young player in high school and college, there was a confidence factor with Bonds that was unbelievable. It didn't border on arrogance. It *was* arrogance.

I recall a conversation I had with Gene Thompson, the old Cincinnati pitcher and longtime scout who had pitched in two World Series. He was an amazing man, one of those guys liked and admired by everybody. I think he spent over sixty-five years in organized baseball. Think of that. I've had occasion to talk with him over the years about different old-time players. Gene has made comparisons between the players in days gone by and the players now.

I think the comparison he made is a fair one. He said, "As good as Bonds is, I will tell you one thing. When I played at Cincinnati when Bill McKecknie managed the team in the late thirties, early forties, there was no way in the world he would have let Bonds stand in on the plate like that and take basically three quarters of the plate away from the pitcher without flipping him. If he took a hack and hit one out of the park, then posed at the plate like he does, McKecknie would have yelled out of the dugout, 'The next time that SOB comes up to the plate, see how he swings the bat from his ass!'" That's the way they played the game then.

And I've been told this by others who played in that era. There's no way you can let a guy take that much of the plate away from the pitcher without making some effort to move him off the plate. And I've noticed in recent years that it's something today's big league pitchers rarely do. They seemed to let McGwire and Bonds alone. It's as if they're going to lose a pitch up and in and hurt those guys. They're both big, strong guys and nobody wanted to tangle with them. But that doesn't mean a damn thing to highly competitive pitchers. I buy into Gene's thought process there. I cannot believe that Bonds could have stood in on the plate like that in the old days, especially because he wore a guard for his forearm, one for his shin, one for his wrist, and a helmet ... and God only knows what else.

I have been asked, "What's it like to scout in Texas?" It's very interesting. I can sum this up in a nutshell. When you drive around the country you see a lot of very interesting places. Unfortunately you do not have an opportunity to visit them, simply because you're always working on a tight schedule. When I took Spanish as a high school kid, I was not a very good student. My father was fluent in Spanish. He could speak Spanish before he could speak English, and he told me, "You know what? Spanish is a very important language to know because of our proximity to Mexico." Coincidentally, he was born in Mexico.

But the bottom line is simply that I never thought knowing Spanish would be particularly useful to me in the United States, but I was wrong In Texas it's a predominant language followed, closely by some Middle Eastern languages. It's difficult to get by today just being fluent in English, especially if you're lost and looking for directions. Many people I encountered in Seven-Eleven stores and gas station attendant cashiers were not that fluent in English. That's not to put anybody down or show any disrespect. It's just a matter of fact in Texas. And another thing. There are a lot of pickup trucks in Texas and they all seem to go ninety-five!

Once when I was driving back from Oklahoma City I passed a road sign that said, "Artillery shells—$2.95 apiece." I guess that referred to spent cartridges, but nothing would surprise me in Texas. I've seen a lot of signs along the road in my time. Remember the Burma Shave signs? They were great. And now there are signs for everything else. But I've never seen one for artillery shells. Only in Texas.

Oklahoma is a little bit better. I went to Norman, home to the University of Oklahoma, and found a lot of pickup trucks, but they don't quite go ninety because the roads aren't quite as good. They settle in at about eighty-eight. And you see a lot of people in red because everything is the University of Oklahoma, and everything is football. No question about it.

Another thing I'm asked quite often is, "Who is the best individual you've ever worked for?" Well, as far as clubs go, the best club I've ever worked for, without a doubt, is the Dodgers. The way they treated the people under Peter O'Malley was just great. You couldn't ask for anything better. The treatment we've received subsequent to O'Malley's owning the club, I suppose, has been pretty ordinary compared to the other clubs. Remember, I worked for four other clubs before I came here and experienced a lot of different ups and downs.

The best individual scouting director I had the privilege of working with was Walter Shannon, who was an old Cardinal with Branch Rickey for years and went on to head up the scouting department at Baltimore when they had Frank Robinson, Brooks Robinson, Boog Powell, and that bunch. Then Shannon went to the Angels. We had a lot of players with the Angels in those days. In fact, Nolan Ryan was not even our number one pitcher. Frank Tanana was. That's over thirty years ago. We had a lot of talent but we couldn't seem to get it all together and win anything. Subsequent to that I went to Kansas City and then on to the Dodgers. Walter went to Milwaukee with the Dalton Gang, Harry Dalton and company, and they won a pennant over there when they had Paul Molitar and Robin Yount, two great young players, future Hall of Famers.

Success always followed Walter Shannon of the Angels and a lot of people around him, and I've always had great admiration for Walter Shannon.

To change the subject a little bit, I think everyone associated with professional baseball is asked about one famed player or another, "What's he really like?" That question is mostly asked by people not in the game about players with considerable ability who may be fan favorites. When a player has exceptional ability the fan wants to know what kind of a guy he is.

Why does that question come up? Well, my theory, and I guess it's as old as the game, is that they really want to know about the player's personality and his interactions with people. He's a good or great player, but is he a good or great guy? Naturally they're hoping you'll say, "He's a terrific guy."

I have a general attitude about this. It's a given that baseball probably reflects the rest of society. It's been said and written about enough times. But the reality is that some players are good guys in terms of dealing with the fans and interacting with people, some of them are kind of indifferent, and still others are a first class pain in the ass.

And the same thing applies to experiences I've had with front-office people. And that's why I would like to talk about a front-office individual that I worked for over twenty years, the former owner of the Dodgers, Peter O'Malley. He was a particular joy to work for and over the years

I've stayed in touch with him. Everything he did, in my judgment, indicated class.

I remember the 1994 season, when the baseball agreement between MLB and the players expired. Labor unrest resulted in the longest strike in the game in eighty-nine years and caused the cancellation of the World Series. During all that, Peter O'Malley brought Donald Fehr, the representative of the Players' Union, in to talk to the people who worked for the Dodgers. He had a kind of open conversation and Fehr explained the position of the Players' Union. Whether you agreed with him or not, we got the feeling that what Peter O'Malley was trying to do was draw the different sides together rather than the name-calling and the rest that went with labor unrest that can develop in any professional sport.

Taking care of the employees' concerns was just who Peter O'Malley was. Listening to Fehr was very interesting. He is a sharp individual in his own right. And to the best of my knowledge that was the only time anything like that was ever done. Peter was attempting to draw the sides together.

We have never had a union in scouting. And to be very honest, my own opinion is that for all the years I've worked for the Dodgers and even prior to that, it never concerned me very much. I've always been pro-union. I grew up in a heavily industrialized area and I worked in summers at Curtiss Wright, which was the United Auto Workers. The union was very much involved there, and also the longshoremen to a certain extent. And they were very powerful unions. Of course, we didn't have much of a say as kids because there was a lot of labor unrest at the time.

I've always been pro-union and yet I never worried about needing a union while I worked for Peter O'Malley because we were treated so well by the owner of the ball club. In terms of earning power and wages, we never worried about it because we knew we were going to be treated fairly by the owner. We never worried about getting a bonus because we knew that if the club was making money and doing well, whatever was available would filter down to the working people. And that's the way we were treated all the time.

An example of that is a story I remember hearing many years ago in the early stages of my career working for Peter. I think it was at the conclusion of the 1981 season when I got my first World Series ring. Along with the ring they gave us pendants for our wives which matched the rings. Nobody else ever did anything like that. One scout recently told me the Texas Rangers did it after they won the 2011 World Series. Walter Nash, who ran the ticket department for the Dodgers in Brooklyn and came to Los Angeles with the team, made the statement in a conversation we had about the pendants, "Gee, what a nice gesture on O'Malley's part."

He said that began in the seventies when we had won three National League pennants but didn't win the World Series. At a get-together celebration for one of those pennants, I think it was Tommy John's wife who said that it would be nice if wives were somehow recognized because it can be stressful if you're married to a ballplayer. And the same thing applies if you're married to a scout. There's a lot of separation. There's a lot of difficulty in raising children when the husband is gone a lot, and in some cases it's difficult for the marriage.

Peter listened attentively and decided, "You know, that's a big point." And from that point on, when we won the World Series in 1981 and the last time we won in 1988, Peter gave the World Series rings to the men and pendants to their wives. He was always very generous in how he took care of his people. That's just his MO, as we say. That's the way he was.

Tom Lasorda when he was a young pitcher in the Dodger system. Notice the "B" on his cap.

Another classy guy who they say "bleeds Dodger blue" is Tommy Lasorda. Over the years he has done so much for me and for scouting. He turned eighty-six years old in 2013. Most people don't know it, but he was originally signed by Phillies scout Jocko Collins in 1945 and in November of '48 the Dodgers selected him from the Phillies in the minor league draft after he returned from the service. So he's been with the Dodgers sixty-five years! And, to the best of my knowledge, the two longest employees of the Dodgers are Tommy and Vin Scully, who came to the organization one year later.

As you can well imagine, I am often asked about Tommy Lasorda. Is he what he pretends to be? Let me tell you that Tommy is the best ambassador for baseball who has ever lived. He's a scout's best friend. Some of his stories are difficult to believe, but I can tell you this. They get your attention all the time. He's got a great sense of humor. He's a great baseball guy.

I've seen this firsthand: When he got the Olympic team I was one of the people who told him, "Tommy, that's not a very strong club. You're going to have to beat Cuba."

And when he read the list of our players he said, "I don't know who any of them are." And not only did he beat Cuba, but the team came home with the gold medal. His team included Ben Sheets and Roy Oswalt, who both became very successful major league pitchers. But at that time I don't think there was a person around who gave them even a slight chance to compete for the gold in the Olympics with the bunch of kids they had on that club. The problem that the opponents had was Lasorda didn't care what they thought.

I saw him in 1988 when we were in the playoffs with the Mets. They had beaten us maybe ten out of twelve that year and nobody gave us a chance. We lost the first game at Dodger Stadium on a misplayed base hit in a great game pitched by Orel Hershiser. Now our number one pitcher gets beat in a heartbreaker. We knew the Mets had a far superior hitting club. And I bet you at that point in time you could have gotten a hundred to one odds that we couldn't beat them.

But we not only beat them in a great playoff series, we then defeated Oakland in the World Series. Nobody was more excited than Tommy when Kirk Gibson hit his now-famous ninth inning home run to give us victory in the first game, then we kicked Oakland's ass in that series! They only won one game. We just outplayed them and their bash brothers, McGwire and Canseco, in every way. We outhit

Kirk Gibson hit a home run that still gives me goosebumps.

them; we outpitched them; and we outdefensed them. Tommy outmanaged a great major league manager, Tony LaRussa.

As far as Tommy Lasorda is concerned, the facts are these. He is the scouts' best friend. He is the little guy's best friend. He is the underdog's best friend. He is a beauty! "Sleep is my enemy," is one of his favorite statements. I used to ask him, "Tommy, how can you get away with sleeping four or five hours a night?"

"Hey, Gib, sleep is my enemy."

"What's the matter?" I'd asked him. "Are you afraid you're going to miss something?"

"Exactly. You're finally right about something," he grinned.

Lasorda is a peach of a guy. In my lifetime I have met many people in and out of baseball. And quite often when you meet someone who makes an impression on you, you may say, "This guy reminds me of so and so." In all the years I've known Tommy I've never met anyone who reminds me of him. He's an original. There is no gray in Tommy's life. Everything is in black and white. He's one of a kind.

I've asked him on occasion, "Why do you have such a warm spot for scouts?"

His honest answer was, "I think it's because I did it. I scouted the East Coast for the Dodgers for a couple of years and I know how hard the work is. I know how much time you guys are separated from your families, and more often than not over the years, your contributions can be overlooked very easily." And as a result he has always been wonderful to us. It is a fact that he's a Hall of Famer, and rightfully so. He's done so many things over the years in terms of anything you can possibly think of. He's done all kinds of charity work. He did it when he was much younger and he still does it.

Jim Muhe initially introduced me to Tommy. Those two were very close friends. Jim and I then became friends because in those days, in November and December, I took a bag of balls and a fungo stick and hit ground balls to local kids that I may have signed. Jim usually went with me for that.

So he introduced me to Tommy and I'll never forget how it went down. He said, "Hey, Tommy, meet this guy. He's not one of 'America's guests.'" That phrase was one of Muhe's favorites. The phrase "America's guests" had a twofold meaning. It was a ballplayer who didn't realize his own potential and didn't put out too much, or maybe an individual who was a front-office person, or a scout that he didn't think worked very hard. And that was my introduction to Tommy when I joined the club in 1979. And over the years I've gotten to know Tommy quite well. He's done so many wonderful things not just for me, but also for others like me. Tommy and I have known each other for over thirty years now and I consider him one of my closest friends. He's a hell of a guy.

I remember one occasion when my oldest son's wife had a relative in the hospital. She was a huge Dodger fan and a huge Tommy Lasorda fan. So I explained it to Tommy and asked him if he would sign a picture for her.

"Well, what's her name?"

And I told him and he signed a picture.

"Where does she live?" And I told him the town and so forth.

Then, not only did he give me the photos to give to her, but he took it upon himself to call her in the hospital. Needless to say, it was a terrific experience for her.

Over the years, I've kept up my interest in old-time ballplayers, guys who were playing when I was a kid. I had occasion to meet Pete Coscarart. You have to be an old-timer to know who Pete was. He was a shortstop-second baseman who played in the big leagues for nine seasons with the Dodgers and Pirates from 1938 to 1946. He was a particularly interesting guy to me, first of all because he was accessible. He lived about thirty miles from me and when I got to meet him he was probably in his eighties, but he was still active in a regular golf group.

I knew about his playing history because Pete was on the field with the Dodgers in Game Four of the famous 1941 World Series in Ebbets Field when catcher Mickey Owen missed the third strike that gave the Yankees a "second life." It went down with two outs and nobody on, and they came come back to beat the Dodgers 7–4 in a game that looked like the Dodgers easily had in the bag. They closed the Dodgers out 6–4 the next day and clinched the Series in five games.

Well, that's how I got to know Pete. Now Pete's career did not cross Tommy Lasorda's. He played in the major leagues earlier and was gone from the Dodgers organization by the time Tommy was a young player pitching at Montreal and then arriving on the scene with the Dodgers.

At any rate, this must have been a year or two later. And I recall this quite well. I got a phone call from a lady in Escondido, California, where Pete lived. It was his daughter telling me that her father had a very serious heart condition and was in the hospital and feeling kind of blue, and they were trying to buck up his spirits. When I asked what I could do, she said, "My dad knows you work for the Dodgers, and he didn't ask for this, but I know you spoke highly of Tommy Lasorda. He's always admired what a feisty guy Tommy is and what a good manager, and I wondered if you could possibly get Tommy to drop him a note."

"Sure," I took it upon myself to say, "I'll try to get ahold of Tommy. He's doing quite a bit of traveling for the club since he had quit managing."

I was able to contact Tommy and mentioned Pete Coscarart. He said he remembered Coscarart's career well. So I explained the story to him and Tommy immediately got on the telephone and he called Pete. He called him once. And he called him twice. And then Lasorda got a call from Pete's daughter and she said, "You won't believe this, but even my dad's doctor said his general attitude and overall approach to his problems went out the window after he talked to Tommy Lasorda. My dad's coming home in another day."

And that's who Tommy is. I don't ever remember Tommy telling that story to anybody. I really don't. It was just part and parcel of who he is. Here was an old Dodger, Pete Coscarart, possibly not remembered by many people, but to Tommy it was good enough that he was an old Dodger and Tommy was going to do all he could to buck up Pete's spirit. And he really did.

But the point is that Tommy Lasorda is a role model. I've been with him in different parts of the country, and no matter where you go or what part of the country you're in, when people see him they immediately smile and they want to interact with him. It matters not whether they're little kids or thirty years old or sixty years old. He is a terrific ambassador for baseball. He is absolutely the best!

Tommy has four living brothers. They are all up there in age and every one of them served in the military at one point or another. One of his brothers was a career Air Force guy. In recent years Tommy has spent a lot of time in children's hospitals and at Walter Reed Hospital in Washington, which is a military facility. Others talk about it. He goes. When he was eighty-two years old he went to Afghanistan and Iraq. It was not a chore to him. He enjoyed every bit of it.

He's such a piece of work. The thought of not being involved during the draft has never crossed his mind. He flits in and out of the draft room in the days preceding the draft and on draft days. He loves to eat and he loves good food and he's constantly bringing in stuff for breakfast and the rest for all the scouts. And that's the one and only Tommy Lasorda. And there absolutely is nobody like him, no matter how you cut it.

Some of my favorite guys over the years, mainly with the Dodgers, have to be included here. You have to remember I worked close to ten years with other clubs before I joined the Dodgers in 1979.

One in particular is Bob Welch, the right hand pitcher the Dodgers had who was later traded to Oakland, where he won a Cy Young Award in 1990 with a 27–6 record. Nobody has won that many games in a single season since.

He's one of my favorite major league players. He was a free-spirit guy, good-natured, and he initially had some off-the-field problems with alcohol. He eventually wrote a book about it called *Five O'clock Comes Early*, in which he discussed his battle with alcoholism. I got to know Bobby quite well. We used to play golf occasionally. There was Bob, Ed Roebuck, and myself. There was no getting away from it. Of all the big league players I've known over the years, I felt Welchie was just the absolute most fun guy just to be around. He loved life and he was a terrific competitor and a terrific pitcher.

As a matter of fact, in 2001 he was a pitching coach for the Diamondbacks when they upended the Yankees in the World Series in seven games. Subsequent to that, he went on to become a sort of assistant coach at Arizona State University. He's had his ups and downs, but he never lost his feeling for people. He always interacted well with young players. Once Welchie was established as a major leaguer he was always giving gloves and spikes and anything you can name to young players. He made a lot of money in baseball and hopefully he still has it.

Something that has crept into the business over the years is the question of how to deal with writers and electronic media people. How to answer their questions. That's why you see a lot of ex-players on the pregame and postgame television shows. The theory on that is, simply, that they can draw out other players to talk by the questions they ask in the interviews. And, in my opinion, most of the questions they ask are pretty infantile.

One of my favorites, 2011 Cy Young Award–winning pitcher Clayton Kershaw, is a youngster who handles interviews well. He's a straightforward and honest guy. There's nothing artificial about him. He answers all questions in his same easy way. You can see this youngster is not trying to be more than who he is. He knows he's good, and he's smart, and he really works hard at getting better and better and better.

I heard one interview when

Bob Welch, a fine pitcher.

somebody asked him to compare himself to Sandy Koufax. He answered that very well when he said, "That's a whole different world. I'm just trying to be as good as I can be and help my team to win." He's a first-rate competitor. And another interesting thing about Kershaw is that he's a team representative and he's twenty-three years old. Normally that selection is made by the collective voting of the players on the team, and in spite of his youth, he is certainly looked at as a key member of the team and is very well respected.

Another guy who comes to mind who has always been very much a favorite of mine is a coach on the Seattle Mariners now, Dave Hansen. I signed David back when I was an area scout. He had a scholarship to play baseball at USC, but we signed him in 1986 in the second round. From the first day I walked in and attempted to sign him, I really enjoyed his family, his mom and dad and three sisters. From his interaction with the family, I could see this was a kid who came from considerable means, but he was very unspoiled. He was the oldest kid in the family. He was a good student who wanted to be a baseball player. And actually, Dave was a good football player, a high school quarterback who had some Division One offers. He played on a very good team, Rowland High School, which was a big school at that time.

He played in the big leagues for fifteen years, 1990 through 2005, but he never quite achieved regular status. He became a key bench player and became one of the leading pinch-hitters of all time, not only in terms of number of hits, but in terms of home runs. In fact, in 2000 he led the major leagues with seven pinch-hit home runs in one season. He was a very good hitter, but not what I'd call a home run hitter. But that achievement in itself is special. When you pinch-hit in the major leagues it is so difficult because they face specialists who air out everything they've got in the last inning or two of a game. The guys who work the last couple of innings in the major leagues always have premium stuff. There isn't any coasting there. They come in and attack the hitters.

Dave never changed. Even when he was classified as being a pinch-hitter, he would go out and take 250 ground balls a day. He worked hard and enjoyed every minute of it. He's a terrific competitor and he was a very good hitting coach for the Dodgers, and now with the Mariners.

Things didn't go exactly David's way as a player because he wanted to play every day. But I remember him saying, "You know, Tommy Lasorda and the staff think maybe my defense isn't as good as it should be. I'm going to work at it. But in the meantime they have me classified as a pinch-hitter. Gib, I'm going to make myself the best pinch-hitter in baseball." And for several years he was.

I remember teasing him about how he could really manage his money when he was a young player. When he was playing with our A Ball club in Bakersfield, California, and I took him out to eat after a game one time and he had plenty of money on him. And I said, "You know, these other guys are having some difficulty paying their bills. How do you come up with a pocketful of money?"

"Oh," he says, "I cut hair." He was the team barber. They had a dress code on that team and they had to have short hair and no facial hair. "I do it a lot cheaper than the local barber." He was eighteen years old and had that all figured out. And I thought to myself, "He is a special kid." And he has always been that way.

Today we live in the same town and I see him once in a while. How time flies. I remember his oldest daughter when she was just a little tyke and he took her to the ballpark occasionally. She's in college now. And he has another daughter in high school and a son around ten. "Dave the Dude Hansen." I don't know if that nickname ever officially caught on, but when he was a youngster starting out, he had a habit of calling to different players "Hey, dude." Dave Hansen has always been one of my special favorites and he always will be.

I'd like to recall some chance meetings and conversations which sort of reflect on some of my experiences in the game. In the course of seeing literally thousands of games and traveling hundreds of thousands of miles either by air or automobile, you run into peers of yours to some extent who have scouted or been very well-known players. You don't see it as much now as you did years ago. It has to do with economics, really, because years and years ago it was natural for former major league players to gravitate to scouting. It still exists to some extent, but it is not nearly as prevalent as when I started to scout.

Just from the standpoint of who was around and who wasn't, we had Sloppy Thurston. There was Dutch Reuther, who had pitched in the 1919 World Series for Cincinnati. And many others like Larry Barton, Sr., and Jackie Warner, who had played extensively in the twenties and thirties against Babe Ruth, not to be confused with a player with the same name who came along decades later. And there was Glenn Wright, who had been a terrific shortstop for the Dodgers and Pirates; he played in the twenties and thirties and lived up in central California.

People always wonder what happens to certain major league players after baseball. But to a certain extent you have the same situation in scouting. I can remember seeing those guys over the years, and when I first started to scout with guys like Joe Stephenson and Bob Zuk and Rosey Gilhousen, the old time scouts who had been around forever. And there is a connection there, of course. As time goes by you call on your own experiences and you're looking at your peers now who are far younger. It's kind of like when you're growing up or when you're a young adult and the police are older and the guys in the service are older. Then you reach a point where you're older than they are. And then you're even older than the president of the United States! It's just a progression of a natural course of events in a person's life.

Then I think of guys like Dick Hanlon, who I worked with many years ago, briefly with the Angels and then for a long time with the Dodgers. Dick and I joined the Dodgers at about the same time, but he had pitched in the organization for many years. He never got to the big leagues, and actually made his name in the Pacific Coast League. He was one of the best scouts I ever worked with and he was a consummate workaholic. He loved being around young players. As a result, that rubbed off on the young players.

You don't always get the players you love. In fact, the odds are greatly against it when you're competing against twenty-nine other teams who also have large scouting staffs. But over the years, quite often, players who went on and had good careers as major leaguers would approach other scouts and ask how Dick Hanlon is doing. I remember him well.

Dickie was a very successful scout. He signed a sort of raw-boned catcher from the San Francisco Bay Area. Dickie noted, "He's not going to hit enough, I don't think, but he's got a great arm. I'd like to put him on the mound." And that was Dave Stewart. He was right on the money on that one. He signed Stewart and John Wetteland and several others over the years. Both Wetteland and Stewart were considered to be down-the-line prospects.

He had considerable success not chasing high visibility prospects. Over the years he constantly furnished us with good prospects. That's when I started cross checking players. He was the scout of record who signed pitcher John Wetteland, who went on to have a great career. How great was Wetteland? By the time he went to the Yankees after we traded him, he became their closer and was named 1996 World Series MVP when the Yankees defeated Atlanta. At that time the Yankees had a young pitcher who was his setup man, a guy by the name of Mariano Rivera.

This is a good place to touch on the realities of scouting, player development and the rest from a personal standpoint. Over the years I found this experience to have taken place. Organizations change. There may be new ownership and quite often the new people who come in are not very complimentary regarding the efforts of the previous administration. It almost never happens that they come in touting the players and so forth of the prior administration. Generally it's just the opposite. They say things like, "Why did they get this guy? Why did they get that guy? This guy can't play." That's just a reality of the game.

Or ownership remains intact but they're unhappy with the general manager. So frequently the general manager goes, and when he goes, often the scouting director goes. And when the scouting director goes, often some of his key people go. You have new people come in and a different emphasis is placed on scouting. I experienced this as a young scout with the Angels when Gene Autry was not happy with the way things were going on the field. He wanted a pennant. But we all landed on our feet with different organizations.

Another scout who became a friend of mine, Steve Gruwell, scouted for Cincinnati, where he signed RHP Paul Moskau out of Azusa Pacific University, and then scouted for the California Angels for approximately twenty years. We were good friendly competitors and were always competing for players. I think during his long tenure with the Angels he was involved with many good players like Wally Joyner, Tim Salmon to some extent, Jim Edmonds, Garrett Anderson and others.

I used to play golf with him occasionally and about ten or twelve years ago we were out on the links in September and I remember him telling me, "I don't think they're going to offer me a contract."

And I said, "Aw, come on, don't be ridiculous. You have a good record there. You're a front line scout."

"Well, they're kind of distant and these are new people."

And I'll be damned if a short time after that he called me and said, "They let me go. They called me and told me they were going to go in a different direction."

A different direction was the term he used. So he lost his job. At the time I would say he was probably in his very early sixties, and he tried to get another job. Unfortunately he didn't get one right away. Then he had some health problems, and eventually his kidneys shut down and he was put on dialysis, which took a lot of time out of the day. After a couple of years he had a seizure and he died. Were the people who let him go evil? I would say that's not the best way to describe them. But they were part of a system that is far less than perfect. They came in with new people and dusted aside individuals they considered expendable. I don't think Steve was exceptionally highly paid, but he was probably in the so-called upper status end of it in terms of salary. So they just dismissed him. Not too long after that Steve died.

Now, what kind of success did these new people have? Not very much. Actually, next to none. They didn't win anything. They didn't change the program. They essentially stumbled around and within a few years they were gone, ultimately to be replaced by a new scouting director, Eddie Bane, who did a good job but eventually lost his job, too. What happens in this type of situations? Usually when new people are brought in, they have convinced ownership that they can add something to the dance that the previous group didn't. It's that simple.

Whatever happened to these guys? Well, they went in different directions. Several of them are still working, not in the same capacity that they were, but they dismissed a guy like Steve Gruwell, who was a very big contributor to the program that existed. Why you would just come along and dismiss this guy is difficult to understand and I never could figure it out. I really don't have an answer for it because I've seen it done before, more often than you would think.

I don't feel a scouting director should be appointed for life like a Supreme Court Justice. I'm not suggesting that at all. But when a scout has a list of success and has performed well, there isn't any question. I think that what you should do it look at his performance like you would a ballplayer. If you have a .300 hitter, the fact that you pay him a little bit more money than the guy who hits .260 for you makes sense. In the case of Steve Gruwell, he was successful. And, much like a ballplayer, whether you personally like him or not is immaterial.

I quite often feel that people who have the power to hire and fire don't pay enough attention to performance and work ethic. It's very easy to get scouts to become almost mimics of a scouting director. A good scouting director should not want a scout to mimic or agree with everything he says. Why would the "boss" trust a "yes man," anyway? God knows Hanlon was anything but a yes man. And Steve Gruwell certainly didn't fit that mold.

In some respects, at least in Steve's situation, I think he grew out of favor with management, so they had no problem just dismissing him. Dickie Hanlon wasn't dismissed, but he contracted Alzheimer's and had a problem working. In 2003, Steve Gruwell and Dickie Hanlon died within a month of each other. Sad. Hanlon was a different personality than Steve, but in a way he was very much the same. He was very successful and a good competitor. If you were a good scout in Northern California you sure as hell knew who Dick Hanlon was. If you were in Southern California you sure as hell knew who Steve Gruwell was.

This is a reflection of one of my pet peeves, and I hate to say it. Over time, especially after a scout passes on or retires, all of a sudden people start claiming credit for players that scout signed. Actually, it's just a manipulation of information to make themselves look better. It's an unfortunate thing that exists in the game. To combat it, the Scouting Committee of the Society of American Baseball Research (SABR) has been focused on which scouts signed which players. It's the result of situations where some scouts who are not comfortable in their own skin decided to dress up their history by taking credit for players other scouts found and signed.

In a different tone, I recall a comment Steve Gruwell made to me about an experience he had and I think all scouts have similar things happen from time to time. His wife was involved in the medical field. He told me he went to some function, "And there were all these doctors around. I was trying to blend into the woodwork, but my wife had mentioned I was involved in baseball and I ended up getting cornered by several doctors. It's amazing how these very sharp medical people talked and talked, trying to convince me how much they knew about baseball. I realized how universal the game is and how these medical people had an interest in the game."

I ran into Eddie Mathews in central California at Channel Islands High School, which is near Santa Barbara, where Eddie went to high school. He was a great football and baseball player. He signed out of high school and came to the major leagues two years later at age twenty. At a high school game I was able to talk with Mathews and he told me he was uncomfortable scouting kids in high school. He said, "When I was this age, I was in the Southern League trying to catch two ground balls in a row. I was a pretty good hitter but was told early on by Billy Jurges, 'Look, if you can't catch it and you can't throw it, you're going to be a liability every time the ball comes in your direction. Half the game you play is in the field.'"

We talked a little more and he emphasized again, "I'm just uncomfortable trying to figure out kids at this age. I know guys that do it well and I give them credit for it. But I'm just not comfortable doing it." I thought what he had to say was interesting. I enjoyed him. I thought he was a real good guy, and, as we all know, he was one of the top third basemen in the game. It's not difficult for good baseball fans to remember Eddie Mathews.

I saw Pete Reiser play quite a bit in the 1940s. He's another one of those players that's always fun to talk about. Pete had a ten-year major league career with the Dodgers, Braves, Pirates, and Indians from 1940 to 1952 with time away for military service during World War II. It's pretty commonly accepted that in his prime he was absolutely one of the best young players that had come along in many years. In 1941, his first full season in the majors, he won the National League batting championship with a .343 average. At age twenty-two he was the youngest player to ever win the batting title. Many say he did all the things Mickey Mantle could do, and yet his career was cut drastically short because he collided with cement walls while trying to catch long fly balls and suffered numerous serious injuries such as a fractured skull, concussions, and broken bones.

In fact, I believe that on one occasion he was given Last Rites by the Catholic Church because of a fractured skull he suffered in a game. But that didn't stop Pistol Pete! As a player, he had it all. Yet, in all the years he played, he only appeared in 861 games. In 1946 he stole home seven times and many believe he was "robbed" of his eighth that would have tied the all-time record set by Ty Cobb in 1912 on a poor call by the umpire.

I recall running into him roughly thirty years ago. I think he was scouting for the Cubs at that time. It was in Apple Valley, California. They had a very big high school that served four or five surrounding towns. I was up there during Easter week making the rounds of the high school showcase tournaments. Scouts are sometimes known to glance around to see if there are other scouts, especially at an out-of-the-way game. When you do what I do now and go around the country cross checking the top prospects reported by your own scouts, you see as many as twenty or thirty scouts at a game.

An area scout could go as much as two weeks and not see another scout if he's doing his coverage. But this particular day in Apple Valley I happened to look over behind third base and there was a chunky guy who was taking a lineup from the coach. I looked at him and thought, "I've seen this guy somewhere before." Then it dawned on me that it was Pete Reiser.

Once I recognized him I went over to say hello to him. At first he was a little guarded, probably wondering who I was and what I wanted from him. I told him I was scouting for the Dodgers and we had a nice conversation. I had also seen him play in Brooklyn and later when he coached for Walter Alston, 1960–64. He had also coached for Leo Durocher when "Leo the Lip" managed the Cubs, and later for the Los Angeles Angels for a year or two.

I asked him how he enjoyed scouting and he said he liked it. We must have talked baseball for an hour or an hour and a half. At any rate, Pistol Pete was as nice a guy as you could imagine. I feel really fortunate that I got to see him as a player because he was terrific. Had he been able to stay injury-free, there is no question he would have been a Hall of Fame player. He could do everything.

One of the things we talked about that day was the difference in the players in the major leagues during his era. He had originally been signed by the St. Louis Cardinals in 1937, just after his eighteenth birthday, but was among a group of players declared free agents the following spring when Commissioner Kenesaw Mountain Landis discovered some sort of shenanigans. At that time Branch Rickey was the general manager of the Cardinals and arranged for the Dodgers to sign Reiser and hide him in the minor leagues, then later trade him back to St. Louis. But Reiser performed so well Rickey's plan backfired because the Dodgers decided to keep him until Rickey became general manager of the Dodgers in 1942.

He was certainly an interesting guy to talk to and he said he loved being connected with baseball, no matter how it was. He said he loved doing it. And he had an interesting comment and I think I picked it up over the years. Quite often you see so-called old-timer scouts who don't want to retire, and your first thought is, "I wonder why he is still scouting." It's because they have experience that has exceptional value and they are still big contributors.

Pete said, "Gib, I think it keeps you young. No matter how old you get as a former player, and I don't care at what level you played, the products are the players and you look on yourself as still being able to play. Now subconsciously you may think, 'Boy, would I love to hit against this guy.' Or, 'I wouldn't want any part of this kid. He's got tremendous stuff.' You never lose that and I think it's the advantage of having been a player that someone who never played can never experience, I don't care how smart he is. The one area he can't share is the area of actually playing the game." .

As many times as I saw him play, each time was a thrill. He was an absolutely great player. When he died in 1981, Leo Durocher said, "Pete Reiser had everything Willie Mays had, except luck." When you see major league games now and you see the padded outfield fences you can thank Reiser for that.

But times have changed, and the scouting world has changed compared to when I started. One obvious condition when I started in 1969 was that scouts had a different dress code that presented a more professional image. I won't say they wore ties, but I've seen those who did, and sports jackets and slacks, shined shoes, and some wore fedoras. One guy I worked with, Dale McReynolds, took a shoeshine box with him on the road, and after shuffling around in the dirt at ballparks he shined his shoes. But it was a different era. As times changed attire changed. I never ever saw a scout with a goatee.

Nowadays I think the dress code in scouting has deteriorated greatly. I was at a game yesterday watching the University of Arizona have their fall program scrimmage, and there were probably forty-five scouts there. I was looking at guys wearing rumpled jeans and sneakers with goatees and their hair not neatly trimmed or anything. They looked like they had fallen off the turnip truck somewhere. They walked around spitting into an empty water bottle and the rest, which was just a total no-no when I started scouting.

I was never a sports-jacket guy, but always wore a clean sweater and tried to be presentable because you represent your club and don't want to look like some sort of a bum if you run into the parents of a player. You want to create the best possible image you can because if you do run into a prospect and have occasion to meet the family, you want to have a professional appearance.

And that's actually where I think the game has gone in terms of a negative aspect. I don't like it. I don't like seeing it, and I think there should be an effort made by directors of organizations to tell their guys, "It's pretty simple. You don't have to dress up like you're going to a wedding, but certainly you don't want to create the impression that you're some sort of an unkempt bum."

Saying that, I must add that of the group of goateed, sloppy looking scouts that I've seen, I'd venture to say there is not one of those guys who has ever heard of Sloppy Thurston or Joe Stephenson or Rosey Gilhousen or even Eddie Mathews as a scout. They may know Eddie Roebuck to some extent because he scouted for a very long time, but they never interacted with him, or for that matter, Pete Reiser.

In the final analysis, the game loses there. It lacks the former structure that told scouts to be low-key, do your job, make your notes, and present a presentable image when you're at any high school game. Today you have quite often the opposite. Many times these guys are loud. They'll see a player that, for obvious reasons is not a prospect, and often you'll hear a comment that's far too loud and says something like, "This kid's ridiculous, or this kid's terrible. Or this guy can't play so how in the hell did he make this team?"

I remember one experience in particular when I was at a game probably twenty years ago during Easter vacation week in the Anaheim area. There are many games going on each day. There were several scouts there to see a player, but because there were quite a few games going on you often had to see one game before you could see the other.

Several of us were there to see a particular hitter, a position player. He struggled in his first at bat, and in his next at bat he wasn't any better. It was probably fair to say that to a large degree his ability had been exaggerated. As a result some smart ass scout made the loud comment, "This guy is terrible. This guy is a joke. He can't play."

At that point the lady who was sitting behind him took her purse and blasted him over the top of his head. I kid you not! I can still remember her. She was kind of a tall redhead and she said, "Next time, Buddy, keep your mouth shut when you're sitting around me whether you think my son can play or not." A lot of people laughed over it. And you know what? It did my heart good to see that.

The reason I'm mentioning this is there needs to be some sort of code of conduct for scouts at the ballpark. No matter who the player is, he's somebody's son. Remember, mom and dad think he's the best. Why? They love him, and that's as good a reason you can think of. And make no mistake about it, that same scout with the big mouth might be sitting in a park where his son is playing. The boy may not be nearly as good as he thinks. How will he react if a scout makes a comment like those he made?

It's a sad commentary on what has happened and what can happen. And one of my biggest beefs is when they draw attention to themselves as being representatives of professional baseball.

I was originally taught to be careful, even when you leave a ballpark. Don't make a big issue out of leaving the park even though you may have two other games to see that day. Remember often people are aware who is a scout. And if you have to leave in the fourth inning to go to another game and you walk out, the first concern is that you may be leaving the game to go home and you won't see Junior hit again. And it's not the right thing. Just ease out of the ballpark and don't make a big issue out of leaving. I used to know one guy who always made the comment, "I'm out of here." As if the general public should know or even cared whether or not he was leaving. That becomes another issue and another negative. It's just a condition that exists now.

I don't like to live in the past and I enjoy what I think I've accomplished in the game and my love of the game. I'm not trying to reinvent what happened forty years ago. All I am trying to do is draw some conclusions that I think are valid.

But this is not a critique about what's wrong with baseball. There are a lot of things wrong with baseball as a business. But it's not the game itself. It's the people in the game. That's why I try to dwell on positives, people who have impressed me, who they were and what were they really like.

One of my favorite positive memories goes all the way back to a game I attended with my buddies at Yankee Stadium when I was a youngster. I somehow got separated from them at the end of the game. After wandering around a while looking for them I realized I was lost. Luckily an usher saw me and saw the distress on my face and took me to the Yankee clubhouse to decide what to do next. Joe Gordon talked to me for a couple of minutes and then gave me a Coca-Cola to make me feel better. He was my favorite player from that point on. I met him years later when he was doing some scouting and told him about that adventure and how I never forgot how nice he had been or that he had given me a Coca-Cola. He got a big kick out of that.

He said, "I got you a Coca-Cola?"

And I said, "Yes you did."

"How old were you then?"

"About ten," I said.

"Thank the good Lord I didn't offer you a cigarette!"

We both laughed.

Former Cincinnati pitcher and longtime scout Gene Thompson once told me, "Joe Gordon had the greatest personality of anybody in the game. And did you know he played the violin in a symphony orchestra in Portland, Oregon, when he was only fourteen? He was also a licensed pilot, a skill he had prior to World War II, and one he used during his military service."

In 1979 when I joined the Dodgers, the presence of Roy Campanella, affectionately known as "Poochie" by the Dodgers, was still very evident. He was certainly a great catcher. He was one of very few players named MVP three times; he played on seven all-star teams, 1949–1956; and he was inducted into the Hall of Fame in 1969. But his career ended suddenly one rainy night when he broke his neck in an auto accident. He was a very jolly guy, even though he had that impairment, and was very involved in community activities and worked with young catchers for the Dodgers at Vero Beach in the old days and offered thoughts and suggestions on how they could improve their game.

I've gotten a lot of what I call background material from Buddy Kerr, the old Giants shortstop who was traded to the Boston Braves. Buddy lived in New Jersey and was a scout for many years. I remember scouting in the International League and running into him several times. What a nice guy. As a matter of fact, at one point I mentioned that I had run into Vin Scully. Apparently Kerr was from the same general area where Scully grew up in New York City because Scully remembered going to the same church that Buddy Kerr attended. They had lived near the medical center in New York City, up around the George Washington Bridge. I first saw Kerr play in or around 1947. I also saw him once in Arizona when he was visiting Gene Thompson. He was such a nice guy.

Another was Spider Jorgensen, who was a longtime scout and played for the old Brooklyn Dodgers. He was a teammate of Jackie Robinson's in Montreal and they both played their first major league game with the Dodgers in 1947. Jorgensen always said he was glad that he and Jackie Robinson made their major league debut in the same game because all the press focused on Jackie, which made Spider's debut a lot easier.

I want to share this anecdotal story about Spider Jorgensen. I got to know him quite well over the years when he scouted for the Cubs and then the Philadelphia Phillies. He was one of those guys you couldn't help liking. The year was probably 1997, which would have made it fifty years since Jackie Robinson had come to the major leagues. Writers started popping in and looking Spider up because he came to the big leagues with the Dodgers the same year as Jackie Robinson. I remember him telling me, "Oh, God, I hate those guys. They all want to know so much trivial stuff. Jackie was a great player and everything, and we were friendly. We got along well. I used to play cards with him occasionally."

I said, "Spider, tell me about that infield you had then."

"Well, the infield we had in Brooklyn was really pretty good when I got there. Jackie didn't play second base."

"You know," I said, "I had forgotten about that."

He said, "Yes. Jackie played first that year, Eddie Stanky played second, Pee Wee was at short, and I played third. We got into the World Series that season and I'll remember that my whole life."

Knowing that Stanky had a reputation of being a highly aggressive battler-type guy, I asked him, "How'd you get along with Stanky?"

He said, "You know, Gib, Stanky was really a smart baseball man. But I think to some extent he was deranged. I didn't realize it when I was playing with him. He was a little guy with a big mouth and he was one of Leo Durocher's favorites."

And I recall this very well. Spider said, "But then he gets traded to Boston. I'm playing against him. What he lacked in speed and power he made up because he was smart. He was a good little player. I think he was on first, somebody got a hit to right field, and Furillo fielded the ball. You know Carl had a great arm and he threw it to third base. We had Stanky out by two and a half miles, but he came in there sliding with one spike up around my face, and as he was sliding he threw two hands

Spider Jorgensen played his first major league game on the Dodgers with Jackie Robinson in 1947, and later was a longtime scout.

full of dirt in my face. He had been running the bases with both hands full of dirt! Of course we started rolling around and swinging at each other and we both got kicked out of the game. I really couldn't understand it."

Two of my all-time favorite memories are much more recent, and both involve the two Dodger World Series–winning clubs, 1981 and 1988. Before there was Kirk Gibson's unbelievable two-run homer on a 3–2 count with two out in the bottom of the ninth that gave the Dodgers a come-from-behind 5–4 victory over Dennis Eckersley and the Oakland A's in Game One of the 1988 World Series that still gives me goose bumps, there was the Rick Monday home run in Game 5 of the NLCS against the Expos in Montreal that got us into the 1981 World Series. I'll never forget either one of those beauties!

And I can't mention Rick Monday without alluding to perhaps the greatest moment of his 19-year major league career. On April 25, 1976, in a game

Jean and I with the 1981 World Series Trophy.

at Dodger Stadium when he was with the Cubs prior to joining the Dodgers, the Dodgers were at bat when two individuals ran onto the outfield grass and attempted to set the American flag on fire. Rick Monday charged them from his center field position and snatched the flag before they could ignite it. Today that play is remembered as one of the top one hundred moments in major league history.

My Two Cents

This chapter contains some random thoughts on things that I feel are important in my profession.

Here is a sixty-year-old scouting report you may find interesting:

Fielding. He can't stop quickly and throw hard. You can take the extra base on him if he's in motion away from the line of throw. He won't throw on questionable plays, and I would challenge him even though he threw a man or so out.

Speed. He can't run and he won't bunt.

Hitting vs. right hand pitcher. His reflexes are very slow and he can't pull a good fast ball at all. The fast ball is better thrown high, but that is not too important as long as it is fast. Throw him nothing but good fast balls and fast hard curve ball. Don't slow up on him.

Hitting vs. left hand pitcher. Will pull a left hand pitcher a little more than a right hand pitcher. Pitch him the same. Don't slow up on him. He will go for a bad pitch once in a while with two strikes.

That report was written about the Yankee Clipper Joe DiMaggio in 1951, the last year of his career before he retired at age thirty-seven. It was a scouting report by the Brooklyn Dodgers, who had been scouting the Yankees at that point in time for about five weeks in preparation to face them in the 1951 World Series.

At the time the Dodgers had taken a thirteen-and-a-half game lead into the National League pennant race, but were hotly pursued by the New York Giants.

I wouldn't say the Dodgers rolled over and played dead, but they played about .500 baseball the last six weeks or so of that season and the Giants, caught them on the last day of the season. They had a best of three playoff set with the Giants, and the Giants won that playoff series on the shoulders of Bobby Thomson's famous home run, which was called "the shot heard 'round the world."

Somehow this scouting report is a matter of record and I didn't have to get into the archives to get it. It was not leaked by the Dodgers, but it had been leaked by the Giants. Now it's a fair question to ask, "How in the world did the Dodgers get the Giants' scouting report?" I don't know the inside story to that, but here is what I was told. Because the Giants did basically no advance scouting of the Yankees during their attempt to catch the Dodgers, the Dodgers had concluded the Yankees were going to win the American League pennant, and volunteered to turn over the information they had garnered to the Giants. The DiMaggio report above was part of that information.

The reason I bring it up is that it is essentially a negative report showing that DiMaggio's skills had diminished by this stage in his career. The report actually left a bad taste in everybody's mouth because he was an icon in the game, a great player who, by 1951, was no longer the great player he had been. He had suffered many injuries and decided if he couldn't be the great DiMaggio of days gone by, he wouldn't play at all.

Everyone who loves baseball knows about his amazing career and his legacy. That scouting report was perhaps the last one about him, and it stands.

My point is this. It's no surprise to anyone that the skills of all players diminish as they get older. The competitive juices may still be there, but the "law of diminishing returns" kicks in with age. Are clubs chasing players whose skills have diminished rather than taking a chance on young players who may come up through their farm systems?

I guess the era of the DH and the recycled big-name free agent power hitters is answer enough to that question. But it seems to me an organization's farm system has to be greatly depleted if it doesn't have anybody who can perform up to the level of a big-name player in that declining phase of his career. My logic is biased because I'm in a business that says to get good young players to replace the older players in your system who may not be as productive as they once were. Previous experience tells me that chasing players who were formerly great when they're past their prime does not work in the long run. Why chase retreaded players? Why not give a minor league youngster a chance?

Are the youngsters up to the task? Perhaps not right away, and I'll share one shining example of this very thing. The great Hall of Fame outfielder Al Kaline, a Baltimore youngster, signed a contract with Detroit and went from high school right to the major leagues. The first year, 1953, he played sporadically and he struggled. They say pitchers just knocked the bat out of his hand. The next year he was a regular because he had an outstanding arm that was both strong and accurate, and he batted .276. In his third season, 1955, he was twenty-one years old, and won the American League batting title. Think of it. Just twenty-one years old. He played 152 games and led the league with an astounding .340 average at the plate. To the best of my knowledge, that has never happened again. He became a great all-around player for the Tigers for twenty-two seasons and was a very key player in All-Star and World Series games. He led the American League in hitting nearly sixty years ago at age twenty-one. His last season was 1974, when he played 147 games and saw his batting average slip to .262. He was forty years old. He's almost eighty now.

As I said, this is an extreme example that proves my original premise here about giving young players a chance rather than chasing older players past their prime.

I'm reluctant to say this because it may appear on the face of it that I'm setting myself up to seem smarter than general managers, but that's not my point at all. What I am saying is there really is no reason in the world not to give a promising young player an opportunity to play in your organization at the highest level. There isn't any getting away from it. At twenty-one a player's reflexes and hand-eye coordination are superior to those players who are mid-thirties or older. There's no question about that. Does that make him a better player? Obviously it doesn't. But it does go a long way toward making him a better player.

Here's another thing worth discussing. There's always so much attention paid to the current salaries of major league players. It has been fodder for sportswriters and talk radio gurus in their constant discussions of the subject. Since I work in baseball, I can only assume the position of somebody who's in the game, as opposed to what a fan's reaction may be. Personally I have no qualms about the money players make. But unfortunately there are many misconceptions that are totally out in left field as far as I'm concerned.

Often people who follow baseball complain about the money these guys make. "I could do that and I would play for much less." But I don't want to get into that because it's a ridiculous argument. The market was created by ownership. You can argue it any way you want, but the Players' Association has no leverage at all to force any owner to pay a player any amount of money.

In 1966 there were twenty big league teams. I'm not implying all players played for the minimum which, prior to 1966, was $6,000 a year, but the average salary for players in both the American and National League was $19,000. In 1973 Rod Carew made $60,000, and Reggie Jackson $70,000. In 1981 there were twenty-six teams and the average major league salary went to $241,400. As of 2012 we have thirty teams, and roughly 250 more big league players than we had in 1966, and the average annual salary is around $3.5 million.

A large amount of the credit for the increase goes to Marvin Miller, an economist and labor organizer who was the primary figure in the foundation of the Major League Baseball Players' Association in 1966. Organization came about after many attempts were made to do it for more than a hundred years, dating back to when owners were completely in charge of salaries and the players had no recourse. If they protested, they were blackballed from the game.

This union was a huge step forward for the players. Over time it created the first collective bargaining agreement, arbitration, free agency and other milestones for them. Miller, who died in 2012 at age ninety-five, served as the union's first director for seventeen years until he retired in 1983. Today many consider the MLPBA one of the most powerful labor unions in the country.

A hobby of mine has been researching 1919 and 1920, and the Chicago Black Sox. One of the stars for that infamous team was Buck Weaver, the great third baseman. He was probably the best third baseman in both leagues at that time. Most people don't realize this, but there were multiyear contracts handed out even in that era, and Buck Weaver had one. Buck was making $7,250 per year in 1919. Since the Black Sox scandal did not come to light until almost the end of the 1920 season, he also played for that salary in 1920. If you want to compare dollar earnings per se and the cost of living, I'd have to say that he was doing better than the average player was in 1967 who was making $19,000.

As I already mentioned, major league clubs vastly underpaid players for many years. I know the argument that is thrown out: "But what about the players during the Depression?" Babe Ruth was the highest-paid ballplayer during those years. As he signed his contract with the Yankees for 1930–31 with a salary increase from $70,000 to $80,000 a year, he was asked if he realized he made more money than President Herbert Hoover, who got $75,000. He gave what has become a classic answer: "Well, I had a better year than he did."

To put it back into perspective, in 1936 Lou Gehrig signed for $31,000, which made him the highest-paid player in the game since Ruth, at a time when approximately twenty percent of the country was out of work. Then, as now, there's a general attitude by the working guy that if he were playing he would play for less and not be as selfish as the players of the day.

In 2011 Albert Pujols, at age thirty-one, turned down a nine-year contract from the St. Louis Cardinals. Everybody likes Albert Pujols. He's a good guy and a great player. But no right-thinking baseball man thinks he or any other player will play the same at 40 as he does at 31. It's just not logical. But again, it's all relative because the salary structure that is currently in effect is entirely created by the club owners and not the players. Pujols ultimately turned it down and the Cardinals let him move on.

Metal bats is another thing I have issues with, and I'm not the only one. For the most part, I don't think manufacturers were honest when they introduced them by saying they would be the same as wood bats. That's my number-one problem with them.

During the duration of my scouting career, metal bats were introduced. History says aluminum bats were "invented" in 1924, but it wasn't until the seventies that the major manufacturers like Hillerich and Bradsby and others started producing them in the United States. The bats were introduced by a statement from companies which said the use of metal bats would not liven up the game to any extent, hitters would not hit the ball further, but they were just much more economical. But that did not apply.

The first metal bat I came in contact with was a fungo, one that's used to hit infield and outfield. I was working for Montreal, and in those days we used to work players out that were drafted in the winter. They were all California kids: Ellis Valentine, Gary Roenicke, Gary Carter, and others who made up a good bunch of young players, plus numerous minor league players. We used to work out in October, November and early December.

A big part of that workout regimen was that I hit a lot of fungos. The ball came off hotter than it did with a wood bat. Now once the determination was made, the manufacturers could no longer say it was just an economical instrument. They had to acknowledge that they were hotter, that the ball went further. Hitters had a terrific advantage. A pitcher could make a good pitch, jam him, throw the ball on his hands, and normally with a wooden bat you break the bat and the hitter certainly could not hit the ball hard when the pitch was in on his fists. With metal bats, more often than not, the ball would be hit over the infielders' heads. Manufacturers had to acknowledge the metal bats propelled the ball further.

Then they approached the situation on an economical basis and they said you never break a metal bat, which initially wasn't quite true. There were some defectives. But at any rate, you don't break metal bats like you do wooden bats, and it's expensive to replace wooden bats. As a result, metal bats entered into the realm of amateur baseball at almost every level from Little League, pony league, colt league, American Legion, Connie Mack, high school and college ball. Metal bats were on the scene.

In the last thirty-five or so years we've seen a terrific change in the metal bats. And there have been modifications, and the tin bat used at this time in college baseball and the rest is not nearly as lively as those being used for the past twenty-five years.

Of course, accidents happened with the wood bats. Sadly, baseball lost a first base coach, young Mike Coolbaugh, a couple of years ago when he was hit in the head by a line drive foul ball during the course of a ballgame. And I noticed just the other day Luis Salazar, a former major league infielder whom I remember quite well, was standing at the rail by the dugout observing a spring training game in March 2011 when the catcher for Atlanta hit a line drive that hit him in the face above the eye socket, and he lost his eye as a result. You have to acknowledge that he was standing on the top step of the lip of the dugout watching the action on the field, but the ball probably came off that wooden bat at maybe a hundred-ten miles an hour and he couldn't react quickly enough to get out of the way.

If that can happen with a wooden bat, you can imagine the velocity that a baseball would come off a tin bat. It's kind of difficult to figure out the rationale that's used, but my question is simply, why can't colleges go back to wood bats? After all, a wood bat is used universally in professional baseball at every level starting with the lowest rookie league. Organized baseball all over the world uses wooden bats. A wood bat is the instrument used by professional players. And yet college baseball and all amateur baseball down to Little League uses metal bat with economy as the reason. It's much less expensive than when kids were breaking bats at different levels.

Certainly I'm not aware of the financial condition of these different amateur leagues where kids play. But I cannot believe that it makes a lot of sense to use a bat they will never use at any professional level. It doesn't make any more sense to me than to take a peach basket glove to start out when you really want them to use something that would introduce them to the game that's played.

I'm not talking professionally. I'm talking about the wood bat because when you're a young kid playing baseball, at least in my generation, you'll learn to play pepper. Pepper is a compressed group of players throwing the ball to a hitter who meets the ball and hits it to each one of the different individuals that he's facing. You don't really see it much in baseball any more but we used to see it all over the big leagues. It's great reflex training for defensive players and a great key for the hitter to get a feel where the barrel of the bat is and learn that you don't want to be hitting the ball from the label down to the handle. Not only does it sting, but the ball doesn't go anywhere.

I've been dealing with metal bats over three-quarters of my scouting career, but I don't think it's a wise decision to continue to use them. Certainly not at the college level, where the focus is on winning. In fact, it's reduced the situation for college pitchers who really want to pitch away from the bat. Pitch away, away, away. They never want to come in and jam a hitter. Why? Because the metal bat will propel the ball over the infielders' heads, even if the pitch is in on the hitter's hands. And that doesn't happen with a wood bat.

Basically that's my beef about metal bats. I don't like them. I never have. And in my judgment, if that's the difference between balancing the budget and not, then something's wrong with the budget. I just can't help but think baseball has been convoluted to some extent at the amateur level by using metal bats. Personally I'd like to see them discontinued.

In all good conscience, I need to mention some personal thoughts about things I feel are lacking in the professional game today, namely respect for the military and concern for many old timers.

Our society for the most part has a great respect for our military personnel. We honor them on Sundays at ballparks. We play "God Bless America" and the "Marine Corps Hymn" and other patriotic music and quite often end this by saying, "If you are in uniform and come to games on Wednesday of each week, you can get in for half admission."

I find that comical, and irritating, actually. In my opinion, I wonder why there isn't free admission for anybody who is on active duty in the military whether they're wearing a uniform or not, and regardless of the day of the week. If they produce a military ID card, why not let them into the ballpark for nothing? Almost all ballgames are on TV every day. Are the parks filled up? Rarely. The Dodgers draw quite well and have done so over the years. Surely baseball can afford to do this as a small tribute to our military personnel for the sacrifices they've made for our country. Baseball is a big business.

As a kid growing up during World War II, at Yankee Stadium, the Polo Grounds, and Ebbets Field, I saw many men in military uniform in the ballparks. I wouldn't swear that they got in free every time, but in a lot of instances they did. And they should have. And I even recall foul balls hit into the stands that were returned so they could be sent to military teams across the world in combat zones and elsewhere.

Here's something else to think about. Why in the world is it legal for some old-timers who played before the formation of the Players' Union to be excluded from the benefits that are inherent with that union? I'm talking about players like Early Wynn, who pitched in the major leagues from 1939 to 1963 and accrued three hundred victories, and the many others who pushed to get a union started way back when at the conclusion of World War II.

I remember Jesse Flores, a wonderful scout for the Minnesota Twins and a terrific guy who was liked and admired by everyone. I knew Jesse quite well. He was a very good pitcher in the American League in the forties and fifties and then scouted for the Twins for years; he signed Lyman Bostok and thirty-two others who played in the major leagues. Because of the time frame that he played in the big leagues, his pension was ridiculously low, maybe something in the neighborhood of a hundred dollars a month. But he never complained.

Today's players are walking millionaires, and I cannot understand why some of these guys who are in the upper echelons of earning power could not set up something to help the old timers who had gone by the boards. By now many of them have passed away, and in some cases they almost had to pass the hat to bury a few of them. It's a damn shame!

Often the old-timers have problems making ends meet as retired individuals in their eighties, and in a few cases some have lived into their nineties. They are not getting any help other than trying to scrape by on Social Security.

I am confused as to why some individual doesn't take advantage of this situation and convince a player or a group of players to do something for these guys. Why would that be a problem when it's the right thing to do? Sadly, the right thing to do often gets overrun by people who say, "Well, that's not my problem. What are we supposed to do, take care of everybody who was born too soon and missed out on the big-time contracts?"

In all fairness, today some clubs are very considerate in trying to take care of the old-timers on and off the field. I know this to be the case with the Dodgers, and I know it to be the case with the Yankees. George Steinbrenner and Company were always very considerate of old-timers. That does not mean all other organizations have not done anything. Jerry Reinsdorf of the White Sox is a real force in trying to get help for the needy.

But I think something should be done at the top level of the game, and the champion of this cause should be the Commissioner of Baseball, regardless of whether it's Bud Selig or his successor. Somebody should pick up the gauntlet and run with it in terms of taking care of the old-timers who have spent their lives in the game.

However, there are some wonderful people in baseball who have done much to correct some of this. Dennis Gilbert is one. Just to give you an illustration, in 2003, a scout in his fifties passed away. It turned out he was not very well off financially and left his family with not very much. Enter Dennis Gilbert, an agent and a highly successful executive with the Chicago White Sox. Dennis Gilbert is a very wealthy man. He is a former player, incidentally, who was signed by Joe Stephenson many years ago. But Dennis went on and had a great career in insurance, and then he became a highly successful agent.

He established the Professional Scouts Foundation to help out scouts and other baseball people who might be in need due to poor health or retirement or other circumstances. He invested a great deal of effort and got all kinds of celebrities in and out of baseball to contribute memorabilia to be used in a silent auction at what became an annual dinner at a big Los Angeles hotel. Collectors from all over the country participated in the auction and raised a tremendous amount of money.

Willie Mays got up and spoke. He captivated the people there and turned around and donated fifteen thousand dollars. He said, "I got fifteen thousand bucks to sign a contract when I was a young player and I've gotten so much out of baseball all of these years, and I want to give something back." I felt it was wonderful. Tommy Lasorda made a big cash contribution. And all the ballclubs were asked to donate by buying a table for the evening. I forget what the going rate was for a table, but I want to say somewhere around five thousand dollars.

Think of it this way. We have players playing now who make more money in one ballgame than some Hall of Famers have made in fifteen-year careers. Think of that. We're talking about thousands of ballgames that were played by these old–timers to make as much money as an individual today may make by playing just one game. Somebody owes something to somebody here, that's for sure.

I think the salary structure is interesting because there are all kinds of ways to view it. I'm not outlining these things just to be controversial or just to defend the position of the players, but to a degree you have to look at some form of rationale when you're saying players at this point in time are making $3.5 million a year as an average

But in terms of the average fan who is getting annoyed because the players make too much money, forget it. I started to allude to what we used to do when we went to baseball or golf tournaments and we got all kinds of questions. I remember one that really resonated well with me. I didn't really think much about it, to tell you the truth. I was a scout. My job was to procure players. I wasn't really thinking about how much money the players were making. My general attitude was, "Well, we had a good year. We were in the World Series or close. We drew three million fans." The fact that Steve Garvey was making fifty times the money I was making as a scout never entered my mind. It didn't bother me. It didn't affect me one way or another. I knew I couldn't play. And decades ago when I did play I wasn't good enough to play in the big leagues.

However, I remember Al Downing, a clever pitcher who pitched for the Yankees and then the Dodgers. He gave a talk at a dinner after a golf tournament where he answered questions from the floor. To a degree he outlined a concern about money. He said when fans complain about how we pay players, it was interesting because they didn't complain about actors like Kevin Costner or Robert Redford making fifteen or twenty million dollars for one movie. Thinking back on that, why didn't that happen? And when fans read about the movie salaries, the first reaction isn't, "Well, I would do it for less," or "I would do it for half of that." It's simple. The average guy can't relate to being in a movie. Why? Because the fan likely never was an actor. However, he did play baseball and maybe thought he would become a major leaguer some day.

In doing some reading the other day I learned that a man by the name of Frank Scott, credited with being a pioneer of the concept of agents, was one of the game's first agents in the fifties. But instead of negotiating contracts, he was more of a promoter who sought and got lucrative endorsements for big-name players like Mickey Mantle, Yogi Berra, and Roger Maris. But by the late seventies, more agents appeared on the scene with the self-designated purpose of negotiating player contracts. One of the leaders was Scott Boras, who demanded and got huge signing bonuses for unproved drafted players and professionals. I will discuss this in more detail later.

Nowadays almost every young player in each draft who is a possible first- to fifteenth-rounder seems to have an agent. If Junior turns out to be a very good player as a high school boy, he had some scouts come into the house to talk with him and his folks and will ask a lot of questions. That's just standard procedure. But the interesting feature to me is the appearance of the agents. Do youngsters need agents at that point at time? Some people may think they do.

Realistically, as things are now, I'd say every youngster needs an agent as he is approaching the big leagues, sure. And I'm not opposed to agents for higher-level players once they have progressed through minor league ball; an agent may be in order. But for kids just starting in professional baseball, I think agents are totally unnecessary.

As a high school player or a young college player, if you have parents who are available and can advise you, signing bonuses are a matter of record that can be easily accessed. Any team that wants to draft a youngster really wants to employ him. Those in the business that evaluate players, the scouts, think junior has a chance to become a major league player. So why would anybody think that organization is trying to cheat that youngster? And yet, that's what agents often thrive on. A lot of them go in and ingratiate themselves with the family and the player and then tell him, "You need me, and if you don't have me, they're liable to short you money, and I'll make sure you get it. Here. Sign on the dotted line."

Professional baseball has a rule that if an amateur player gets an agent, he automatically loses his amateur status and becomes a professional. Think of that. Without being too specific, it's the individual and the jockeying around of terminology that bothers me about all this. So how do agents survive with each succeeding draft? They hang out a different shingle when they call on the youngster and his parents. He becomes a "friend of the family," or tells them, "I'm an advisor." It's a subterfuge, really, and gets around the rules. Boras is excellent at convincing the young player that the family needs the advice that he's going to get from him.

Normally their fees, I'm given to understand, are somewhere around five percent, and they vary insofar as some agents don't collect anything until the player gets to the major leagues, but some get their cut right away. "For what?" is my question. Are we to assume that the drafting takes place because advisor/agent B represents the player?

Unfortunately, that's not a general attitude in the industry. And I do not believe there is one club in all of organized baseball that is trying to cheat a young player. They're trying to hire him. And really, what they're saying is, "We're trying to hire you, and if you sign your name, we're going to pay you for signing your name and allowing us to develop your skills to see how far they will take you in this game." It's that plain and simple.

At this time the most successful agent is Southern California–based Scott Boras, who claims to have signed seventy major leaguers and another seventy in the minor leagues, and some of the biggest names in the game. And he works at it. He has a beautiful setup in Newport Beach, California. I've seen it on TV, but have never been invited there.

I can just tell you this from a practical standpoint. When Fred Claire was our general manager with the Dodgers, there was a youngster playing in Hawaii by the name of Sardinia. I don't know if he's still playing, but I think he has a couple of brothers who may be. Anyway, he was a good-looking high school catcher. I cross checked him and I liked him. He was a thick, strong kid with a plus arm. He caught very easily and had some power. He looked like he was going to be a high-round draft. We kept asking our scout who covered Hawaii, Hank Jones, "Who's the agent?"

And he kept saying, "I'm trying to find out, but the parents are very tight lipped and they won't say."

Well, frankly, we suspected the family had been told not to disclose who the agent was.

Hank is one of our best scouts and he always has been, and he's a very diligent worker. I told Hank to stay after the player and the family because it is very important for us to know this and we didn't want to go in blind.

The draft approached and we got ready ten days ahead of the actual draft date. That's when we go over and review reports and film of every player and then prepare our preferential list. It's a very thorough process in which we spend a lot of time evaluating every player report submitted and often as much as eighteen hours daily on the players we may select.

The whole concept of preparing for the draft is not necessarily conducive to being bright-eyed and bushy-tailed each day. It involves long, drawn-out days and we're trying to compartmentalize players by position. Finally we get a call from Hank, probably a week before the draft, and he said, "His agent is Boras. I stayed and talked with Mom and Dad. The father was not very communicative but the mother was. She said her son had been instructed not to say anything."

But his mother asked Hank, "Why are you folks so concerned about who my son's agent is?"

And I felt Hank's answer was a very solid one. He said, "Well, we like to know this because some agents are a lot easier to deal with than others." End of comment.

Now, maybe two or three months later, Boras was in touch with Fred Claire and they were discussing one of our major league players who has Boras as an agent. As it happened, I was in scouting director Terry Reynolds' office with him at the time. Terry got a call from Fred Claire and talked with him a few minutes and then hung up. He looked at me and said, "Jesus, we might be in some trouble."

"What kind of trouble are we in?"

Hank Jones is a very bright and successful scout for the Dodgers in the Northwest (P.J. Dragseth Collection).

He explained that he had a conversation with Fred Claire, who revealed that Scott Boras had apparently complained that one of our scouts had told the mother of a player, and he named Sardinia, that he as a representative of the Dodgers was not very fond of dealing with Scott Boras.

I didn't believe it, not for one second. Basically, I've known Hank for many years and knowing him, he may have said that to me privately, but he sure as hell wouldn't have said that to the mother of the player."

Reynolds said, "I hope we're not in trouble."

"What disappoints me," I said, "is that Fred didn't tell Scott Boras to take a long walk off a short pier! He should have said that straight away. Look, that's not what our people do, and if you're going to claim it, prove it. Period. Other than that, let's get down to business on the other issue."

That didn't sit too well with Reynolds, but we called Hank and he repeated what he had been told. "I just told her that we would like to know this because some agents are more difficult to deal with than others."

"Did you make any comment about Scott Boras when she said it was Boras?"

"No. I'm not that dumb. Why in the world would I do that?"

To me, no matter what she told Boras one way or the other, you're just playing around with minutiae. For my part, I wish Claire had backed up our scout and said, if he doesn't like it, let him lump it. That's too bad. But nobody seems to want to do that with this guy simply because of leverage. Boras has a large number of big league players and he's highly successful. Apparently Claire didn't want to dispute the claim out of hand. I knew the claim to be untrue. Why? Because I knew Hank Jones.

In my mind the whole agent/advisor process is a manipulation to try to beat the system. Are the agent and the advisor actually the same guy? Of course. Is he performing the same tasks? Yes. Does he get a cut of the kid's earnings? Yes. How much and whatever manipulations are taken to get it is something else. But it's there.

Another beef concerns something we find all too often in the game at this point. We have a lot of people who start scouting but have next to no background in the game as players, coaches, or managers. We have a lot of people entering the game from what I call "the side door." They are fans; they're very interested in baseball; they're well read about the subject; they're statistically oriented, and often come in as statistician type people.

Here's how that happens. They may have worked as interns for a couple of years. And the next thing you know they may start getting paid. Then they convince somebody that they would like to be a scout. They do that for a year or two and after four or five years they feel qualified to become a general manager. This may seem like a reach but it certainly is not. It's a fact. Throughout all of this one question lingers. Does the guy know anything about evaluating players? In my judgment many times the answer to that is a resounding, "NO!" In my view, it's a slap at the integrity of the entire scouting process, and that is a weakness to the game.

I want to share a recent experience I had talking with a very sharp scout by the name of Tim Wilken, who had been scouting director and is now a special assistant to the GM with the Chicago Cubs. Before that he worked for Toronto and was a key individual in the procurement of some players who became part of World Series–winning teams. Then he went to work for Tampa Bay and was very successful there. He has been successful every place he has ever worked in baseball. I recall a recent conversation when he asked me, "When you were a kid growing up, how did you learn who the players were?"

The first thought that came to my mind was simply, "By following the game on the radio and in the papers." Television was not available when I was a kid growing up just prior to and during World War II, and we listened to the games on the radio. But I got very interested as a young kid in getting *The Sporting News*, and that carried over for a big part of my life. When I was a GI overseas my family sent it to me and I read it cover to cover. Tim Wilken said that's how he learned about the ballplayers, too. And I think most in my generation were exposed to players the same way. *The Sporting News* gave us everything we needed to follow our favorite teams and their minor leagues as well. You read every box score to keep up with daily progress of players.

But now we have people entering the game through what I call "the side door," which in baseball means someone who didn't play, someone who didn't coach, but quite often the leverage that allows them admittance through the side door is an educational background. They may have taken quantum physics in a major university. They love baseball. That's always the key. They tell you, "I love baseball," yet almost none of them know anything about baseball history. They're sharp academically and often play around with different numerical equations and say things like, "This guy can hit on Tuesday but not above six thousand feet, and is very capable of hitting at sea level."

That means nothing to baseball people like me who came in via the front door. Certainly we use some statistical data. But the way my generation was scouted and the one that preceded me in scouting, was visually. We went to see the kids play. Not only did we see how they handled themselves in competition and saw what their tools were, but we also got to know inclinations, tendencies, mental makeup and other vital things.

But this current generation, and they're a victim to some extent, will say,

"Well, my television set shows six games at once." And if they're not looking into the television set, they're looking into the computer. That seems to be a widely accepted practice in bringing these people into the game. Personally I think it is a very dangerous practice.

No matter how you cut it, it's not a feeling that a person who comes in through the side door can get looking at a computer. Sorry, but that just does not exist. Does the individual who scouts that way add value to a club? Probably, to some extent. But you have to temper everything he says by asking, "Wait a minute. Does this guy really have the feeling of playing the game?" And you ask that because he never played. "Is he apt to know what the statistics are on a given team in terms of their ability to win and how to win?" He may know that, but that is not what scouting is about.

No matter how you analyze it, I don't think there is any doubt that there is a tendency in the game to be attracted to this type of individual nowadays. Saying that, I certainly think it is worthwhile mentioning that if I had my options to pick somebody I wanted to add to a scouting staff, my first priority would be somebody who had the experience of playing the game. There is not a question about that in my mind. That is the first individual I would pick. There could be a place for the side-door scouts, but I sure as hell would not want to send them out in the middle of nowhere to scout a kid where they had to make a judgment on their own!

It's very easy for this current group to run to a game to see one of the twenty or thirty most talked about and widely known players. They're right at home when they get in among a bunch of scouts. They feel they must be in the right place. That isn't real scouting; it's just following the crowd.

Here's a question for you. Who was Jimmy Kelly? He was a professional baseball player who was signed when he was just thirteen years old in 1984. That's right. Thirteen. Obviously he was an advanced player at that tender age. Where did he come from? He may have an Irish name, but he was a Dominican player. The reason I'm talking about him here is that many Dominican youngsters were brought to the U.S. and some made it to the big leagues. Vladimir Guerrero; the Martinez brothers, Ramon and Pedro, both excellent pitchers; Sammy Sosa; and so many others have enriched our game.

We all know of some Dominican players, but certainly not in the numbers that the general public thinks exist. The issue of Jimmy Kelly is particularly interesting because it gives some history in terms of the conditions and the guidelines that were set up after he was signed.

Kelly was originally signed by the great Latin American scout Epy Guerrero, who was working for Toronto at that time. Why did he sign a kid so young? Kelly was not very physical at that age, of course. But still, the agile little shortstop was so advanced that Toronto's general attitude was to sign him and put him into their academy in the Dominican Republic and play him there probably for two or three years until he developed and got stronger. Then, theoretically, by the time he was seventeen or so, he may become a front-line prospect. But that never really happened for him.

Instead, in 1985, at age fourteen he was sent to play in the Gulf Coast League, a rookie league, with the Blue Jays. It was his first venture into the United States and it was very difficult. He was homesick and he had problems with the language. At the same time, his abilities were overwhelmed by competition averaging four years older than he was. But he didn't give up. He played in the Toronto system through the 1989 season before he was traded to the Mets in 1990, where he spent his sixth and final season. His best season was 1988, when he played 118 games with Knoxville in the AA Sally League. Altogether he played in 431 minor league games.

George Washington High School in the Washington Heights area near the famous George Washington Bridge has produced many outstanding professional players. Probably the best known today is Manny Ramirez. Quite often these Spanish-speaking youngsters come into the U.S. from the Dominican Republic and gravitate to that area because they have relatives living there. They're at home there. Spanish is spoken there. When you go see a game at George Washington High School, the primary language of the players is Spanish, but most of them can speak English because they've learned it by living here.

The problem that Jimmy Kelly experienced is geographical to a point. The Dominican Republic is a very difficult place for a kid to grow up. There's almost no education program there. No schooling. The Dodgers have had a couple of cases over the years where we have signed players that we felt were very promising youngsters, and we knew going in that they were illiterate. It wasn't just that couldn't speak English; they could not read and write Spanish. Of course the Dodgers tried to make allowances for that and set up some kind of education for these kids so they could survive here, at least socially.

Just to give a brief outline of what happens in the Dominican Republic, the Dodgers were the first organization that was very active there in signing players. In addition to that, many organizations had academies there which were like spring training facilities that had many baseball diamonds, places for the youngsters to play the game, workout facilities, and cafeterias. Today there is even one Japanese academy in the Dominican Republic. Baseball is everything for Dominican children who are interested in sports.

There is no middle class there and there is an unbelievable amount of poverty. The country was originally an attractive vacation paradise until Rafael

Trujillo, who was the dictator of the country since 1930, was assassinated in 1961. Since then they have had terrible problems economically. As a result, American baseball has struggled with Dominican players to a degree. There have been a lot of activities over the years where players who wanted to be considered younger swapped birth certificates and the rest so that maybe a twenty-three year old could pass himself off as nineteen.

When Jimmy Kelly signed in 1984 he received five thousand dollars. At that time major league baseball realized there were no age limitations for players who were being signed out of the Dominican Republic, so they eventually established an age requirement saying any players signed out of the Dominican Republic had to be seventeen years of age by the conclusion of his first professional season.

It's very tough for young kids who sign out of the Dominican Republic even to get off the island, and many young players quite often do not leave the place. They may remain there and play in the academy of a given major league team. After they have him for a certain length of time and realize he is not a prospect, they release him. There are all kinds of anecdotal comments about that. How does a Dominican player get off the island? He either swims or hits his way off. Baseball offers him an opportunity to accomplish the latter.

The number of players I'm referring to here is pretty easy to check. It covers the period of 2003–2010. What it averages out to is roughly four hundred players were signed out of the Dominican Republic each year. If there's four hundred signed, that certainly does not mean anywhere near that number even leave the island. That's really where the confusion can take place. Less than two percent of the youngsters who sign there make it to the major leagues. Out of each draft we have in the U.S., as many as eight to nine percent of those drafted each year get to the major leagues. That doesn't mean that they stay there. But there isn't a strong correlation between the numbers of Dominican players who get there as opposed to the number of American kids.

Incidentally, in the 2012 World Series, commentators reported there were seven Latin players involved. But they were not all Dominicans. Many were from Venezuela, which is a very difficult place to scout because there is a lot of violence there. There's a lot of political unrest and a lot of shootings. You can understand why players want to get out of there. We have a terrific scout down there, a former right-hand pitcher for the Washington Senators and the Minnesota Twins, Camilo Pascual. He had one of the best curve balls anybody has ever seen. He is an excellent scout who has operated there for many years.

The Dodgers Academy in the Dominican Republic was started by Ralph Avilla, a genuine legend in the scouting world, who is the grandfather of

Detroit's catcher Alex Avila. It's very tough for these kids at the academies who first play with each other and then compete at a higher level of competition when they come to the United States as players in the minor leagues. Only the best kids are able to move through the system.

And if you are one of those kids trying to make it, the biggest negative is simple. The biggest negative is that the competition gets awfully tough as they progress. And that is what happened with Jimmy Kelly. There's a mentality for dealing with players from Latin America and there is a thought process that goes in it that does make sense. They want to make sure that youngsters are prepared for the competition level that is placed by the major league baseball teams. It becomes terribly difficult when a kid comes from a society where there is next to no education, where kids do not read and write. And, as I said, that is quite often the case in the Dominican Republic. I cannot speak for Venezuela because I don't know that much about the program there.

So my hat is tipped to any of the kids who come out of these programs where English is not their primary language and they have often learned it on their own by watching television. I've learned from Dominican players that the Dodgers have had. Jose Vizcaino is one, and another is Jose Offerman. Then of course we had the Martinez brothers and Pete Guerrero. And as time passes, they do pick up sufficient English to get by.

Some things have changed for the kids out of the Dominican Republic. As I said, a minimum age requirement of sixteen-going-on-seventeen was instituted. Players would say the biggest thing is the signing money. When Jimmy Kelly signed in 1984 he received five thousand. Today the average signing money for them is up around twenty thousand.

In my readings about U.S. history I found an excerpt from a short speech made by Theodore Roosevelt over a hundred years ago. Though obviously not directed to sports, I think it is a fitting conclusion to this book:

> It is not the critic who counts; not the man who points out how the strong man stumbles, or where the doer of deeds could have done them better. The credit belongs to the man who is actually in the arena, whose face is marred by dust and sweat and blood; who strives valiantly; who errs, who comes up short again and again, because there is no effort without error or shortcoming; but who does actually strive to do the deeds; who knows the great enthusiasms, the great devotions; who spends himself in a worthy cause? Who, at the best, knows in the end the triumph of high achievement, and who at the worst, if he fails, at least he fails while daring greatly, so that his place shall never be with those cold and timid souls who know neither victory or defeat.

Epilogue

Writing this book has given me the chance to reflect on my love of baseball and my long career in the game. From 1969 to the present as a professional scout I have worked with and learned from some of the best and most colorful scouts in the business, been employed by good organizations, played a role in the careers of several successful major league players, and had the thrill of watching two Dodgers teams win world championships in 1981 and 1988. Great pride belongs to special scouting staffs that contributed to those championships.

Interwoven with all of that, of course, was the business of baseball that included expansion to thirty major league franchises and changes in club ownerships and philosophies. As in every profession, some things were more palatable than others, but we always kept looking forward.

In 2012 the Frank McCourt ownership of the Dodgers ended after a long process of negotiations and protocol, not to mention media attention and speculation. During the spring of 2012 the Dodgers were purchased by the Guggenheim Group.

Currently Mark Walter, one of the owners, has been quite vocal in expressing what he wants to do with the club. I recall the final weeks of the 2012 season when the prospects of the Dodgers' getting to the playoffs were grim and ultimately we did not make it. There is no question at all that the Dodgers ball club was far better than we were playing at that time. The question became, "How much better would we get under the brand new owners?" I believe a lot better.

Why? Because that group of business people came in and introduced a new condition that said, "We're going to spend money. We're going to try to get the best available players from the free agent market and hopefully this will get us to the Fall Classic now or in the near future." That was ambitious after just a couple of months at the helm. But baseball is played on the field, not on paper, and the result was that things didn't quite come together for that 2012 season. Despite having a lot of very fine offensive players, the team struggled to produce runs.

To be perfectly honest, when I learned the Guggenheim people were going to purchase the Dodgers, it was really a sense of relief. That's because the general thrust of what the Dodgers were trying to do under the McCourt leadership was to be competitive, which, in my judgment, is just a nice way of saying, "We are not able to compete from a financial standpoint so we're hoping to be spoilers for another club trying to get to the postseason."

That position never became formally used but it was the general attitude. If you're in player development, if you have been evaluating players as long as I have, you would look at your club and say, "You know what? This is not a contending club." This is a club that, on any given day, can beat anybody. World Series winners. Pennant winners. Great teams in major league baseball win a hundred games. That still means you may get beaten sixty-two times.

Generally speaking I feel there was a sense of relief and a new hope for the future when all of that went down because it meant the club would be able to compete monetarily. When you can compete monetarily in conjunction with having a competent scouting department and player development personnel, and the Dodgers certainly have that, then the future looks bright. I think the future of the Dodgers is bright.

So basically that's my attitude in terms of where we were then and where we will go. I don't think there's any question that when this club comes together it will be an exceptional club in the National League West for some time to come. Of course, one must realize that to sustain an organization, a scouting department must feed the system with quality players. Just signing highly priced free agents alone is only part of the puzzle to become a true contender. Developing your own players over the long haul is even more important.

Looking back through my life as a baseball scout, the best summary I can give is this: I have a special pride in being called "scout," and would eagerly do it all again.

Index